A Metaphorical Study of Saundarananda

A Metaphorical Study of Saundarananda

LINDA COVILL

MOTILAL BANARSIDASS PUBLISHERS
PRIVATE LIMITED • DELHI

First Edition: Delhi, 2009

ISBN: 978-81-208-3367-8

MOTILAL BANARSIDASS
41 U.A. Bungalow Road, Jawahar Nagar, Delhi 110 007
8 Mahalaxmi Chamber, 22 Bhulabhai Desai Road, Mumbai 400 026
120 Royapettah High Road, Mylapore, Chennai 600 004
236, 9th Main III Block, Jayanagar, Bangalore 560 011
Sanas Plaza, 1302 Baji Rao Road, Pune 411 002
8 Camac Street, Kolkata 700 017
Ashok Rajpath, Patna 800 004
Chowk, Varanasi 221 001

Printed in India
BY JAINENDRA PRAKASH JAIN AT SHRI JAINENDRA PRESS,
A-45 NARAINA, PHASE-I, NEW DELHI 110 028
AND PUBLISHED BY NARENDRA PRAKASH JAIN FOR
MOTILAL BANARSIDASS PUBLISHERS PRIVATE LIMITED,
BUNGALOW ROAD, DELHI 110 007

Contents

PREFACE

The *Saundarananda* exerted a strong pull from the first time I came across it. It is a beautiful and compelling poem which manages to maintain a concentrated focus on the theme of spiritual reorientation, dramatised through the experience of the reluctant convert Nanda and his changing relationships with his wife Sundarī and his half-brother, the Buddha. Discovering it as I did at a time when I had been thinking a great deal about the process of transformation and conversion, it could not fail to enchant. I decided not only to translate the entire text of over a thousand verses, but also to make it the subject of my doctoral research, conducted at the University of Oxford between 2001 and 2005. Although I knew from the outset that I favoured a literary and broadly cultural approach to the text over a narrowly doctrinal one, my work remained rather fragmentary until Richard Gombrich, my supervisor at Oxford, gave me the name of George Lakoff. Thereafter my ideas very quickly fell into place. I began to notice metaphors everywhere; even the most simple and practical communication seemed rich with layers of coded meaning. Lakoff's understanding of metaphor illuminated the *Saundarananda*, a text from a far-off time and a different culture.

This book, then, is about metaphors, specifically Buddhist metaphors. In particular, it examines how one highly skilled transmitter of his culture, the *kavi-bhikṣu* Aśvaghoṣa, used Buddhist metaphors to convey his understanding of spiritual reorientation. The book therefore aims to provide a comprehensive examination of the content, function and background of the *Saundarananda*'s conversion metaphors. That he was both a *kavi* (poet) and a *bhikṣu* (monk) must have been an enduring source of tension for Aśvaghoṣa, balancing the creative impulse with the Buddhist principles of restraint and disengagement. We cannot know for certain if Aśvaghoṣa was a very good *bhikṣu*, but he was undoubtedly a great poet and a convincing evangelist of Buddhism.

Given that the *Saundarananda* is a remarkable product of the literary and religious imagination, it is quite surprising that this is the first book-length study of the poem published in English. It seems to me that the time is ripe for the promotion of the *Saundarananda*, and Motilal Banarsidass Publishers are to be commended for undertaking to do so. Scholars working in the academic discipline of Buddhist Studies will be the primary audience of this book, but readers whose interests lie in early Indian culture, the development of Sanskrit literature, the use of metaphor for religious purposes, and the wider application of Lakoff's theories of metaphor will also find much relevant material within these pages. The broader audience may well include Buddhist practitioners and those fascinated by the interior process of religious conversion, for the *Saundarananda* is after all a spiritual biography. The book is intended to be accessible to those readers with limited or no Sanskrit, since an English translation is always provided for any Sanskrit quotation. There is also a glossary which supplies brief definitions of key Buddhist terms and other technical expressions. All quotations are given in the Roman script, and compounds are hyphenated (*kāvya-dharma* for example), though not when *sandhi* conventions have fused the compound with one vowel (*kāvyopacāra*). For those who would like to read the entire *Saundarananda*, my *Handsome Nanda* (2007) has been published by New York University Press and Clay Sanskrit Library in a handy format, with Aśvaghoṣa's Romanised Sanskrit text and my English translation on facing pages.

This book is based on my D.Phil thesis, "Metaphors for Conversion in Aśvaghoṣa's *Saundarananda*", which was accepted by the University of Oxford in 2006. I am very glad to have the opportunity to thank my supervisor, Richard Gombrich, for his enduring kindness, his faith in me, and his linguistic rigour. Jim Benson at the Faculty of Oriental Studies in Oxford has been a gifted, humane and extraordinarily generous teacher of Sanskrit. I am also grateful to those who read all or part of this work, including David Smith and Ulrike Roesler, for their encouraging remarks and their help in weeding out errors and inconsistencies. My mother, who read the entire text with the vigilant eye of a non-native English speaker, helped to minimise the number of typographical errors. I thank my father for his deep pride in me as well as his financial support. Finally, I am enormously thankful to the members of my family for their tolerance and love.

This book (especially the glossary) is for my friend B.K.

ABBREVIATIONS

AN	*Aṅguttara Nikāya*
AśvBC	Aśvaghoṣa's *Buddhacarita*
AV	*Atharva Veda*
BhāKA	Bhāmaha's *Kāvyālaṃkāra*
Car	*Caraka-saṃhitā*
DN	*Dīgha Nikāya*
Dhp	*Dhammapada*
Dhp-a	*Dhammapada Aṭṭhakathā*
It	*Itivuttaka*
J	*Jātaka*
JAOS	Journal of the American Oriental Society
JASB	Journal of the Asiatic Society of Bengal
KA	Kauṭilya's *Arthaśāstra* ed. Kangle
Khp-a	*Khuddakapāṭha Aṭṭhakathā*
Lal	*Lalitavistara* ed. Vaidya
Mil	*Milinda-pañha*
MN	*Majjhima Nikāya*
Mvu	*Mahāvastu* ed. Senart
MW	Sanskrit-English Dictionary ed. Monier-Williams
PED	Pali-English Dictionary ed. Rhys Davids & Stede
PTS	Pali Text Society
Pv-a	*Petavatthu Aṭṭhakathā*
SN	*Saṃyutta Nikāya*
Sn	*Sutta Nipāta*
Suśr	*Suśruta-saṃhitā*
Th	*Theragāthā*
Th-a	*Theragāthā Aṭṭhakathā*
Thī	*Therīgāthā*
Ud	*Udāna*
Ud-a	*Udāna Aṭṭhakathā*
VāgAH	Vāgbhaṭa's *Aṣṭāṅga-hṛdayam*
VāgAS	Vāgbhaṭa's *Aṣṭāṅga-saṃgraha*
Vin	*Vinaya*

VinMV	*Vinaya Mahāvagga*
Vism	*Visuddhimagga*
WZKS	Wiener Zeitschrift für die Kunde Südasiens

CHAPTER ONE

CONCEPTUAL METAPHORS

Once upon a time in the city of Kapilavāstu[1] there was a young man named Nanda who was very much in love with his pretty young wife. One day the Buddha came to Nanda's house and led him away to be unwillingly ordained. Nanda was unhappy with his life as a monk and longed to go home to his wife. Hearing of this, the Buddha took him to heaven and showed him an ugly monkey and a group of beautiful celestial nymphs. Nanda, declaring that the difference in beauty between the celestial nymphs and his wife was as great as the difference in beauty between his wife and the ugly monkey, forgot all about his wife and was filled with desire for the nymphs. The Buddha promised the nymphs to Nanda if Nanda persevered in his life as a monk. Nanda agreed, practised diligently and soon achieved liberation, whereupon he released the Buddha from his pledge concerning the nymphs.

This core Nanda legend, part of the Buddhist cultural environment since early times, provides the narrative framework of the great poem or *mahākāvya*, the *Saundarananda*. The *Saundarananda* was never, as far as we know, translated into Tibetan or Chinese, and no commentary was ever written on it; thus H. Shastri's discovery of the complete Sanskrit text in a Nepalese library in 1908 was a fortunate event indeed.[2] The *Saundarananda* consists of 1063 verses over eighteen cantos, and was written, according to the colophon, by the poet Aśvaghoṣa. Estimates of Aśvaghoṣa's date have generally been tied to those of the Kuṣāṇa king Kaniṣka I ever since Lüders (1911) first postulated, on palaeographical grounds, that Aśvaghoṣa can be placed in his reign.[3] Palaeographical

---

[1] Aśvaghoṣa's preferred spelling of the town more commonly known as Kapilavastu.

[2] The discovery was announced to the world in Shastri, Haraprasad (1909). 'The Recovery of a Lost Epic by Aśvaghoṣa'. *JASB* 5, pp. 165-6.

[3] Lüders (1911:7-11) undertakes a letter-by-letter analysis of manuscript fragments of Aśvaghoṣa's drama *Śāriputra-prakaraṇa* and compares his results with inscriptions from the Kuṣāṇa period. He concludes that the handwriting

arguments aside, several surviving Chinese translations of lost Sanskrit works would seem to support the Kuṣāṇa association. For instance, the *Śri-dharma-piṭaka-nidāna Sūtra*, an anonymous history of 23 Buddhist patriarchs, relates how Aśvaghoṣa, through the power of his music and teaching, persuaded 500 princes of Pāṭaliputra to renounce the world. Meanwhile, the king of Pāṭaliputra was defeated in battle by Kaniṣka, who demanded 900,000 gold pieces in war tribute. The king of Pāṭaliputra no doubt saw in Kaniṣka's demand an opportunity to rid himself of a persuasive monk whose powers of conversion threatened to further reduce the ranks of the city's nobility. He handed over Aśvaghoṣa, along with the Buddha's wooden bowl and a naturally compassionate cock that wouldn't drink water containing insects, reckoning each to be worth 300,000 pieces. Aśvaghoṣa became Kaniṣka's spiritual counsellor, while the renowned physician Caraka is named as the king's medical attendant. The *Saṃyukta-ratna-piṭaka Sūtra*, a collection of stories about Buddhist history and legend, relates that King Kaniṣka had three friends, his prime minister Māṭhara, the physician Caraka, and the poet Aśvaghoṣa, who were his constant companions and advisors.[4] Should the connection between Aśvaghoṣa and Kaniṣka prove valid, Aśvaghoṣa's date could be ascertained with some accuracy, since recent epigraphical discoveries[5] have pinpointed Kaniṣka's reign to a period of 26 years beginning at some point between 107 and 120 CE.

E. H. Johnston, who in the 1920s and 30s edited and translated both the *Saundarananda* and Aśvaghoṣa's other *mahākāvya*, the *Buddhacarita*, has also been Aśvaghoṣa's major interpreter. His translation of the latter is prefaced with a

---

on the fragments undoubtedly originates in the Kuṣāṇa period, and more specifically, in the time of Kaniṣka.

[4] The Chinese texts are described by Sylvain Lévi (1896). 'Notes sur les indo-scythes.' *Journal Asiatique*, pp. 444-484. Lévi's article is translated by W. R. Philips (1903). 'Notes on the Indo-Scythians'. *Indian Antiquary*, 32, pp. 381-389.

[5] This is the 1993 discovery of the Rabatak inscription in northern Afghanistan, described in Cribb (1999).

substantial introduction[6] which considers Aśvaghoṣa as a Buddhist, scholar and poet, acknowledging that he should "start with that one which he himself [i.e. Aśvaghoṣa] would have held to be alone of significance." Johnston is particularly interested in Aśvaghoṣa's emphasis on devotion, his handling of legendary material and his exposition of doctrine. He asserts that the poet's works are "invaluable to us, not for their originality of thought, but as giving us a complete and coherent picture of the faith of a typical Buddhist at a particular epoch." As far as his subject's skill as a poet is concerned, Johnston deems Aśvaghoṣa inferior to Kālidāsa, though readily admitting the appeal of both the *Buddhacarita* and the *Saundarananda* which, he believes, derives mainly from the enthusiasm and conviction of their author. He cites *Saundarananda* 4:1-11 and 10:8-13 as the high point of Aśvaghoṣa's poetic technique. With regard to the question of Aśvaghoṣa's date, Johnston remains unpersuaded by the Chinese texts, feeling that East Asian tradition has confounded Aśvaghoṣa with the poet Mātṛceṭa; his best estimate for Aśvaghoṣa's date, the first half of the first century CE, is a century earlier than the date now fixed for Kaniṣka. Johnston's work remains the single most important contribution to Aśvaghoṣa studies and as an all-round approach has yet to be superseded.[7]

Other scholars who have ventured to study the *Saundarananda* have generally used a narrower focus than Johnston. One group of scholars is interested primarily in questions of a linguistic and textual nature. Hakeda (1962), for instance, uses Edgerton's Buddhist Hybrid Sanskrit Dictionary to find a total of 124 non-standard Sanskrit words in Aśvaghoṣa's two *kāvyas*. Likewise Salomon's (1983) main interest is in the language of the *Saundarananda*. He tries to establish its place on a scale ranging from pure classical Sanskrit at one end to Buddhist Hybrid Sanskrit at the other. He gives several

[6] Johnston (1936:xiii-xcviii).

[7] Johnston (1936:xxiv, xxxvii and xix) for comments on Aśvaghoṣa's technique reaching its "high-water mark"; pp. xiii–xvii summarise the arguments for Aśvaghoṣa's date.

examples of vocabulary, syntax and usage that are characteristically Buddhist, adding several more non-standard Sanskrit words to Hakeda's original list. Sen (1930) is another writer seeking to evaluate the extent to which the language and grammar of the *Saundarananda* deviate from standard usage. He notices features such as the number of repetitions, and the preference for the perfect over the aorist and imperfect in denoting past action. Sen merely observes, and offers very little by way of interpretation. He is struck by the frequency of desiderative forms, but fails to relate this pattern to issues of volition and passivity, an important concern in the poem. Passi (1982) has translated the *Saundarananda* into Italian, during the course of which he offers some emendations to Johnston's text. His later work (Passi 1996) reflects on the translation process and proffers a translation of the first 28 verses of Canto 4 in blank verse in which he attempts to approximate the rhythms and verbal patterns of the original.

A second group of *Saundarananda* scholars consists of those whose interest lies in Buddhist thought and practice. Thus Bennett (1964) focuses on the *Saundarananda* mainly as a source of teaching on meditation. Conze (1959) includes much of the poem's material on meditation in his well-known compendium *Buddhist Scriptures*, as does Strong (1995) in his sourcebook *The Experience of Buddhism*. Ghose (1999) is preoccupied with the idea of emotional health, and seeks in the poem an indication that an affective component can be found in meditational practice and in the enlightened state of a Buddhist sage. He wonders whether Aśvaghoṣa perceived a conflict of interest between his message of Buddhist renunciation and the goal of heightened emotivity dictated by the medium of *kāvya* (Ghose 1999:24). Nevertheless, Ghose largely ignores the stock descriptions, ornaments and other features characteristic of *kāvya*, drawing by far the greatest proportion of his quotes from the more Buddhistic second half of the *Saundarananda*.

Scholars in the final group focus on the *Saundarananda*'s place as the earliest example (along with the *Buddhacarita*) of the *mahākāvya* form of Sanskrit poetry. Bohn (1973) bravely essays an analysis of the poem using the categories of the

Sanskrit poetic theorists. Thus he devotes separate chapters to examples of various figures of speech that occur in the poem, including similes, metaphors, and embellishments of sound such as alliteration and rhyme. He also considers how Aśvaghoṣa communicates the dominant flavour (*rasa*) of peace (*śānta*), and the secondary flavours of love (*śṛṅgāra*) and heroism (*vīra*). Bohn (1973:143) feels that Aśvaghoṣa's "careful and skillful use of different figures of speech such as the *utprekṣā* shows him to be a man who was as interested in composing a poem as in preaching." Warder (1974:142-81) too hunts the *kāvya* elements in the poem, noting that the plot development, topics and stylistic devices of the *Saundarananda* approximate the dictates laid down in the various treatises on poetics. Warder, however, is noticeably more open to the Buddhist elements of the poem, and for him the exposition of the Four Noble Truths in Canto 16 is the climax of the poem. Gurner (1927) detects in Aśvaghoṣa's poetry the influence of epic, particularly the *Rāmāyaṇa*. Bhattacharya (1976), though considering Aśvaghoṣa's philosophical position and school affiliation, values Aśvaghoṣa's poetry above all, coming "to the irresistible conclusion that he was more a *kavi* than a philosopher. In other words, Aśvaghoṣa's contribution to Buddhism in the role of a philosopher pales into insignificance beside his legacy to the Classical Sanskrit literature in the part of a poet" (Bhattacharya 1976:249). Lienhard (1984:165-9), for whom the most interesting thing about the *Saundarananda* is its place in the transitional period between epic and fullblown *kāvya*, almost entirely ignores the Buddhist sections of the poem. Thus Lienhard singles out for mention some features typical of *kāvya*, such as ornate descriptive passages, similes that have lotuses or creepers as their objects of comparison, the artful use of the aorist in Canto 2, and the impressive number of metres. Canto 6 receives particular praise: "Aśvaghoṣa's poetry reaches its height in, for instance, the sixth canto of the *Saundarananda*, which describes Sundarī's despair" (Lienhard 1984:169).

One notes from the above a divergence in critical focus, evident even from the range of the *Saundarananda*'s verses selected for quotation by the various scholars. Those who see the poem as a Buddhist tract quote mainly from the second half of the poem, while those for whom the poem's importance lies in its belletristic aspects are wont to quote primarily from the first half. So pervasive is this tendency that one cannot avoid the impression, in reading these evaluations of the *Saundarananda*, that one is dealing with a poem of two disparate halves somewhat unsuccessfully fused together. However, splitting off parts of the *Saundarananda* and studying those parts independently results in a false impression of inorganic heterogeneity. The *Saundarananda* is a remarkably focused work, and has but one central theme. All the features of the poem - the plot, setting, characterisation, narrative flow and imagery - are marshalled in support of this theme and remain subservient to it. There are no sub-plots. The poem's central theme, as I see it, is a movement towards a condition of spiritual perfection, and away from an inferior condition of worldliness. This drama of spiritual reorientation, or conversion, is centred in the character of Nanda. Doubtless Aśvaghoṣa hoped that his reader or auditor, having imaginatively participated in Nanda's deepening commitment to the Buddhist goal of liberation, would be inspired to go and do likewise in actuality. It is evident from the last two verses of the poem, in which Aśvaghoṣa speaks of slipping his audience a pill of liberation coated with the honey of poetry,[8] that he had no wish merely to entertain his hearers, but to change their lives. Hence much is at stake, and Aśvaghoṣa uses all his skill as a poet to bear on his central theme of conversion.

This book is a study of the metaphors that convey the *Saundarananda*'s theme of spiritual change. These metaphors, or better, root metaphors, are miniature versions of the conversion story. They illustrate the conversion process by plotting movement from one spiritual and psychological condition to another. In doing so they provide useful navigational aids. The individual offshoots of the *Saundarananda*'s root metaphors criss-cross the text, functioning

[8] *Saundarananda* 18:63-4. Hereafter all verses cited without reference to a specific work are from the *Saundarananda*.

as connectives between the two apparently disparate 'halves' of the poem. Thus the metaphors help to structure the poem and to organise it into a coherent whole. Furthermore, they concretise and enliven a largely invisible and potentially dull topic, the process of conversion. The root metaphors reflect the main theme; for instance, from the concept of a journey Aśvaghoṣa develops a metaphor for spiritual evolution as a journey undertaken by Nanda as the traveller, while he uses the sphere of medicine to depict Nanda's spiritual progress as a gradual recovery from illness. These are of course well-known Buddhist metaphors, but Aśvaghoṣa also uses others which are less familiar; the training of elephants, for example, or the refining of gold. In each case an entity regarded as deficient (a wild elephant, unrefined gold) evolves into something altogether finer and more valuable (a fully-trained war elephant, refined gold).

Additionally, many of the root metaphors illustrate not a spontaneous or self-initiated conversion, but one that depends for its momentum and successful conclusion on an outside source. The *Saundarananda* portrays Nanda's evolution from libertine to liberated man as dependent on the assistance and direction of an external agent of change – the Buddha. Aśvaghoṣa gives us a hero who is brought to liberation by the Buddha because he would have been unable to attain it on his own. With regard to the ultimate goal of attaining liberation, Nanda's dependency on the Buddha's agency is evident, particularly in the first eleven cantos of the poem, though the remaining seven cantos depict a Nanda increasingly able to direct his own spiritual progress. The root metaphors that Aśvaghoṣa chooses to incorporate into the poem reflect this tri-nodal structure of the **agent** (the Buddha) causing the **progress** of the passive **object** (Nanda). So in the metaphor of a journey, the Buddha appears as a guide who indicates the direction of travel, while in the medical metaphor he is cast as the physician who heals the sick. It is noteworthy how frequently the poem's figurative language casts the Buddha in the role of helper and advisor to Nanda, as though to offset any negative impression that Nanda's forced ordination may have on the reader. Thus the theme of conversion includes an insight into both the internal psychological experience of conversion from Nanda's point of view, and into the external instigation and manipulation of the experience. This book will show how the *Saundarananda*'s metaphors support both aspects of its conversion theme.

In setting about this task my strategy has been straightforward. I initially read and translated the *Saundarananda*, taking as my text Johnston's critical edition published in 1928 by the Oxford University Press. All translations from the poem presented in this book are my own, as are those from other works unless otherwise stated. I then noted all the *Saundarananda*'s similes and metaphors, looking out in particular for clusters or patterns of imagery. I subsequently categorised this material and drew up charts demonstrating which root metaphors are used to illustrate the central theme of the poem. I then selected for further study those root metaphors which featured most prominently and which held the greatest interest for me. The richness of Aśvaghoṣa's metaphorical thinking meant that some selection had to be made, a process which was inevitably subjective. Secondly, I proceeded to investigate these selected root metaphors more fully by turning to other literature. In many cases the Pali Canon offered stimulating parallels, while Sanskrit technical literature provided the necessary facts and much useful background information. Thus I consulted a work on elephantology when researching metaphors of elephant training, and Āyurvedic treatises when researching ancient Indian medicine. Armed with the knowledge thus gathered, my final step was to interpret the similes and metaphors created by Aśvaghoṣa, and to apply this interpretation also to the target of the similes and metaphors. My assumption throughout has been that the more thoroughly one understands the area of human activity or thought from which Aśvaghoṣa derives his imagery, the better one understands the target area for which they function as conceptual models. Thus a bald metaphorical statement such as "The Buddha is a doctor" may reveal little, but in reading Āyurvedic treatises or the Pali accounts of the famous doctor Jīvaka one builds up a comprehensive idea of what the ancient Indians would have understood by such an equation.

1.1 Western Theories of Metaphor

Establish a terminology to suit my purposes has been less straighforward. Both India and the West have long and venerable traditions of literary criticism. Aristotle discusses metaphor in chapters 21 and 22 of his *Poetics*, starting with his definition that "Metaphor is the transference of a term from one thing to another: whether from genus to species, species to genus, species to species, or by analogy." Aristotle is certain that metaphor, along with expressions such as compounds and foreign terms, is non-standard language. For Aristotle, clarity is the fundamental requirement of good poetry, but while ordinary unembellished language has the most clarity, poetry must be garnished with non-standard language in order to add a certain grandeur and to avoid banality. Too much metaphor, on the other hand, makes for incomprehensibility; the poem will read like a riddle.[9] Aristotle's conception of metaphor as something of an obstruction to lucidity arises from a dichotomy of style and meaning, or form and content, a dichotomy that has prevailed over many centuries and which has been challenged only in relatively recent times. Thus Aristotle's thought marks the start of a long debate over whether metaphors are merely ornamental, serving to heighten the pleasure of reading poetry, or whether they serve a cognitive function by helping the reader to understand difficult abstract concepts. A second contentious issue is whether a metaphor can be restated in literal language, or whether it remains essentially untranslatable.

Such questions, and in particular the question of whether metaphor deviates from truth or conveys truth, have been particularly important in religious discourse, though they have aroused considerably more debate amongst Christian theologians than amongst Buddhist scholars. Those with an interest in theological aesthetics have long disputed whether a reader's understanding of a text can ever be truly objective, whether the author's intention can ever be truly known, and the extent to which metaphor is a valid means of speaking of God. Such disputes have taken place within the framework of a wider

---

[9] Halliwell (1987:55-7). For Aristotle's definition of metaphor see p. 55.

concern with the correct interpretation of Biblical texts. Many have concluded that metaphors, and indeed all other modes of expression, are inherently inadequate to convey religious truths. Samuel Johnson was particularly suspicious of the use of metaphor in prayer and worship, declaring that he did "not approve of figurative expressions in addressing the Supreme Being" (Boswell 1791:1293). Others, like Aquinas, believed that one could speak of God by analogy. In his study of the Bible as literature, the literary critic Northrop Frye (1982:54) observes that "metaphor is not an incidental ornament of Biblical language, but one of its controlling modes of thought." Most Biblical scholars now appear to accept the inevitability of metaphorical language in religious discourse, while acknowledging its inadequacy in conveying divine truth.[10]

The traditional Western view of metaphor, dating from Aristotle and followed by certain thinkers such as Hobbes and Locke, takes metaphor to be a stylistic decoration of language and an obstacle to understanding. Metaphor, in this traditional view, is considered one of those figures of speech called tropes because it deviates from the meaning of words. Instead of using the proper name for something, the writer chooses to use a different name. According to the traditional view, all one has to do to understand the metaphor is to restore the original term. Underlying the traditional view, then, is the assumption that metaphors exist at the level of the individual word. Those who shared the traditional view that metaphor is simply a device to make poetry more attractive were often preoccupied with how one might distinguish a metaphor from other non-literary figures such as metonymy and synecdoche, and how different types of metaphor could be distinguished form each other by their subject matter. They were also concerned about the aesthetic value of the metaphor, judging whether it is strained, mixed or inappropriate.

I. A. Richards initiated a move away from the position of traditional rhetoric when he noted, in his *Philosophy of Rhetoric*

[10] For general discussions of the interplay between Christian theology and literary criticism, see Soskice (1985) and Jasper (1989).

(1936), that a word alone cannot be metaphorical. Frustrated by the lack of technical terms to analyse metaphor, he devised the terms 'tenor' to denote the original topic under discussion and 'vehicle' to denote the new topic, while the 'ground' refers to their common characteristics. Richards holds that metaphor proceeds from a tension between tenor and vehicle. Other 20th century thinkers, such as Max Black and Monroe Beardsley, also challenge the traditional view of metaphor as the substitution of one word for another. Paul Ricoeur (Valdes 1991), a philosopher who turned his attention to the theoretical problems of literary criticism, follows Richards in recognising the sentence as the primary unit of meaning. He broadens the debate by arguing that not only do metaphors have emotive value, but they also create new meaning. Ricoeur and others have posited the primacy of metaphor as a cognitive tool, an aid to understanding. In general, the 20th century has seen a shift in emphasis away from the aesthetic aspects of metaphor, and towards its cognitive role.[11].

In the last few decades, the study of metaphor has increasingly taken place within the contexts of disciplines other than the traditional one of literature. For instance, psychologists have noticed that metaphor acts as a common linguistic currency, fostering intimacy between people in much the same way as technical jargon, slang and jokes. Susan Sontag (1988) has written about the invocation of war metaphors in discussions of illnesses such as cancer and AIDS. Rohrer (1995) is one of several researchers to investigate the metaphors used by politicians to conceptualise the political situation and sway public opinion in the first Gulf War. Environmentalists[12] have developed a number of influential metaphors that have had a powerful impact on the popular imagination. Thus research in the last quarter-century has focused not only on how metaphor

[11] The growing interest in the cognitive content of metaphor is charted by Cooper (1986:1-44).

[12] For example, Hardin (1974) uses the metaphor of the earth as a lifeboat to emphasise the fragility and limited resources of the environment.

can aid understanding, but also on how it can distort understanding and manipulate its recipient.

In this book I have not adopted the traditional approach of Western rhetorics towards metaphor. It has long been realised that metaphor is rarely as simple a matter as one word being replaced by another. Instead, a metaphor may well refer to a whole scenario and may even describe a story in miniature. Furthermore, the traditional view that metaphors are deviant, detracting from lucidity rather than increasing it, seems patently untrue with regard to the *Saundarananda*. This is not to say that Aśvaghoṣa leaves his metaphors to do all the work of making sense in his poem. He frequently states his meaning in unadorned language as clearly as possible, and then reinforces his message with a figurative expression.[13] Those challenging the traditional view, such as Richards and Ricoeur, while accepting the cognitive role of metaphor, nevertheless still deal with metaphor largely within the context of creative writing. These later theorists often devote much thought to the question of when a metaphor can be said to be live, dead, novel, established or just an idiom, which are valid concerns when judging the aesthetic worth of a piece of writing, but are not so pressing when the aim is to tease out the thought behind the metaphor. Furthermore, the concentration on metaphor in recent cross-disciplinary studies diverts attention from elements that metaphors have in common with similes, allegories and other forms of non-literal expression.

1.2 Indian Poetics

Sanskrit literary theorists, meanwhile, turned the manufacture of figures of speech into something of a national industry, quite dwarfing the meagre output of the traditonalist poeticians of the West. A proliferation of ever more finely differentiated stylistic devices, or *alaṃkāra*s (ornaments), resulted from their endeavour to provide an exhaustive taxonomy of non-literal expressions. The Sanskrit poeticians hoped

[13] This pattern is particularly noticeable in later cantos in which the Buddha imparts teachings to Nanda. Examples are at 5:17-8, 14:4-5, 15:29, 16:39-40.

thereby to provide objective criteria for measuring aesthetic value. Hence they developed a precise vocabulary for the dissection of any given figure of speech, labelling the constituents of a simile, for instance, the *upameya* (the subject of comparison), the *upamāna* (the object of comparison), the *sadṛśya-dharma* or *sādhāraṇa-dharma* (the shared element) and the *upamā-vācaka* (the word denoting comparison). The earliest surviving document of *alaṃkāra-śāstra* (as the discipline of Sanskrit poetics is generally known) is the *Nāṭya-śāstra* of Bharata. Its date is uncertain. S. K. De (1960:14-17) uses stray references in the *Buddhacarita* to adduce the existence of *alaṃkāra-śāstra* learning at the time of Aśvaghoṣa, and so concludes that this discipline began at around the beginning of the Common Era. He further supposes the core of Bharata's work to date from the last two centuries BCE. Bharata's work concerns itself mainly with drama, but it does mention four figures of speech – *yamaka* (repetition or chime), *rūpaka* (metaphor)[14], *dīpaka* (illuminator) and *upamā* (simile). By the time of the next surviving work on poetics, Bhāmaha's *Kāvyālaṃkāra* (which is almost certainly much earlier than the mid-8th century date assigned to it by De), the number has swelled to nearly forty, a few of which are further classified. He lists two types of *rūpaka*, for example. Daṇḍin, the next prominent name in the field, enumerates 33 figures of speech in his *Kāvyādarśa*, many of them further sub-divided into very precise types. Thus he differentiates some thirty or so different kinds of *upamā* alone.[15] Both Bhāmaha and Daṇḍin spend much effort in defining and exemplifying figures of speech.

The close scrutiny and definition of *alaṃkāra*s is the main preoccupation of Indian poetics. Another powerful current running through Indian poetics is the theory of aestheticised emotion or 'flavour' (*rasa*). *Rasa* theory has its roots in the

[14] 'Metaphor' has become the common translation for *rūpaka*, though a *rūpaka* is actually a simile lacking a word indicative of comparison (excluding compound-based similes).

[15] Bhāmaha discusses *rūpaka* at *Kāvyālaṃkāra* 2:21-24. Daṇḍin lists his *alaṃkāras* at *Kāvyādarśa* 2:4-7 and discusses *upamā* at 2:14-50.

Nāṭya-śāstra. The *Nāṭya-śāstra* concerns itself with the technical demands of theatrical presentations, hence the eight *rasas* that Bharata identifies - the erotic (*śṛṅgāra*), the comic (*hāsya*), the tragic (*karuṇa*), the cruel (*raudra*), the heroic (*vīra*), the fearsome (*bhayānaka*), the gruesome (*bībhatsa*) and the wondrous (*adbhuta*) – are envisaged as an indication of a play's emotional effect on the spectator. Bharata discusses what factors, such as the setting and the season, stimulate an emotional response in the spectator, how an actor can portray emotion through tears, shuddering and the like, and the 33 transient emotional states that an actor might portray. Such factors all serve to trigger the experience of *rasa* in the audience. The experience of *rasa*, or generalised emotion, is considered a pleasurable experience, even when it is triggered by the enactment of frightening or sad events. The *rasa* concept remained relatively undeveloped until the Kashmiri critic Ānandavardhana drew attention to the significance of *rasa* for poetry. Ānandavardhana held that *rasa* could be experienced through the medium of poetry as well as drama. However, *rasa* cannot be engendered simply through the use of words that directly express emotional states. Indeed, *rasa* can only arise by suggestion (*dhvani*). Ānandavardhana and his commentator Abhinavagupta attribute to language a third semantic power, that of suggestion, which operates in poetry over and above the primary semantic power of denotation and the secondary semantic power of indication. *Dhvani* is that suggestive power of language that brings out a certain nuance, resonance or meaning that is not found in dictionary definitions. Furthermore, Abhinavagupta gives great prominence to a ninth *rasa*, peace (*śānta*), which had been added to Bharata's original list of eight *rasas* by Udbhaṭa in approximately the 8th century. For Abhinavagupta, the *śānta rasa* takes on a transcendental dimension, functioning as revelatory experience which is equated with the acquisition of insight and the experience of spiritual bliss. Thus Abhinavagupta incorporates into *rasa* theory the possibility of liberating knowledge. Indian poetics reached a high point with the *rasa* / *dhvani* theory put forward by Ānandavardhana and Abhinavagupta. Later theorists tended more to systematisation and co-ordination than to innovation. Underlying all such later elucidations was the unquestioned belief that the experience of refined, heightened, aestheticised emotions was a delightful one, and that the good poet should strive to evoke these experiences in his listeners.

The *Saundarananda* is a rewarding text for anyone seeking either a display of *alaṃkāra*s or the evocation of *rasa*. Rustomji Bohn undertakes such a search in his 1973 thesis for the University of California at Berkeley, entitled *Aśvaghoṣa's Saundarananda: A Poetic Study*. Bohn analyses the poem in terms of the principles of Sanskrit poetic theory outlined above, in the course of which he devotes seven chapters to the various types of *alaṃkāra*s found in the poem, and one long chapter to *rasa*s. Among the stylistic devices he covers are similes (*upamā*) , metaphor (*rūpaka*) , personification (*utprekṣā*), substantiation and example (*arthāntara-nyāsa*) and *dṛṣṭānta*), and the embellishments of sound (*śabdālaṃkāra*). The seven chapters dealing with *alaṃkāra*s consist of a number of quotations from the poem, each of which fulfills Bhāmaha's definition of a particular *alaṃkāra*. These chapters, with their lists of ornaments quoted out of context, illustrate the technical, mechanical and sterile nature of the *alaṃkāra* approach, and give an overall effect of randomness. As a result of this treatment, Bohn blinds himself to the underlying cohesion in the imagery. He comments that though the same objects appear as *upamāna*s again and again, "they are seldom used to make the same point" (Bohn 1973:77). To substantiate his comment, he mentions all the similes that use an elephant as *upamāna* and sees in them no unity or progression, but only variety and difference. I explore these similes in Chapter Three from an entirely different perspective. Bohn's appreciation of the *Saundarananda*'s elephant motif is hampered by the exclusion from his survey of a series of *rūpaka*s based on war elephants, which, since they are not *upamā*s, cannot be allowed to intrude into his *upamā* chapter. Bohn (1973:13) does his subject a disservice when he writes that the *Saundarananda* "should be treated as a poem regardless of the poet's insistence that it is more the message than the poetry which should be studied."

After a discussion of the *Saundarananda*'s stylistic devices, Bohn proceeds with his investigation of its 'flavour' (*rasa*). Here he outlines his proposal that the dominant *rasa* of the *Saundarananda* is *śānta*, with *śṛṅgāra* and *vīra* as subsidiary *rasa*s. Bohn's commitment to his task of detecting stimulants to emotion in the *Saundarananda* leads him to such ludicrous statements as this one: "The playful love scenes between Sundarī and Nanda, Sundarī's tears and Nanda's lamentations when the two are parted, Nanda's austerities, his hymn of praise to the Buddha, and his final mission to help others, are *anubhāva*s. They are the effects which are manifested by different emotions and which are experienced by the characters of the poem" (Bohn 1973:246). The last two of these, which occur after Nanda has attained enlightenment, are surely not *anubhāva*s - the explicit effects of emotion – but the effects of non-emotion. One problem with analysing the *Saundarananda* in terms of *rasa* theory is that Ānandavardhana, and also Abhinavagupta, state that *śānta rasa* should only be presented as the subsidiary *rasa*, and never appear as the principal *rasa*. It is apparent, of course, that the *Saundarananda* does not conform to this stricture.

The above comments are not intended as a criticism of Bohn's work, but are rather meant to indicate the unsuitability of the principles of Sanskrit poetics for a thematic analysis of poetry. The approach of the *alaṃkāra* school in particular, with its focus on the external, stylistic elements of a poem divorced from their context, does not lend itself easily to interpretative literary criticism. The concept of *dhvani*, with its interest in the capacity of language to suggest meaning without expressing it directly, is potentially a much more fruitful point of engagement with Aśvaghoṣa's poetry. However, suggestion, *dhvani*, was always aligned with the cultivation of refined, heightened emotion, *rasa*. It does not seem plausible that Aśvaghoṣa, who tells the tale of a man weaned off emotional stimulation, would have liked to see his work cast as a wholesale effort to stimulate the emotions of his audience. Sanskrit theorists tended to examine poetry by way of a scholarly analysis of its modes of expressions, rarely taking the content into account. For neither the *alaṃkāra* nor the *rasa / dhvani* school is form held to develop out of content.

Sanskrit critics were preoccupied with how one could determine the worth of poetry. Controversies raged amongst poeticians over many centuries in an attempt to establish the criterion of good poetry and the nature of aesthetic delight. Hence some might judge poetry by its grammatical correctness, others might relate the appeal of poetry to its decorative language, while the *dhvani* theorists would rank *rasa* evocation as the highest goal of poetic endeavour. For Aśvaghoṣa, however, these are all secondary considerations. Instead, he subordinates poetry to his message, pressing it into the service of the Buddhist goal of liberation. He makes of the *kāvya* form a bribe, a sweetener on which his audience can feast while simultaneously digesting less palatable Buddhist teachings. There is no doubt whatsoever that this was Aśvaghoṣa's conscious intention, since it is clearly stated in the last two verses of the poem. "Holding liberation to be supreme", says Aśvaghoṣa, "I have here described the truth in the guise of poetry." (*kāvya-vyājena tattvaṃ kathitam iha mayā mokṣaḥ param iti*, 18:64b). Aesthetic delight is not Aśvaghoṣa's highest aim, and what is more, he also divorces such delight from the Buddhist aim of tranquillity. When he states that "this composition on the subject of liberation is for calming [the reader], not for his pleasure" (*ity eṣā vyupaśāntaye na rataye mokṣārtha-garbhā kṛtiḥ*, 18:63a), Aśvaghoṣa draws a clear distinction between tranquillity (*vyupaśānti*) and pleasure (*rati*). They are not the same thing, whatever the *rasa* theorists might later argue.

1.3 George Lakoff and Conceptual Metaphors

It seems that both Indian and traditional Western literary criticism, while offering a vocabulary suitable for analysing one isolated linguistic expression, struggle to provide a useful critical apparatus for the consideration of a group of thematically linked linguistic expressions. In general, the traditional approaches are geared towards the analysis of figures of speech rather than towards their synthesis. Where a poem's figures of speech are grouped together, as is done by Bohn, they are drawn together on the basis of a shared style rather than on the basis of shared content. Yet in reading the *Saundarananda*, it is soon apparent that many metaphors and similes have so similar a content that they reflect and magnify each other. For example, one characteristic of the poem is a simile-metaphor overlap, in which the metaphor reinforces or clarifies the meaning of the simile, and vice versa. The following verse, with the metaphor given in bold type and the simile in italics, is an example:[16]

> *yathauṣadhair hasta-gataiḥ savidyo*
> *na daśyate kaścana pannagena* |
> tathānapekṣo jita-loka-moho
> **na daśyate śoka-bhujaṃgamena** || (5:31)

> *Just as a snake never bites the wise man who holds herbs in his hand*, so **the serpent of grief does not bite** the man of no preferences who has conquered his delusions about the world.

This verse is based on a Buddhist principle and illustrated by both a metaphor and a simile. The principle at the heart of the verse might be more plainly rendered as "a detached undeluded man does not experience grief". The metaphor dramatises this underlying idea by visualising grief as a snake that bites, enabling the reader to imagine more keenly the shock of pain. The representation of grief as a snake is a conventional one, stemming from the sighing noise made by the snake, hence the metaphor alone (that is, the second line of the verse) would have been sufficient for the audience to arrive at the underlying principle. The simile likens a person not experiencing grief to a wise man holding herbs in his hand, a recognised protection against snakebite that would have been familiar to Aśvaghoṣa's audience. Again, the simile on its own, without the metaphor, would yield the desired meaning: "Just as the wise man who

[16] Verses 5:42, 9:32, 10:52, 11:59, 13:50, 14:16-7, 14:30, 17:45 and 18:9 are other examples.

holds herbs in his hand is never bitten by a snake, likewise the detached undeluded man does not experience grief". The simile emphasises the protection afforded by non-delusion by aligning it with the protective handful of herbs. This additional perspective would remain opaque if the metaphor were considered on its own. Broadly speaking, the metaphor focuses on the pain of grief/snakebite, while the simile focuses on its prevention. The application of both the simile and the metaphor to the basic statement gives it not only additional power and intensity, but also greater clarity. In such cases it seems inappropriate to consider the simile and metaphor separately, simply because they differ formally, when what is most striking is their shared element and the way each of the two figurative expressions enlarges the vision evoked by the other.

The theoretical framework which I have finally adopted is that propounded by George Lakoff, who works within the field of cognitive linguistics.[17] Lakoff's argument is that human reasoning is not abstract, as has been traditionally thought, but derives directly from our day-to-day experience. Our own bodily experience, observation of everyday occurrences and knowledge of cultural models provide the tools whereby we structure our abstract, philosophical thought. The mental leap that we make from saying things about the physical realm to saying things about an abstract concept is via metaphor. Lakoff claims that all of us, even the most illiterate, actually reason about abstract concepts in metaphorical terms, in an automatic and unconscious way. In cognitive linguistics, metaphor is the mechanism whereby something is understood and experienced - rather than just talked about, as in traditional Western rhetorics - in terms of something else. Metaphor is a way of thinking, not just a way of talking. As a result of this insight, Lakoff (1989:50) distinguishes two uses of the term "metaphor", firstly as a particular linguistic expression, secondly as the concept

[17] For a full discussion of Lakoff's thought, see Lakoff and Johnson (1980), and Lakoff and Turner (1989). Lakoff's most recent work (Lakoff and Johnson 1999) claims that the various views of Western philosophers about what constitutes a human being are overturned by the discovery that all thought is embodied, and reason largely metaphorical and imaginative.

underlying such an expression. Where I use the word in this second sense, I will generally speak of a 'conceptual metaphor' or 'root metaphor', or use a qualifier ('the medical metaphor'). I will retain the word "metaphor" to speak of a particular instance of a root metaphor. Conceptual metaphors are basic and easily understood in a particular society, with the most successful conceptual metaphors appearing frequently and unconsciously in everyday speech and equally frequently but rather less unconsciously in literary speech. There is a great advantage in noticing the difference between a metaphor and a conceptual metaphor, and noticing furthermore the dependency of the former on the latter, since it permits the recognition that the same conceptual metaphor may underlie many metaphors and indeed similes. Thus the idea of the conceptual metaphor has allowed me to group together a number of *rūpaka*s and *upamā*s and consider them thematically, even where these *rūpaka*s and *upamā*s appear in entirely different portions of the text. In so doing I hope to overcome the limitations of both the Indian and Western theoretical approaches, with their tendency to reflect on individual isolated linguistic expressions.

Lakoff also uses the term 'source domain' to refer to the conceptual area from which a metaphor is drawn, while the 'target domain' is the topic to which the metaphor is applied. The way that we think about the source domain is transferred, via the strategy of metaphor, to the target domain. The source domain, then, is that area of human experience which lends its categories and structure for the conceptualisation of the target domain, the actual topic under consideration. Each metaphor additionally has a set of correspondences between categories in the source domain and those in the target domain, which Lakoff describes as a source-to-target 'mapping'.[18] The notion of source

---

[18] See Lakoff and Turner (1989:4, 61, 63, etc.). Interestingly, the Sanskrit critic Daṇḍin hints at this kind of idea when he defines the quality *samādhi* in *Kāvyādarśa* 1:93: "Where the characteristic of one object is justly applied elsewhere, in compliance with ordinary usage, that is *samādhi*" (*anya-dharmas tato 'nyatra lokasīmānurodhinā | samyag ādhīyate yatra sa samādhiḥ smṛto yathā* ||). I take this to mean that Daṇḍin's *samādhi* is a superimposition of the attributes of one object on another. He gives as an example "the water lilies

and target has allowed me to sidestep the vexed question of the degree of resemblance suggested by a simile and a metaphor. Both simile and metaphor draw material from a source and apply it to a target. Furthermore, a joint consideration of simile and metaphor cannot be so very far removed from the principles of Sanskrit literary theorists, despite their fondness for exhaustive categorisation of minute differences in figures of speech. The terms *upameya*, *upamāna* and *sādhāraṇa-dharma* were applied to the analysis of metaphors (*rūpaka*) and similes (*upamā*) equally, suggesting the implicit recognition that an object of comparison could lend its properties to a subject of comparison to enable the latter to be conceptualised in a different way. This implies that the difference between a simile and metaphor is not so great – in the case of the former, the similarity of subject and object of comparison is explicitly stated by means of a particle of comparison, while in the case of the latter, the same similarity between the subject and object is unstated but is understood from the context.

To illustrate how Lakoff's terms have proved useful for my purposes, I offer the following two figures of speech as examples. The first occurs when Nanda turns to take one last look at his wife before leaving her:

> *kākṣeṇa paśyan na tatarpa nandaḥ*
> *pibann ivaikena jalaṃ kareṇa* (4:41cd)

> In looking [at his wife], Nanda was not satisfied with a glance, like a man drinking water with one hand.

---

close their eyes; the lotuses open their eyes" (*kumudāni nimīlanti kamalāny unmiṣanti ca*), noting that verbs normally pertaining to eyes are applied to flowers. In Lakoff's terms the expression draws on a bodily-based conceptual metaphor, in which the eyes are the source domain, flowers the target domain, and the action of opening and shutting the eyes maps to the opening and closing of the flowers. Daṇḍin says nothing further about *samādhi*, and in any case his rule against offending ordinary usage would limit *samādhi* to certain stock expressions such as the example he gives.

A quick look at his wife is not enough to satisfy Nanda, just as drinking water with one hand is unsatisfactory for a thirsty man.

The source domain here is the everyday experience of drinking water – in this case, with one hand. The target domain is Nanda's sensory experience of his wife – in this case, he is using his eyes to look at her. According to Lakoff, conceptual metaphors are basic and easily understood in a particular society. An attempt should therefore be made to establish a general understanding regarding the source domain for the period under consideration, namely, the first century or so of the Common Era. To properly interpret this example, though, all we need do is recall our own physical experience of thirst and our observation of thirsty people (especially if we can imaginatively project ourselves through time and space to ancient India). We might then come up with the following elaboration of the source domain: in a hot country, especially when clean drinking water is likely to have been in limited supply, thirst would have been a common and unpleasant experience. The extremely thirsty man would be overwhelmed by his thirst. He would direct all his actions to obtaining water, and on finding it, would gulp down large amounts to quickly slake his thirst, preferably with both hands or a vessel of some kind rather than just with one hand. However, the quenching of his thirst is only temporary, and he will soon feel thirsty again. We now turn to apply this interpretation to the target area; we know that with regard to his wife, Nanda is not satisfied with using just his sense of sight. We can further deduce that instead of merely looking at her, he would wish to use his other senses and converse with her, touch her and make love to her in order to alleviate his desire – this would be the equivalent of using both hands or a vessel to drink water. However, the alleviation of his desire would be temporary, and he would soon feel desire again. The poet's delicacy and the conventions of *kāvya* prohibit an explicit description of Nanda's libido, but the simile hints at all that we need to know.

Much later, when Nanda encounters the Apsarases, the beautiful nymphs of heaven, their effect on him is couched in the same terms:

sa jāta-tarṣo 'psarasaḥ pipāsuḥ (10:41a)

His thirst aroused, he desired to drink the Apsarases.

Here the underlying idea, that Nanda's sexual desire is like a thirst that he wants to slake, is exactly the same. The fact that the word *apsaras* derives etymologically from *ap*, water, only enriches the metaphor. This is just one of the many verbal and figurative echoes that associate Nanda's wife with the Apsarases. The two examples are formally distinct, the first being an *upamā* and the second, while not technically a *rūpaka* , is implicitly metaphorical. Both, however, draw on the familiar Buddhist conceptual metaphor of desire as thirst. By importing what we know about thirst to interpret desire, we are led to understand that desire, like thirst, is very unpleasant, drives out all other thoughts, and can be only temporarily assuaged. The examples also illustrate Lakoff's observation that metaphorical structuring is sometimes partial, such that one aspect of a metaphorical relationship is highlighted, while another aspect may be hidden (Lakoff and Johnson 1980:10-13, 52-55). Hence desire is like thirst in that it is an unpleasant, uncontrollable and insatiable urge. However, the conclusion that drinking water is necessary and indeed good for one's health has no counterpart in the target domain.

The above investigation of two different non-literal expressions is typical of the approach that I have adopted. The general principle is that where the *Saundarananda*'s figurative expressions are founded on a shared conceptual area, those figurative expressions will be considered as a group. Secondly, this common conceptual area (that is, the source domain) will be carefully investigated, since when a poet appeals to cultural models and common everyday experience, he has at his disposal a powerful mechanism that allows him to say more about the area under discussion (that is, the target area). Thus the connotations arising from the source material will inevitably have implications for the target material. The target material is often abstract, the source material mostly concrete. Furthermore, not only is knowledge about the source material concrete, common-sensical and widely known, it also predates the reader's exposure to the target material. The reader can therefore use the knowledge that he already has about the source realm to help him visualise and interpret the target realm. This transfer of the source-oriented knowledge and its superimposition on the target area is effected via metaphor. Each reader has an inbuilt and ready-made database of connotations, associations, prejudices and stereotypes that can be accessed by the poet by means of an apt metaphor or simile and brought to bear on the newly-presented topic. Such a mechanism of course gives the skilled poet considerable persuasive power. If the topic presented to the reader is new, the poet can import into a new topic the reader's pre-existing knowledge of a different topic. (This transfer of information would normally occur spontaneously and unconsciously on the part of the reader, but for a reader separated from the poem by time, space and language, the process is harder work.) If the topic is not new to the reader and he already has conceptions about it, metaphor helps to break down and reformulate these conceptions. Paul Ricoeur (Valdes 1991:84) has noted metaphor's "extraordinary power of redescribing reality". Lakoff and Johnson (1980:145) too ascribe to metaphor the capacity to create reality:

> Many of our activities (arguing, solving problems, budgeting time, etc.) are metaphorical in nature. The metaphorical concepts used to characterise those activities structure our present reality. New metaphors have the power to create a new reality. This can begin to happen when we start to comprehend our experience in terms of a metaphor, and it becomes a deeper reality when we begin to act in terms of it … Much of cultural change arises from the introduction of new metaphorical concepts and the loss of old ones.

For a religious poet bent on proselytism, the mastery of metaphor would prove of unquestionable benefit.

1.4 Metaphors in Buddhism and Buddhist Studies

Conceptual metaphors seem to me to be intrinsic to any kind of thinking and talking about Buddhism. At the same time they are so deeply ingrained in the tradition as to be barely noticeable. Thus the life-changing experience of the Buddha is conceptualised as an awakening or a liberation, adhering to Buddhist teachings as following the path, desire as thirst, and so on. Apart from these fundamental conceptual metaphors, more poetic metaphors and similes have also played an important role in the Buddhist tradition, though on occasion figurative writing has been condemned.[19] Overwhelmingly, though, the texts approve figurative language. Time and again the Buddha of the Pali Canon resorts to metaphors, similes, and analogies of great diversity, in many cases also providing full explanations of his figurative language. He readily acknowledges both the persuasive power of figurative language and its usefulness in illustrating a hard-to-grasp truth. Some of his examples are justly famous, such as the *Māluṅkyaputta Sutta* (MN i.429-430), in which a man who refuses to live as a monk until the Buddha answers ten questions is likened to a man who refuses to have a poisoned arrow extracted from his flesh until he finds out the name, clan and caste of the archer, what the arrow is made of, what bird provided the feathers for the arrow shaft, and so on. In fact, the Pali *sutta*s are so replete with metaphor that later Theravāda *Abhidhamma* scholars deemed the entire early *Sutta Pitaka* material figurative (*pariyāya*, 'a way round').[20] Later

---

[19] See for instance AN iii.107 and SN ii.267, where the Buddha's *suttanta*s are opposed to those which are "created by poets, mere poetry, showy in vowels and consonants, heretical, spoken by disciples" (*kavikatā kāveyyā cittakkharā cittavyañjanā bāhirakā sāvakabhāsitā*). DN i.11 lists poetry as a forbidden occupation. *Aṣṭa-sāhasrikā-prajñā-pāramitā* 328 warns that Māra may try to persuade a bodhisattva that what he has heard is not the word of the Buddha, but the work of poets.

[20] Gombrich (1996:65) and Hamilton (2000:203) both make this point. Underlying the term is a spatial metaphor of literal language as 'straight' and

Buddhist texts are equally rich in figurative language, one particularly well-known example being the parable of the burning house from the *Lotus Sūtra*. On occasion, similes seem to occur spontaneously with no intended target domain, and are even credited with triggering understanding on the part of the person to whom the figure occurs. An interesting passage in the *Mahāvastu* has the Buddha-to-be, having abandoned his erstwhile teachers Ārāḍa Kālāma and Uḍraka Rāmaputra, report this experience:

> While I stayed on Mount Gayāśīrṣa there were revealed to me three similitudes [*tisro upamā pratibhāyensuḥ*], which I had not heard of in former lives, which, indeed, had never been heard of, which were unknown to me, and were, indeed, unknown before.[21]

The three similes concern a man who wishes to light a fire (*jyoti-arthiko*). In the first simile he uses damp wood and stands in water; in the second he uses damp wood, but stands on dry ground. In the third simile, he uses dry wood, stands on dry ground, and is successful in lighting a fire. The bodhisattva, concluding that the similes describe a man desiring insight, with firstly neither his body nor mind withdrawn from sensual pleasures, secondly his body but not his mind withdrawn, and thirdly with both withdrawn, determines to pursue the course of action illustrated by the third simile. It is apparent that the spontaneously occurring similes reveal an underlying process of abstract thought; furthermore, the impact of similes is evident from their portrayal as the motive for the bodhisattva's subsequent actions.

The Buddha testifies to the converting power of figurative language in the *Danta-bhūmi Sutta*. Prince Jayasena asks the novice Aggivessana to teach the Dhamma to him, but goes away unpersuaded by what he hears. The novice subsequently laments

---

figurative language as circuitous - the *alaṃkārika*s likewise describe non-literal language as 'crooked speech' (*vakrokti*).

[21] Mvu 121, trans. Jones (1952:117).

his inability to explain the Dhamma convincingly. The Buddha responds by composing two analogies, and then says:

> Aggivessana, if these two similes had occurred [*imā dve upamā paṭibhāyeyyuṃ*] to you with reference to Prince Jayasena, he would have spontaneously acquired confidence in you, and being confident, would have shown his confidence in you.[22]

Aggivessana may have had a good understanding of doctrine, but he lacked the ability to convey it in metaphorical terms, and so lost the chance to make a convert. It is clear that the Buddha credits figurative speech with a great deal of persuasive and explanatory power.

The field of Buddhist Studies appears largely to have neglected Buddhist 'literariness' in favour of a concentration on doctrinal and philosophical matters. There are exceptions, of course, a particularly honorable one being Joel Tatelman's (2000) study of the *Pūrṇāvadāna*, which does an excellent job of proving that literary analysis is a valid approach to Buddhist narrative texts.[23] In the main, though, neither the figurative language nor the conceptual metaphors of Buddhism have received much scholarly attention. An initial effort in this direction was made when C. Rhys Davids (1906-7:52-151) compiled a list of Pali similes nearly one hundred years ago, but though Rhys Davids's work covers just the *Sutta Piṭaka*, and is accompanied by only a rudimentary analysis of her data, it has never, to my knowledge, been updated or expanded. Steve Collins (1982:165-76) was the first scholar to undertake a more detailed exploration of imagery patterns in the Pali Canon, as part of his investigation into the conceptualisation of the human being in early Buddhism. Thus he notes that the house is a consistent metaphor for the person, with the result that the image

---

[22] MN iii.131, trans. Ñāṇamoḷi and Bodhi (1995:991).

[23] In his Introduction, Tatelman (2000:2) states his intention to study the story of Pūrṇa "as a work of literary art, not unlike a literary critic might study a novel by Conrad or Woolf."

of 'leaving home for homelessness' takes on a wider soteriological significance. Collins (1982:166) argues that Buddhist imagery plays a unifying role: "patterns of imagery give us access to fundamental and unconscious structures of the imagination in Buddhist culture; and … these structures unite all Buddhists, from the meditators and scholastics to the ordinary peasant, into one cultural world."[24]

Richard Gombrich has frequently written of the puns and metaphors used by the Buddha in debates with his opponents. He notes (1996) that while the Buddha at first adopts the language and definitions of these adversaries, he gradually moves to an allegorical reinterpretation of their language and a redefinition of their terms in order to win them over. Similarly, Gombrich has pointed out that the Buddha pokes fun at brahminical values through the non-literal language of jokes and satire. As well as noting the primacy of the purification metaphor in Buddhism, Gombrich has also drawn attention to the metaphorical reinterpretation of brahminism's three ritual fires as Buddhism's three fires of desire, hate and ignorance. Gombrich (1991) has also discovered in the name of the *pātimokkha* ceremony a medical metaphor for the purging of faults. Sue Hamilton (2000) too makes considerable mention of Buddhist metaphors, exploring, for example, the metaphorical significance of the Māra figure, whom she takes to be representative of negative states of mind as well as death. She notes some common and consistently used metaphors of early Buddhism, in particular how the world (*loka*) often signifies the life of an individual, rather than the universe as a whole. Hamilton also considers how cognitive functioning is perceived as a stream, and she builds on Collins's work on house imagery.

Cooper's (2002) creative exploration of emptiness *(śūnyatā)* is a rare example of an author attempting to come to grips with a decidedly Buddhist concept through a systematic consideration

---

[24] Collins also interprets vegetation imagery (1982:218-24) and river imagery (1982:247-61). Collins's more recent work includes a consideration of the Pali conceptualisation of *nirvāṇa* as the quenching of a fire (1998:216-221), and as a city (1998:224-229).

of metaphor. In doing so Cooper puts on a literary rather than a philosophical hat, allowing his own free associations with the word 'emptiness' to suggest various interpretations of the term. David McMahan (2002) has also explored the concept of emptiness, but from a position firmly within the tradition. He is the only scholar, to my knowledge, to import findings from cognitive linguistics into the field of Buddhist Studies, finding in Mahāyāna Buddhism's dominant visual metaphor an excellent example of Lakoff's notion of a conceptual metaphor that is basic to a particular culture. McMahan's work is a comprehensive investigation of sight as a metaphor for wisdom and insight. Since he believes that a culture's dominant metaphors are realized in objects, myths, symbols and other cultural products, McMahan further argues that the visual metaphor finds expression in the visionary literature and visualisation practices of Mahāyāna Buddhism, and even in the eyes painted on the Swayambhunath stūpa in Kathmandu. McMahan (2002:62) is certain that anyone wishing to understand a society "should benefit from the study of the prevalent metaphors of that cultural world".

Happily, work of the type described above seems to have gathered momentum in the last decade or so, a trend that I hope will continue and to which I hope this book will contribute. The book consists of an exploration of the *Saundarananda*'s key conceptual metaphors. Some of them are drawn from the cultural experience of Aśvaghoṣa's contemporaries – Chapters Three, Four and Five are devoted to conceptual metaphors deriving from fields of elephant management, medical practice and gold production respectively. Also included are two chapters that examine conceptual metaphors drawn from basic bodily experience. Metaphorical expressions based on bodily experience tend to be less visible than metaphors based on cultural models, requiring a close reading to locate them in the text. The spatial concepts of up and down are tackled in Chapter Six, while movement from source to destination is covered in Chapter Seven in a consideration of the path metaphor. Before a full encounter with metaphor, however, Chapter Two prepares the ground by providing an overview of the poem's storyline, and by relating the *Saundarananda* to other versions of the legend. These preliminary remarks will set the scene for the ensuing five chapters on metaphor. The final chapter summarises my findings and offers some concluding thoughts.

CHAPTER TWO

SOURCES AND STORIES

The purpose of this chapter is twofold: firstly, it functions as a necessary prelude to the following chapters by providing a canto-by-canto overview of the poem's storyline. As well as relating the plot of the *Saundarananda*, the summary below draws attention to several key metaphors and principal motifs, points out some of Aśvaghoṣa's poetic techniques, and highlights the emergence and resolution of certain important issues. Secondly, this chapter explores Aśvaghoṣa's creative engagement with the traditional Nanda fable by contrasting the *Saundarananda* with other versions of the Nanda story. The tale of the lovelorn Nanda, a reluctant recruit to the Buddha's order, was well-known to the Buddhist tradition and appears several times in Buddhist literature. Existing scholarly writing on the *Saundarananda* has largely failed to take any notice of different versions of the story, beyond simply citing sources.[1] However, while Aśvaghoṣa invented neither the characters nor the plot of the *Saundarananda* and is clearly indebted to traditional material, his version is no mere repetition. Instead he moulds the story, highlighting some episodes, inserting others, and leaving out certain features entirely. Such variations often support and magnify the poem's central theme of conversion.

2.1 The Story of the *Saundarananda*

Canto 1: Description of Kapilavāstu

(*kapilavāstu-varṇana*, 61 verses)

The poem's opening canto at first glance appears to have little to do with its later preoccupations. We start far back in the mythological past with a description of the sage Kapila, his disciples and his ashram (1:1-17). Aśvaghoṣa is at pains to establish an appropriate spiritual ancestry for his heroes, providing a vision of the renunciant, ascetic strain of brahminism

---

[1] Shastri (1939:xx) mentions a few of the most obvious differences between the *Saundarananda* and the Pali sources.

as a backdrop for the story that he is about to unfold. Thus the sage Kapila is rigorously ascetic (1:1), encourages his disciples (1:3), and is high-minded, wise and disciplined (1:4-5). The hermitage that he founds on a mountainside (1:5) provides shelter to animals (1:12-3) and is peopled by ascetics disciplined in their performance of ritual (1:11) and austerities (1:16). The mood of religious observance and piety changes at 1:18 when the Ikṣvāku princes arrive and take Kapila as their preceptor (*upādhyāyaḥ*, 1:22). They possess typical *kṣatriya* qualities – they are great-armed and lion-chested, of great splendour and renown (1:19) - and they have come to the forest as a result of dynastic politicking at home:

> *mātṛ-śulkād upagatāṃ te śriyaṃ na viṣehire* |
> *rarakṣuś ca pituḥ satyaṃ yasmāc chiśriyire vanaṃ* ||
> (1:21)
>
> They could not stomach the rank that had come to their [younger half-brother] as his mother's dowry, and observing their father's vow, had retreated to the forest.

Sheldon Pollock (1986:28) submits that Aśvaghoṣa is here alluding to the incident in the *Rāmāyaṇa* in which King Daśaratha's agreement to accept Kaikeyī's offspring as his heir forces his older son Rāma into exile. Pollock is mistaken, however. In the *Rāmāyaṇa* only two brothers, Rāma and Lakṣmaṇa, retire to the forest, while the plural forms in the *Saundarananda* indicate that the Ikṣvāku princes are at least three in number. The real source of the story is *Mahāvastu* 1.348-9, which recounts that King Ikṣvāku had five sons, but had promised his kingdom to a sixth son due to the machinations of the latter's mother. The five sons leave the city in order to honour their father's promise. The *Mahāvastu* also mentions, very briefly, that Kapila donates his hermitage as the site for the future city of Kapilavāstu, signifying his consent by handing over a pitcher of water to the princes (Mvu 1.352). Aśvaghoṣa has an extended version in mind, for he has Kapila fly through the air sprinkling water on the ground from a pitcher while the princes follow in their chariots. The grooves made by their chariot wheels are to be the new city boundaries (1:28-33). There is one subtle but telling difference in Aśvaghoṣa's version: he has Kapila initiate this action, "with the intention of securing their prosperity" (*teṣāṃ vṛddhi-cikīrṣayā*, 1:28), whereas in the *Mahāvastu* the princes approach Kapila and ask his permission to build a city (Mvu 1.351). In the story that it is about to be narrated, the Buddha's actions may seem heavy-handed, so it is important from the outset that a figure of spiritual authority should be seen to have his disciples' welfare as his primary consideration. Indeed, Kapila's act of flying into the air for the benefit of the princes presages the Buddha's similar act on behalf of Nanda in Canto 10.

After Kapila's death (1:34), the princes go astray, indulging in hunting (1:35-36) to such a degree that the ascetics are forced to retreat into the mountains (1:37). In time the princes discover treasure (1:39-40) and build an attractive town full of fine buildings, pleasant gardens and virtuous citizens as per the usual *kāvya* criteria for the description of a city (1:42-58). The eldest of the royal brothers is crowned king (1:61). The canto closes with a simile typical of epic poetry in which the king's guardianship of the city is compared to the rule of Indra in heaven (1:62).

It would be a mistake to dismiss this canto as an accretion of irrelevant Buddhist mythology and *kāvya* convention. Aśvaghoṣa has chosen to place this account of the origins of the Śākyas at the beginning of the *Saundarananda*, not at the beginning of the *Buddhacarita*, where it might seem more appropriate if his purpose were simply to narrate the Buddha's lineage. The account serves a number of purposes. Firstly, it establishes the spiritual credentials of the Buddha's and Nanda's heritage. The zealous asceticism of the brahmin Kapila and the warrior ethos of the *kṣatriya* heroes combine in the making of the Śākyan race. Secondly, the guru-disciple relationship between Kapila and the Ikṣvāku princes to some extent foreshadows the story of the Buddha and Nanda. Both the Buddha and Kapila are great sages seeking to guide and tame the behaviour of their charges, and Nanda bears certain resemblances to the princes. When Kapila dies and his controlling influence is removed, the princes revert to type, like tiger cubs (1:37), and it is emphasized that this is no good thing. When the brothers finally do what Kapila has told them to do, that is, build a city, they grow in wealth and virtue. Furthermore, the catchy anecdote of the sage marking out the city limits concerns boundary-setting. The sage orders the brothers not to overstep (*anatikramya*) the boundary (*dhārā*, 1:29). Later, Nanda too will attempt to live by the disciplinary rules without transgressing them, and he will also discover that when he eventually follows his teacher's advice he will make great progress. Canto 1 therefore provides a fitting introduction to the poem's major theme of transformation, or conversion – the princes are transformed into wise rulers, while nature, within the demarcated area at least, is transformed into a teeming city with fine mansions, highways and public gardens. The remarkably concrete vision of a city springing up in the space laid out by the sage is a vivid demonstration that flourishing best occurs within the prescribed limits set by a wise and authoritative guide.

Canto 2: Description of the King
(*rāja-varṇana*, 65 verses)

In a manner that was to become typical of *kāvya's* introductory scenes, the wide-angle view of the city now shifts to a narrower focus on the figure of King Śuddhodana, who in the course of time has succeeded to the throne of Kapilavāstu (2:1). King Śuddhodana is described in a long passage (2:1-45) that displays a number of intricate verbal and grammatical patterns, most remarkably the sustained use of the various forms of the aorist. The combination of brahmin and *kṣatriya* values that was evident in Canto 1 continues throughout Canto 2, and is especially noticeable in 2:36, where Śuddhodana is said to destroy his enemies with the brahminical virtue of asceticism (*tapas*) and the *kṣatriya* virtue of brilliance (*tejas*) alike. Though Śuddhodana epitomises kingly *kṣatriya* attributes, his spiritual leanings are much in evidence, as is fitting for the father of the future Buddha. Therefore in addition to orthodox behaviour such as offering sacrifices (2:20), generous patronage of brahmins (2:31) and drinking soma (2:44), he also offers a foretaste of dharma, a word that is freely used in this canto. For instance, he turns his subjects to dharma (2:37), thus ensuring a place in heaven for them, and is in every way a model of restraint (2:25, 2:42).

In verses 2:46-56 the portrayal of kingship, an essential ingredient of *kāvya*, is replaced by the traditional Buddhist material of the bodhisattva's descent from the Tuṣita heavens, Queen Māyā's dream of a white elephant, and the birth of bodhisattva (here named Sarvārthasiddha, as in the *Mahāvastu*). Thereafter Nanda makes his first appearance:

> *devyām api yavīyasyām araṇyām iva pāvakaḥ* |
> *nando nāma suto jajñe nityānanda-karaḥ kule* || (2:57)

> As fire-sticks gives rise to fire, so the younger queen too gave birth to a son named Nanda, a bringer of constant joy to his family.

Although it is commonplace to liken a mother giving birth to fire-sticks producing fire, it is noteworthy that Nanda is strongly associated with fire in his very first appearance in the poem. Fire is a prominent Buddhist metaphor for desire, and this verse is an early indication that desire will prove to be Nanda's chief hindrance on his spiritual journey. We learn too that he is handsome, "like the god of love embodied" (*aṅgavān iva cānaṅgaḥ*, 2:59). The next four verses (2:60-3) are the most interesting of the canto, since they draw a contrast between the bodhisattva and his half-brother Nanda. The two are seen as personifications of dharma and pleasure (*kāma*) respectively (2:60), and likewise of dharma and prosperity (*artha*, 2:61). Their differences in temperament become more pronounced as the boys grow up; Sarvārthasiddha remains dispassionate while Nanda idles away his time in pleasures (2:63). The canto ends with a brief account of Sarvārthasiddha's encounter with a sick man, an old man and a corpse, and his departure from his father's court (2:64-5).

Canto 3: Description of the Tathāgata

(*tathāgata-varṇana*, 42 verses)

The bodhisattva's quest for enlightenment is the initial subject of Canto 3. We learn of his temporary discipleship with Ārāḍa and Uḍraka (3:3), his rejection of asceticism (3:5), his awakening (3:7), and his teaching of the Four Noble Truths at Vārāṇasī (3:10-3). The Buddha guides many people to insight, these acts of conversion being indicated by the use of *vi* + √*nī* (3:13, 3:15). Thereafter the Buddha returns to his home city, and displays his supernormal powers (3:21-4) before preaching to the townsfolk (3:36). The rest of the canto describes the effects of the Buddha's presence on the city of Kapilavāstu and its inhabitants; the king (3:37) and many others (3:39) achieve stream-entry, many leave their homes (3:28), and those who remain at home follow the precepts (3:30-3 – the 5th precept is not mentioned), all grow in insight (3:36), and the entire city is free from disease and calamity (3:42). Doubtless the purpose of this section is to contextualise Nanda's conduct in the next canto, for without the foreknowledge that every other citizen of Kapilavāstu has put the Buddha's teaching into practice, we would not find Nanda's absorption in his beautiful wife out of the ordinary. Verse 3:38 sounds an ironic note, since it declares that nobody (*na kaścit*) desires even a happy rebirth, and that everyone (*sarvam*) understands the danger of continued existence. Everyone, that is, except Nanda, who by Canto 10 is planning a rebirth amongst the Apsarases.

Canto 4: His Wife's Request

(*bhāryā-yācitaka*, 46 verses)

The first half of Canto 4 is justly renowned for its charming depiction of the loveplay of Nanda and Sundarī (4:1-23). The couple's close sexual relationship is evident in the dual forms of 4:8 and 4:10, the frequency of words meaning "each other" (*anyonya*, *paraspara*, 4:7, 4:9, 4:10, 4:11), the ready use of singular words meaning "couple" (*dvandva*, *mithuna*, 4:7, 4:8, 4:9, 4:11), and the mention of individual parts of the body – breasts (4:19), lips (4:20), hands (4:13), moustache (4:14), cheeks (4:20), feet (4:17) and so on. Aśvaghoṣa chooses just one small incident to encapsulate the relationship of the pair, but presents it powerfully enough to carry the weight of Nanda's yearning for the next few cantos. The poet has Nanda hold a mirror for Sundarī, while she playfully draws his moustache on her own face. When Nanda blows on the mirror, she feigns anger and smears some makeup on his face. Nanda pretends remorse and throws himself at her feet, and she raises him up, laughing. Nanda then continues to hold the mirror while she completes her makeup (4:13-23). The short but effective mirror episode is Aśvaghoṣa's invention, appearing in no other versions of the Nanda legend. Though brief, it reveals that Nanda is entirely besotted with his wife. These verses contain a number of features typical of *kāvya* portrayal a happy love affair, such as the standard comparison of the lady's eyes to bees (4:4, 4:21) and the lovers playfully feigning various emotions.

A much more serious note is struck when the Buddha appears at Nanda's house for alms but goes away again unnoticed (4:24-5). One serving-woman catches sight of him as he is leaving and informs Nanda (4:28-30). Nanda becomes agitated and asks Sundarī's permission to go and pay his respects to the Buddha (4:32). She reluctantly agrees, but makes him promise to come back before the *viśeṣaka*, the make-up that she has just applied to her face in his presence, is dry (4:34). The *viśeṣaka* is another of Aśvaghoṣa's inventions, and it is the subject of the canto's title. In making her request that her husband return before the cosmetics have dried (with a possible subtext that this is while she is still fertile), Sundarī is trading on her sexuality. She does so again in 4:35, when she threatens to withhold her favour. The remainder of Canto 4 is a masterly depiction of Nanda's painful hesitation as he is torn between his duty of respect to the Buddha and his longing to stay with his wife. The canto ends when Nanda finally turns from his wife and catches sight of the Buddha being honoured by the crowd (4:46), a clear indication of his eventual spiritual destination.

At this relatively early stage Aśvaghoṣa has already begun to prepare for the poem's turning point and key narrative event, the visit to heaven in Canto 10. From a Buddhist perspective, already encountered in Canto 3, any new existence is transient, unsatisfactory and fraught with danger. Hence a life spent consorting with the Apsarases in heaven is not essentially preferable to a life spent with Sundarī in Kapilavāstu. Aśvaghoṣa makes this point several times, in this case by taking care to confer semi-divine status on Nanda and Sundarī. Thus she is like a divinity walking in the garden of delight (*sā devatā nandana-cāriṇīva*, 4:6) as well as like a *kiṃnarī* (4:10), a half-human creature who also figures in Canto 10. Similarly, Nanda's house is likened to a celestial palace (4:24). Sundarī's identification with the Apsarases is further affirmed in Canto 6.

Canto 5: The Ordination of Nanda

(*nanda-pravrājana*, 53 verses)

Canto 5 opens with an image of the Buddha struggling through a stream of people (5:3), recalling the image of Nanda struggling with opposing feelings like a boat in a current (4:44) that ended the foregoing canto. We are reminded of the fundamental Buddhist metaphor of liberation as crossing the stream; the Buddha has crossed the stream, but Nanda remains trapped in it. Canto 5 confronts the potentially controversial matter of Nanda's coerced ordination. The Buddha is shown separating Nanda from the crowd and leading him down a quiet side-road (5:5), rejecting his invitation to take food at his house[2] (5:10), giving Nanda his bowl to hold despite Nanda's decision to go home (5:11), and blocking Nanda's way when Nanda tries to sneak off (5:14). The Buddha leads Nanda to the monastery (5:20) and tells Ānanda to ordain him (5:34). Throughout these events, Nanda has made his disinclination clear, to the point of announcing "I will not become a monk" (*na pravrajiṣyāmy aham*

---

[2] I know of no other occasions in Buddhist literature on which the Buddha rejected a layperson's invitation to a meal, except because of a prior engagment.

ity uvāca, 5:35). The Buddha exhorts him (5:37-49) and although he finally agrees to do as the Buddha wishes (5:50), he weeps as his hair is shaved (5:51).

At no point does Aśvaghoṣa soft-pedal the Buddha's intervention in the life of a reasonably happy person. Sundarī could have been portrayed as flighty or shrewish, but instead she is charming and lovable. The manner in which Nanda was induced to the monastery could have been glossed over; instead we are exposed to a blow-by-blow account of the event. The point is that Buddhist happiness is better and happier than even the happiest of lay lives. Sundarī's delectableness and Nanda's contentment are intended to strengthen rather than to undermine this position. Thus every aspect of everyday life is redefined in terms of a Buddhist life, so that faith provides the greatest riches, wisdom the best flavour, the best work is for dharma and so on (5:24-5). Similarly, the Buddha tells Nanda that were it not for his affections, desires and passions, bliss would be his (5:28). Those things that Nanda believes are making him happy are in fact preventing his true happiness. The Buddha's actions are justified on the grounds that Nanda's life really can be improved; furthermore, Aśvaghoṣa makes it clear that the Buddha goes out of his way to do a favour for Nanda. His action is described as a favour (*anugraha*, 5:11, 5:48), beneficial (*hita*, 5:46, 5:47, 5:48, 5:50), and an effort (*yatna*, 5:18). However, Nanda does not yet appreciate the Buddha's actions on his behalf, and is pictured at the end of the canto in his faded ochre garment. He has lost his radiance, and is likened to the waning moon at dawn (5:53).

Canto 6: The Wife's Lament

(*bhāryā-vilāpa*, 49 verses)

Of the *Saundarananda*'s eighteen cantos, Canto 6 comes closest to a developed *kāvya* style. Its subject is one of *kāvya*'s favourites, disappointed love (*vipralambha-śṛṅgāra*), since the entire canto is devoted to depicting the calamitous effect of Nanda's departure on his wife. Sundarī's distress is sympathetically and delicately drawn in a series of miniature portraits. First she leans out expectantly from the palace roof, her pearls and earrings hanging down (6:2-3), then she collapses on a couch with her pearls in disarray and her shoes half off (6:5). After hearing the rumour that Nanda has been ordained (6:23), her distress reaches a crescendo; she casts off her ornaments (6:28), howls when she sees Nanda's *vīṇā* (6:32) and tears at her face and clothes (6:34). The canto is embellished with a number of lovely similes employing typical *kāvya upamāna*s such as a moon amongst the clouds (6:37) or a lotus (6:11, 6:26). The comparison of Sundarī's pale face to the pale moon at the onset of winter (6:9) echoes a similar comparison made of Nanda at 5:53, and is particularly poignant in its reminder of the bond between the two.

Sundarī's despair is of course antithetical to the Buddhist tranquillity and bliss advocated by Aśvaghoṣa. Her agitated movements as she sinks down (6:5) and then leaps up and runs across the palace roof (6:7) reveal her distraction, as do her restless eyes (*calākṣa*, 6:4). Her haphazard thinking at 6:13-19 as she berates the absent Nanda and the statement that she seems to have lost her mind (*vibhrānta-citteva*) further indicate her confusion. The images of Sundarī burning with longing and anger (*kāmena kopena ca dahyamānā*, 6:10), assailed by the fire of grief (*śokāgninā*, 6:33) and weeping hot tears (*taptāśru*, 6:47), whilst recalling the *kāvya* notion of love as a fire, draw more heavily on the Buddhist conceptual metaphor of suffering as a fire. Their purpose, and that of the whole canto, is to depict the suffering engendered by desire.

The atmosphere changes when one of Sundarī's attendants gives voice to a Buddhist perspective on her mistress's situation. Sundarī should rejoice rather than grieve over Nanda's ordination, and should herself now take vows of chastity (6:39-43). This sober advice has little impact on Sundarī. She much prefers a second opinion that Nanda will soon return as he cannot live without her (6:45-8). The canto ends by comparing Sundarī among her women to Rambhā, an Apsaras who was comforted by other Apsarases when she lost her lover.

Canto 7: Nanda's Lament

(*nanda-vilāpa*, 52 verses)

After describing Sundarī's reaction to her husband's sudden departure in Canto 6, Aśvaghoṣa now reveals Nanda's response to his changed circumstances. He is found wandering round a pleasant grove, but unlike the monk meditating beside a waterfall (7:20), Nanda fails to apply himself. Instead, the reader is informed straightaway, in a simple phrase embellished with *yamaka* (chime) , that Nanda is not happy (*na nananda nandaḥ*, 7:1). In a sequence of lovely verses (7:2-11) the beauty of the trees, flowers and creatures around him serve only to stimulate Nanda's memories of Sundarī. He leans against an *aśoka* tree, and remembers that his wife loved *aśoka*s (7:5). The white *priyaṅgu* blossom reminds him of his wife's pale face (7:6). A creeper wound round a mango tree makes him think of her embraces (7:8). Whatever Nanda sees, however innocent and natural, he subverts to an image of his wife. In the solipsistic manner common to lovers, he interprets his environment as a reflection of his own state of mind. The language of this section is more ornate than is usual for Aśvaghoṣa, and a series of quite complex visual images are developed, for example:

puṣpāvanaddhe tilaka-drumasya
dṛṣṭvānyapuṣṭāṃ śikhare niviṣṭām |
saṃkalpayām āsa śikhāṃ priyāyāḥ
śuklāṃśuke 'ṭṭālam apāśritāyāḥ || (7:7)

> Seeing a cuckoo alighting on the flower-decked top of a *tilaka* tree, he imagined it as a lock of his darling's hair against her white tunic as she leant from the palace.

Despite the lush descriptiveness of the verse, it contains no formal similes or metaphors. Rather, the comparison is drawn by the paratactic construction, which allows Nanda's fanciful notions to be superimposed onto the natural world. Nanda sees the cuckoo, and imagines (*saṃkalpayām āsa*) it as Sundarī's hair. Similarly, he notices the white *priyaṅgu*, and remembers (*sasmāra*, 7:6) her pale face. The forest fails to calm him, since it irritates his overwrought nerves and oversensitised mind. The appearance of several stock attributes, used in *kāvya* to signify an amorous situation, indicate that Nanda remains firmly embedded in his relationship with Sundarī, despite his physical separation from her. Thus it is spring (7:2), the bees are buzzing in the mango-trees (7:3), and the peacocks are calling (7:11).

Though Nanda's distress is the focal point of this canto, there is a hint that his situation is not entirely hopeless. His journey of conversion inches along with his realisation that the practice of renunciation is very difficult indeed (7:13). This first glimmer of insight deepens when he begins to see that he is in bondage (7:14), and at 7:15 he already speaks of "the steely snare of love" (*sneham ayas tu pāśaḥ*). Nanda continues to let his mind wonder, and his thoughts take on an air of defensiveness and self-justification. Very great sages have abandoned self-control for the sake of women, Nanda tells himself, so how could he be expected to hold out (7:24)? The second half of the canto (7:25-45) is devoted to a series of examples illustrative of this proposition, a *kāvya* technique known as *dṛṣṭānta*. The long list of seers tempted by women, drawn from mythology and containing many euphemisms for sex, is perhaps rather tedious for modern taste. However, since these *dṛṣṭānta*s show men in thrall to women, they are an appropriate precursor to Canto 8, in which women are denounced for leading men astray. By 7:47 Nanda has persuaded himself that he ought to go home, since it would be hypocritical to be a mendicant in appearance only. In the last verse of the canto, recognising that his mind is wavering and that his understanding is fuddled, he declares that he will slip away while the Buddha is out on his alms round (7:52).

Throughout Canto 7 Aśvaghoṣa demonstrates great skill in tracing Nanda's unhappiness and sexual frustration to their culmination in his decision to go home, while simultaneously hinting at the tiny gains in his self-knowledge. Canto 7 also contains several clever echoes of Canto 6, with the result that the two separated lovers seem to mirror each other in their reactions. For instance, they both look around and see reminders of the other, they both begin their laments with the same formula (*vilalāpa tat-tat*, 6:12 and 7:12), and the titles of the cantos parallel each other. Nanda remembers Sundarī's eyes swimming with tears (*pāriplavākṣa*, 7:19), which in turn recalls his swimming eyes (*pariplutākṣa*) during his tonsure at 5:51. They both imagine that someone else is in a better position than themselves; Sundarī imagines a woman with superior looks and qualities who has won Nanda's heart; Nanda sees a meditating monk and imagines that he has no lover to trouble his thoughts. These parallels indicate the extent to which Nanda is still taken up with Sundarī; he has not yet really separated from her.

Canto 8: The Attack on Women

(*strī-vighāta*, 62 verses)

Following Nanda's self-pitying ruminations of Canto 7, his longing for home reaches a climax at the beginning of Canto 8. This is cleverly suggested by the triple *utsuka* in the opening verse, when Nanda experiences "a yearning to go home that was the height of yearning" (*gṛha-yānotsukam utsukotsukam*, 8:1). At this point a certain ascetic (*śramaṇa*) approaches Nanda, asks why he has been weeping, and suggests that he disclose the reason for his unhappiness. Nanda agrees to confide in the ascetic, and in 8:8 they retire to a quiet part of the wood and sit down in a bower of creepers. In a continuation of the eroticisation of nature found in Canto 7, and reflecting Nanda's ongoing preoccupation with his wife, the bower of creepers is said to embrace them with its tender young shoots. Nanda, comparing himself to a lonely *kiṃnara*[3], bluntly states that he cannot be happy without his lover. Normally, when the hero in the throes of a troubled love affair confides in a friend, one might expect the confidant to recommend a course of action to secure the lady's favour. Instead, the *śramaṇa* responds with a set of verses in which Nanda's wish to return to his wife is implicitly likened to animals (and one human) seeking out a dangerous or unpleasant situation on purpose (8:15-21). This sequence of

[3] *Kiṃnaras*, semi-divine beings, play an important role in the imagery of the *Saundarananda* and are further discussed in Chapter Six.

verses culminates in the splendidly anti-romantic, anti-*kāvya* vision of Nanda wishing to return to his wife as a greedy dog wanting to eat its own vomit (8:21). The ascetic then launches into a misogynistic diatribe that identifies the home as bondage (*gṛha-saṃjñaṃ ... bandhanam*, 8:29) and woman as the essence of strife (*kali-bhūtām*, 8:30). Women are dangerous (8:31), ignoble (8:33), duplicitous (8:35) and greedy (8:40). Numerous similes exemplify the female character: women are like poisonous creepers (8:31), they strike indiscriminately like hordes of crocodiles in a river (8:37), and they take their pleasure anywhere, like a cow wandering from field to field (8:41). Having described women's malevolent natures, the ascetic observes the repulsiveness of women's bodies (8:47-54). He stresses in particular that any beauty one might perceive in a woman is not her natural state but a result of skillful preparation. From verses 56 to 59, the ascetic marshalls a different argument to encourage Nanda not to go home, calling on Nanda's noble birth, sense of decorum and the promises of chastity he has made. The canto ends with a final salvo against the defects of women's mind and bodies (8:62).

Johnston (1936:xcvii) recognises the satirical tone of Canto 8, though he also believes that the subject matter was keenly felt by Aśvaghoṣa. He quotes 8:35, 8:39 and 8:40 as substantiation for his opinion that "these are not sparks from the anvil of some wit or courtly epigrammatist, but the outburst of a man in bitter earnest, who has himself suffered from the desires he flagellates." Before labelling Aśvaghoṣa as a misogynist, though, Sundarī's sympathetic treatment at the hands of her creator must be remembered. Furthermore, we can note that this vitriol is put into the mouth of the unidentified *śramaṇa*, and is carefully distanced from the Buddha and any of his named disciples.[4] The *śramaṇa*'s opinions are so fanatical and overstated as to become almost humorous, and are not to be taken at face value. Furthermore, the invective of this canto

---

[4] A harder attitude is evident in the Chinese *Abhiniṣkramaṇa Sūtra*, in which the Buddha himself delivers a denunciation of women.

should be considered in context; it is directed at Nanda's specific fixation with the physical and emotional pleasure to be found in a sexual relationship, and is therefore not to be considered as a *vade mecum* for all men, nor as an encapsulation of Aśvaghoṣa's attitude towards women.

Canto 9: The Denunciation of Infatuation
(*madāpavāda*, 51 verses)

Though Nanda has not been paying attention (9:1-2), the unnamed *śramaṇa* renews his efforts to stiffen Nanda's resolve, now censuring the human body rather than women. The dominant motif of Canto 9 is the fragility of Nanda's seemingly enduring physical person, so that while Nanda is caught up in (*ākṣipta*, 9:4) the myth of his own physical wellness, the *śramaṇa* stresses the impermanence of Nanda's strength, beauty and youth (9:5). He then analyses each of these categories in turn, beginning with strength (9:6-21). The word *bala* appears 27 times in this canto, a statistic that indictes how serious is Nanda's misconception about his physical strength (which is not sheer muscle power alone, but also vitality, robustness and so on). His thought "I am endowed with strength" (*balānvito 'smi*, 9:9. 9:16) is shown to be a dangerous presumption. Bodily strength is sapped primarily by disease (9:6), and indeed sickness, both actual and figurative, appears frequently in this canto. Furthermore, strength is dependent on adequate food (9:9), rest (9:14) and a mild climate (9:15). To bolster his argument, the disciple names several mighty men of legend who were easily vanquished (9:17-20). After the denunciation of physical strength, good looks (9:24-6) and youth (9:27-34) are similarly treated. The relentlessness of the aging process is vividly depicted in several similes, a particularly fine one envisaging old age as a sugar mill squeezing the juice out of a sugar cane stalk (9:31).

The body is the seat of the senses, and the remainder of the canto is devoted to a denunciation of sensory experience (*viṣaya*). The longing for sensory experience is insatiable (9:43) and brings nothing but misfortune (9:46). The canto concludes with the ascetic's failure to make any impact on Nanda (9:50) and his decision to report the matter to the Buddha (9:51). Canto 9's emphasis on the weakness of the body and the perniciousness of the senses is well-placed, occurring just before Nanda reaches the apotheosis of desire in the following canto.

Canto 10: A Lesson in Heaven
(*svarga-nidarśana*, 64 verses)

Canto 10 presents the crux of the traditional Nanda legend, one of the few constant narrative elements through the many versions of the story, and the centre of gravity of the present poem. This is Nanda's visit to heaven and his sighting of 500 nymphs, an occasion engineered by the Buddha in order to jolt Nanda out of his obsession with Sundarī. The canto opens with three desideratives expressing Nanda's wilfulness; he wishes to leave off his vowed observances, see his wife and live at home (*sad-vratam utsisṛkṣuṃ bhāryāṃ didṛkṣuṃ bhavanaṃ vivikṣum*, 10:1). In contrast the Buddha's one intention is to uplift him (*abhyujjihīrṣu*, 10:1). The Buddha's desire to give Nanda spiritual uplift is paralleled by the physical motion of taking him by the hand and flying upwards (10:3).

Their first stop is a Himalayan mountain (10:5) inhabited by hermits (10:7) and various animals delicately described in terms of jewels and colours (10:8-11). The female monkey, when it appears, is not subject to the horrific injuries given in other sources, but merely has a damaged eye and a face red with lac (10:15) – a reminder of Sundarī and her makeup. The Buddha asks Nanda whether he finds Sundarī or the monkey more attractive (*cārutarā*, 10:16). Innocent of the irony of his rhetorical answer, Nanda smilingly responds "What comparison can there be, Lord, between your sister-in-law, the most excellent of women, and this mischief-making monkey in the trees?" (*kva cottama-strī bhagavan vadhūs te mṛgī naga-kleśa-karī kva caiṣā*, 10:17).

The Buddha and Nanda now depart for Indra's realm (10:18), which in keeping with the ancient Indian conception of heaven is a jewelled and artificial paradise. The surface of the water is unmoving (10:24), while the trees (10:19-26) show all seasons at once and bear wreaths, lotuses, fine garments, jewels or musical instruments. Birds too are described in exquisite detail (10:28-31), each verse employing a different word for "bird". Nanda is overwhelmed by the loveliness of his surroundings and decides that his own world is just a cremation ground in comparison (10:34). When the Apsarases appear in 10:36, they are introduced with the phrase *madanaika-kārya* "making love their only concern", which is exactly the phrase used to introduce Nanda and Sundarī in 4:1. Thus Nanda's relationship with the Apsarases, or at least his preoccupation with them, is linked to his preoccupation with Sundarī. Naturally, the Apsarases are utterly ravishing. Like true *kāvya* pin-ups, they pull the leaves off lotuses and their pearl necklaces are disordered by their breasts (10:37). They throw Nanda sidelong glances and generally imply their sexual availability. There is a reminder of the conceptual link between the Apsarases and Sundarī in the comparison of their faces, complete with swaying earrings, to lotuses stirred by a *kāraṇḍava* bird (10:38), which echoes a very similar comparison made of Sundarī in 4:23. We are told that these heavenly women are the reward of austerity (*tapaḥ-phala*) earned during a previous life and that there is no sin in possessing them (*nirdoṣa-parigraha*, 10:36).

The catastrophic effect of the seductive Apsarases on the hapless Nanda is worked out in the remainder of the canto, frequently through images of fire and heat. His heart ablaze with the fire of passion (10:49) and scorched by a fiery ardour (10:52), Nanda would have been burnt up were it not for the Buddha's power (10:46). At this point Aśvaghoṣa inserts a number of statements to explain why the Buddha stimulates Nanda's already passionate nature by purposefully exposing him to the Apsarases (10:42, 10:43, 10:47). The Buddha then asks Nanda if he prefers Sundarī or the Apsarases (10:48). Nanda is quick to declare his wife's inferiority, saying that he no longer cares for his wife after seeing the Apsarases (10:51). The Buddha now cuts a deal with Nanda: the price (*śulkārtha*) of the Apsarases is Nanda's practice of austerities (10:59). The Buddha himself will act as Nanda's guarantor in this matter (*ahaṃ ca te 'tra pratibhūḥ*, 10:63). In the final verse of the canto Nanda agrees and the two return to earth (10:64). The colophon, which entitles this canto "a lesson in heaven" (*svarga-nidarśana*), makes a further defence of the Buddha's shock tactics. The visit to heaven is a *nidarśana*, an example, illustration, or teaching aid, and can therefore be considered part of the Buddha's skillful means (*upāya kauśalya*). Johnston's translation "The Vision of Paradise" fails to capture the justificatory tone of the title.

Canto 11: The Condemnation of Heaven

(*svargāpavāda*, 62 verses)

The beginning of Canto 11 finds Nanda keeping to his promise and forcing himself to submit to a life of renunciation (11:1), though without any real enthusiasm (11:2). Furthermore, he remains dependent on the Buddha, "propped up by the supreme teacher" (*paramācārya-viṣṭabdhaḥ*, 11:4), and, tellingly, his continuing obsession with the Apsarases makes the normally handsome Nanda physically ugly (*vairūpyam*, 11:6). Ānanda approaches him at this point, and with a great deal of delicacy questions Nanda's true motivation (11:9-20). Nanda says nothing, but his expression indicates that he is indeed, as Ānanda has suggested, a hireling for the Apsarases (*apsaro-bhṛtakāḥ*, 11:19). Ānanda is moved to both compassion and mirth (11:23), and the rest of the canto is taken up with his efforts to prove to Nanda that a heavenly rebirth is ultimately as unsatisfactory as any other (11:24-62), since it offers no permanent refuge. He begins with a series of similes (11:24-9) designed to emphasize Nanda's folly, before revealing that the attainment of the Apsarases would in any case be temporary (11:31), and would be followed by a far less pleasant rebirth (11:40). Ānanda substantiates his argument with a series of examples (11:42 to 11:49), citing various legendary heroes who attained heaven but then fell from that state. These culminate in the lovely lament of the denizens of heaven as they fall to earth (11:50), a verse which must have pleased Aśvaghoṣa since it also appears at *Buddhacarita* 14:41. Ānanda produces several more well-developed similes to illustrate the insecurity of life in heaven, some of which are reminiscent of other works. Verse 11:59, for example, with its *upamāna* of a bird bound by string, is reminiscent of *Chāndogya Upaniṣad* 6:8:2, while 11:61, which speaks of fish carelessly swimming into a net, echoes DN i.45. The canto concludes with an exhortation to Nanda to "give up your appetite for that shifting heaven" (*jahihi calaṃ svargaṃ prati rucim*, 11:62).

Canto 12: Understanding
(*pratyavamarśa*, 43 verses)

Following Ānanda's denunciation of heaven in the preceding canto, Nanda now experiences a crisis during which he reorientates himself to a new goal. The word chosen to indicate his agitation is *saṃvega* (12:4, 12:8, 12:9), a term that suggests an emotional shock stimulated by a painful experience.[5] This critical moment in Nanda's career is condensed into a powerful simile of a great chariot turning round (12:5), as discussed in Chapter Seven. Nanda approaches the Buddha (12:11) to tell him that he no longer desires the Apsarases and therefore withdraws from the contract (12:13). He also asks the Buddha to teach him (12:17). The Buddha's response takes up the rest of the canto (12:19-43), and initially applauds Nanda's redirection towards what is increasingly referred to as *śreyas*, "the best". Thereafter he turns to a eulogy of faith (*śraddhā*) that is perhaps more akin to Mahāyāna than to the early schools of Buddhism. In a passage dense with figurative language, the Buddha hails faith as the "chief factor in the arising of dharma" (*dharmasya cotpattau śraddhā kāraṇam uttamam*, 12:40). However, rather than analysing this passage for evidence of Aśvaghoṣa's school affiliation, it is enough to observe that, in keeping with the Buddha's early diagnosis of Nanda as a man whose mind is governed by faith (5:18), the Buddha appropriately commends faith to him as a springboard to further development.

[5] For example, in AN i.280 a dissolute monk experiences *saṃvega* when the Buddha admonishes him. Coomaraswamy (1977) explores how *saṃvega* is elicited and how it precipitates spiritual growth.

Canto 13: The Conquest of the Senses through Discipline (*śīlendriya-jaya*, 56 verses)

The opening two verses of Canto 13 report that Nanda is so gladdened by the Buddha's discourse on faith in the preceding canto that he feels as though liberation is already attained (13:2). Such optimism is premature, however, and much work remains to be done. After a brief aside in which Aśvaghoṣa once again stresses that even the Buddha's rougher methods are entirely motivated by compassion (13:3-8), the Buddha at 13:10 embarks on a long speech of instruction to Nanda which takes up the rest of this canto and the three following cantos, a total of 266 verses. The Buddha's first topic is discipline (*śīla*, 13:10-29), which he expounds using an underlying metaphor of cleanliness. Nanda is 'to clean up his act' by keeping a close guard on his conduct (13:10) and by following the rules of mendicancy (13:15). Verses 13:22-26 form a graduated series of desirable states in reverse order, beginning with liberation at the summit and ending with *śīla* (13:26), which is therefore shown to be the necessary foundation of all them, and which appears three times in that verse to emphasise the point. The Buddha next advises Nanda to control the operation of his senses (*indriya*, 13:30-56). This passage draws heavily on a military metaphor in which the senses are envisaged as enemies. Verses 13:31 to 13:34, for instance, elaborate ways in which the action of the senses is always worse than the action of enemies, while 13:35-37 has an complex allegory of the senses as arrows fired by the attacker, sensual desire (*kāma*). The word *indriya* frequently occurs in the instrumental, because the senses are the means by which a man is destroyed. The Buddha describes the correct way to perceive objects (13:41-44) in order to obtain relief from likes and dislikes (13:45-48). Appropriately, considering his propensity for superimposing fanciful notions upon his environment, Nanda should also avoid using his imagination (*parikalpa*, 13:49-53).

Canto 14: The First Steps

(*ādi-prasthāna*, 52 verses)

The Buddha's guidance to Nanda continues in Canto 14, often in the form of lively similes that counterbalance the canto's tendency to preachiness. However, the generally didactic character of the canto is marked by frequent imperatives, future passive participles and √*arh* with an infinitive as Nanda is robustly told what to do. The Buddha's subject matter is fourfold – eating (14:1-19), sleeping (14:20-34), mindfulness (14:35-45) and solitude (14:46-52). Nanda's instruction begins with the correct way to undertake two very ordinary physical activities. With regard to eating, moderation is key, and the urge to either over- or undereat should be resisted. Since people are more deeply attached to food than anything else (14:10), one should eat with extreme circumspection – as unwillingly, indeed, as a mother and father would eat their own child when starving in a wilderness (14:13). The Buddha's advice on sleep is more austere still; wakefulness through the night should be maintained by recitation (14:23), splashing one's face with water (14:24) or cultivating the fear of death (14:27). Nanda should spend only the second watch of the night asleep (14:32-4). Sleep in this passage is imagined as an enemy who must be combatted.

The endorsement of wakefulness now shades into an advocacy for mindfulness (*smṛti*). *Smṛti* is a prominent concept here, with the term appearing more frequently in this canto than in any other. Aśvaghoṣa uses military language to explain that mindfulness, functioning as armour or a guard, should remain protectively focused on the body (14:38, 14:39). As the canto draws to a close its recommendations become progressively more ascetic. Seeking out company is like walking over thorny ground (14:47) and, in a repetition of this image, Nanda is told to avoid the company of others as he would a thorn (14:50).[6] The last verse refers back to Canto 10 and the vision of the Apsarases that so tempted Nanda; it explicitly states that the state of bliss

[6] The metaphor of the path that underlies these two images is more fully explored in Chapter Seven.

available to the renunciant who likes to live alone is superior to the sensual delights of Indra's heaven.

Canto 15: Leaving Notions Behind

(*vitarka-prahāna*, 69 verses)

In this canto the Buddha introduces Nanda to meditation, though his instructions on the physical aspect of meditation are limited to the first two verses and 15:64. The bulk of the canto is devoted to the perils that obstruct the meditator's progress, all of which are thoughts (*vitarka*) of varying degrees of unskillfulness. Such thoughts are conceptualised as places where one mistakenly lives or settles (*adhi* + √*vas*, 15:3 and 15:43). The English metaphor coincides with the Sanskrit here, since Nanda ought not to dwell on such thoughts. The hindering thoughts are presented in a graduated list from the most obvious to the subtlest and are accompanied by exhortations to abandon them. For each unskillful thought the Buddha offers Nanda an alternative, more beneficial thought on which to concentrate. The structure of the canto appears to be closely modelled on AN i.253-6.

As is appropriate in Nanda's case, thoughts of passion (*kāma*, 15:3-11) appear at the top of the list of thoughts to avoid. The passions are a cause of unhappiness (15:8) and should be brushed off like dust from one's clothes (15:3). Thoughts of malice (*vyāpāda*, 15:12-17) harm the thinker more than the person at whom they are directed (15:16), and they should be countered by cultivating loving-kindness and compassion (15:13). Unwholesome (*akuśala*) thoughts should be given up because a man's character takes on the imprint of what he continually thinks about (15:18-25). After a series of similes that stress the danger of backsliding posed by such thoughts, the Buddha exposes the delusion of family feeling (15:30-41). Thoughts of family and friends should be abandoned no less than thoughts of passion and malice, since kinship ties are temporary and dominated by self-interest. In a particularly effective simile, human beings are envisioned as grains of sand temporarily held together in a fist. Verse 15:36 expresses a bleak view of human relationships; a mother lavishes affection on her son not out of disinterest, but with a view to future support, while the son only honours his mother out of duty. Thoughts of one's home region (15:42-49) are also to be avoided, since in truth no part of the world is better than any other, all countries being subject to sickness, old age and death (15:46). Finally, and echoing the subject matter of Canto 9, Nanda is to avoid egotistical thoughts of his own youth and strength (15:53-63) by remembering the certainty of death. The subject-matter of the canto is summarised in a gold refining metaphor that appears in the last four verses (15:66-69); it is analysed in detail in Chapter Five.

Canto 16: Explanation of the Noble Truths

(*ārya-satya-vyākhyāna*, 98 verses)

In the first half of this canto the Buddha instructs Nanda in the Four Noble Truths, giving an initial definition (16:3-6) before discussing them individually (16:7-16, 16:17-24, 16:25-9 and 16:30-9). The exposition on the First Noble Truth equates suffering (*duḥkha*) with birth and the physical body (16:7-8) and reaches a crescendo in a skillful verse in *upajāti* metre:

> *pratyakṣam ālokya ca janma-duḥkhaṃ,*
> *duḥkhaṃ tathātītam apīti viddhi* |
> *yathā ca tad duḥkham idaṃ ca duḥkhaṃ,*
> *duḥkhaṃ tathānāgatam apy avehi* || (16:14)

> Having seen the suffering of birth in front of your eyes,
> understand that suffering was the same also in the past.
> Just as that was suffering and this is suffering, recognise
> that suffering will be like that in the future too.

The word *duḥkha* appears five times in this verse, including two pairs occurring on either side of the *yati*.

The discussion on the Second Noble Truth includes the assertion that one's particular faults persist from life to life (16:20-4). The description of *nirvāṇa* in verses 16:25-29 is interesting for the contrast it provides with the idea of heaven imagined in earlier cantos. For instance, 16:29 stresses the non-spatial nature of *nirvāṇa*. The Noble Eightfold Path is recommended in 16:30-39 as the way to peace. The Four Noble Truths are summarised by the well-known medical metaphor in 16:40. Interestingly, the section on the Four Noble Truths, which makes up the first half of Canto 16, pays special attention to the importance of worthy companions. A man finds peace if travelling with good friends (*kalyāṇa-mitraiḥ*, 16:39) or if attended by knowledgeable friends (*mitrair abhijñaiḥ*, 16:40 – this could also refer to 'friends conversant with the supernormal faculties').

The second half of the canto emphasises the importance of choosing the right time and method of meditation. This topic is illustrated by two metaphors, one based on the medical treatment of the three humours (16:59-64, discussed in Chapter Four), the other envisaging the meditator as a master goldsmith (16:65-7, discussed in Chapter Five). As the canto moves to a close the quality of heroic endeavour (*vīrya*) receives particular mention, which appropriately paves the way for the battle scenes of the next canto. The end of Canto 16 marks the end of the Buddha's lengthy discourse to Nanda; it has occupied most of the last four cantos. Canto 16 is the longest of the poem, and perhaps the most technical in terms of its presentation of the Buddha's teachings. The fact that fifteen out of the eighteen occurrences of the word *samyak* (meaning 'perfectly', 'completely' or 'correctly') are found in this canto points to the perfection of the doctrine that is being taught as well as to the importance of its being perfectly understood.

Canto 17: The Attainment of Deathlessness

(*amṛtādhigama*, 73 verses)

Spurred on by the Buddha's exhortations, Nanda goes to war in Canto 17 and fights a battle with himself in the battleground of his own mind. This basic allegory is spun out in stanza after stanza of military imagery. Thus he has such weapons as a bow of true knowledge (17:23) and the four arrows of the foundations of mindfulness (17:25) as well as a division of fighting elephants (17:24, 17:26, 17:58), the significance of which is explored in

Chapter Three. With these he destroys his enemies passion (*rāga*, 17:38) and malice (*vyāpāda*, 17:39). However, the imagery of this canto draws not on actual combat alone, but also on the wider context of skillful government and political shrewdness (*nīti*). Thus in 17:11-2 a yogin seeking liberation is compared to a king seeking new territories. The king achieves his aims by such strategies as fortifying his city, just administration and forming alliances as well as by fighting his enemies, while the yogin fortifies his mind, abides by his code of conduct, fosters his virtues and fights his faults. In such imagery we find a fulfillment of the concept of *vīrya* that was named as an essential quality of the liberation-seeker at the end of the Canto 16, as well as a full flowering of the *kṣatriya* mores introduced in Canto 1. Then, the princes went hunting with their great quivers bristling with arrows (*śarādhmāta-mahā-tuṇāḥ*, 1:35) before establishing the city of Kapilavāstu; now Nanda slays malice with arrows of loving-kindness kept in a quiver of constancy (*maitrī-pṛṣatkair dhṛti-tūṇaiḥ*, 17:39) prior to acquiring the 'city' of *nirvāṇa*. The Buddhist practitioner is revealed as the true *kṣatriya*.

With his new-found resolution Nanda advances swiftly along the Buddhist path, achieving the stage of the first fruit (17:27), the second (17:37) and the third (17:41) in quick succession. It is at this point that he is said to stand at the gateway of the city of *nirvāṇa* (*dvārīva nirvāṇa-purasya tasthau*, 17:41). Nanda now undertakes *jhānic* meditation (17:42-56), abandoning each level of meditation for a progressively higher one as he detects subtle faults in it. Finally he delivers the coup de grâce and completely severs the last five fetters with his sword (17:57), thereby winning arhatship (17:60-2). Nanda announces his achievement in the traditional manner by uttering a hymn of celebration (17:64-73), incorporating a storm of similes – a total of eight in two verses (17:68-9) – that describe his experience of awakening. Canto 17 presents the final stage in the metamorphosis from Nanda's passive acceptance of the Buddha's interventionist policy to his active control of his own spiritual future. Three strongly-worded phrases in verse 17:13, each containing a desiderative and all pertaining to Nanda, are indicators of his increased volition and focus. The aggressive language of the military metaphor, as Nanda throws off (√*kṣip*, 17:8), breaks (√*bhañj*, 17:26), splits open (√*dṝ*, 17:25), kills (√*han*, 17:39) and so on underscores his newly-acquired independence and sense of purpose. We are told that he attains arhatship by means of both the Buddha's instruction and his own valour (*svena ca vikrameṇa*, 17:62). Nanda has put aside his passivity once and for all, and his energetic participation is as important in his own salvation as the Buddha's agency. Despite Nanda's mastery of himself, he is nevertheless able to perceive the Buddha's influential role in guiding him to this pass, and the last eleven verses (17:63-73), in which he celebrates his liberation, are also a paean of praise to the Buddha.

Canto 18: His Instructions Revealed

(*ājñā-vyākaraṇa*, 64 verses)

Much of the last canto consists of a dialogue between Nanda and the Buddha, beginning with Nanda's testimony (18:7-19) in which he acknowledges his indebtedness to the Buddha and describes how his insight developed. Thus he fully understands the teachings on no self (18:14), the five *skandha*s (18:15) and the doctrine of dependent origination (18:16). At the end of his speech Nanda throws himself at the Buddha's feet (18:20). Nanda's prostration reflects his genuine reverence for the Buddha, in contrast to his mock prostration to Sundarī in 4:17. The Buddha bids him rise and responds with a celebration of Nanda's achievement structured around the two words *diṣṭyā* 'how wonderful' and *adya* 'now' that underscore the congratulatory tone and sense of immediacy of the passage (18:22-38). Nanda's continuation of the dialogue (18:40-8) refers to his utter freedom from desire. Averring that he no longer desires either his wife or the Apsarases (18:42-6), Nanda subsequently asks what he could possibly do in return (18:48). The Buddha's recommendation that he go forth to help others (18:50-60) includes a prediction that Sundarī will be inspired to follow Nanda's example (18:59). The story of the *Saundarananda* ends with the vision of Nanda entering the city of Kapilavāstu for alms and preaching to those in need (18:62). In the final two verses of the poem Aśvaghoṣa speaks directly to us, his readers, instructing us on the correct interpretation of his work. The purpose of his poem is not to entertain us but to calm us; we should therefore ignore the populist, *kāvya* elements of the work and dwell only on those elements that relate to tranquillity (18:63-4).

2.2 Comparative Survey of the Nanda Legend

Aśvaghoṣa's *Saundarananda* is the longest, most complex and most convincing formulation of a popular legend that engaged the Buddhist imagination for many centuries. The versions range chronologically from the very early Pali *Udāna* to Sinhalese versions of the 14th century[7], and stylistically from the simple prose narrative of the Pali *Jātaka* to the highly developed *kāvya* form of Kṣemendra's Sanskrit version included in his *Bodhisattvāvadāna-kalpa-latā*. The early *Udāna* version was subsequently elaborated, several centuries later, in the *Udāna* commentary. The *Dhammapada* commentary recounts the Nanda story as an explanation for two verses in the *Dhammapada* that have traditionally been associated with Nanda. Nanda himself is held to be the author of two verses of the *Theragāthā*, and the *Theragāthā* commentary additionally provides a partial version of his story. There are also several Chinese and Tibetan versions of the story. The appendix lists all the versions of the Nanda story I have come across, though it is probably incomplete; further versions of the story will no doubt continue to emerge. The Nanda story has also attracted the attention of artists and sculptors. Notably, it is depicted on the left wall of Cave XVI at Ajantā[8]; the fresco of Sundarī fainting in distress, painted in muted colours and showing a despondent peacock, has become known as "The Dying Princess". The

---

[7] Translated by Hardy (1880:210-211). Hardy lists a number of chiefly 13th and 14th century manuscripts as his sources, but unfortunately gives no references.

[8] The argument that the Ajantā frescoes are based on the *Saundarananda* is presented by Schlingloff in his article "Aśvaghoṣa's Saundarānanda in Ajanta" (*sic*) (1975).

museums at Lucknow and Mathura contain engraved panels of the Kuṣāṇa period showing Nanda handing his wife a garment and holding a mirror for her.[9]

The Pali *Udāna* contains the earliest version of the Nanda story. It is set in the Jetavana, a pleasant grove that had been donated to the Buddha and his order by the wealthy merchant Anāthapiṇḍika. We find Nanda, the Buddha's brother, telling a number of other monks that he does not enjoy the celibate life of a recluse (*brahmacariya*, Sanskrit: *brahmacarya*), and that he intends to give it up and return to the life of a householder. The Buddha hears of this, summons Nanda and enquires the reason for his dissatisfaction. Nanda replies that the beautiful Janapada-kalyāṇī, her hair half-combed, had seen him leaving the house and had called out to him to come back quickly. It is this memory that has caused his dissatisfaction with his life as a monk. The Buddha then takes Nanda by the arm, and the two immediately travel to the heaven of the Thirty-three gods. There they behold five hundred celestial nymphs (Pali: *accharā*, Sanskrit: *apsaras*) and the Buddha asks Nanda who is fairer, Janapada-kalyāṇī or the nymphs. Nanda replies emphatically that the nymphs are the more beautiful. The contrast between the two is as great, he says, as that between a mutilated monkey, its ears and nose cut off, and Janapada-kalyāṇī. When the Buddha promises that he can earn the five hundred nymphs through ascetic practices, Nanda agrees to persevere with the *brahmacariya*. With that they swiftly return to the Jetavana, where the other monks soon come to hear that Nanda is practising *brahmacariya* in order to obtain the nymphs. They taunt him, calling him a hired servant (*bhataka*) and hawker (*upakkitaka*). Nanda, humiliated, practises diligently and attains arahantship, whereupon a deity informs the Buddha of Nanda's achievement. Nanda himself then comes to the Buddha and releases him from his pledge regarding the five hundred nymphs. The Buddha replies that he already knew that Nanda had achieved release from the defilements (*āsavas*), and that at that

---

[9] Putri (1946:166).

moment he (the Buddha) was released from the pledge. The Buddha then utters the *Udāna* proper:

> *yassa nittiṇṇo paṅko, maddito kāma-kaṇṭako |*
> *moha-kkhayaṃ anuppatto, sukha-dukkhesu na vedhati ||*
> (Ud 3.2)

> He who has crossed over the mud, crushed the thorns of desire, and attained the destruction of delusion does not tremble in happiness or sorrow.

Other than these metaphoric expressions of the attainment of arahantship, the language of the *Udāna* confines itself for the most part to a simple, repetitive rendering of the events, with little attempt to provide characterisation or motivation for the action.

Much later, and some four centuries after Aśvaghoṣa, Dhammapāla provided a commentary for the *Udāna*. He inserts an independent episode at the beginning of the story in order to relate the circumstances under which Nanda joined the order, and to provide a motivation for Nanda's subsequent reluctance to continue his *brahmacariya*. He recounts that the Buddha enters Nanda's house on his wedding day, which also happens to be the day of his consecration as king. He places his bowl in Nanda's hand and then leaves. Nanda follows with the bowl in his hand, thinking that the Buddha will take it back at the head of the stairs, or at the foot of the stairs, and so on. When Janapada-kalyāṇī is interrupted at her toilette with the news that the Buddha is taking Nanda away, she rushes to the top of the house with her hair half-combed and calls out to him to return soon. We are told that her words become lodged in Nanda's heart as though they had landed sideways (*tassa hadaye tiriyaṃ patitvā viya ṭhitaṃ*). The Buddha leads Nanda to the *vihāra* and has him ordained. Dhammapāla also adds an actual sighting of a mutilated monkey as the Buddha takes Nanda to the heaven of the Thirty-three. For good measure, the monkey has now lost its tail, as well as its ears and nose, and is sitting on a burning tree-stump in a burning field. Thus Nanda's later comparison, that the nymphs are as superior in beauty to Janapada-kalyāṇī as Janapada-kalyāṇī is to a mutilated monkey, is given a basis in actuality. In the *Udāna*, the monkey features only as a hypothetical object of comparison. In a final addition, the commentary explains that the monks taunt Nanda because they are instructed to do so by the Buddha.

The *Udāna* commentary differs markedly from other versions of the Nanda story in the extent to which it feels obliged to justify the Buddha's actions. For instance, in addressing the question of why the Buddha leads Nanda from his home despite his unwillingness, Dhammapāla explains that the Buddha knows that Nanda will not be persuaded of the dangers of sensual pleasures unless separated from them first through the Buddha's skillful means. Secondly, when explaining why the Buddha shows the lovely nymphs to the already lustful Nanda, Dhammapāla uses a medical model in the Buddha's defence. He explains that a physician, when treating a patient suffering from excessive humours, first exacerbates the symptoms of his patient in order to thereafter purge them completely. So too does the Buddha exacerbate Nanda's symptoms of lust in order to purge them with the medicine of the noble path (*ariya-magga-bhesajja*). Dhammapāla also provides justification for certain other actions of the Buddha, such as the Buddha's promise to stand surety for Nanda's attainment of the nymphs, and the Buddha's instruction to the monks to taunt Nanda.

Verses 13 and 14 of the *Dhammapada*, a text which like the *Udāna* is very old, traditionally pertain to Nanda:

yathā agāraṃ ducchannaṃ vuṭṭhi samativijjhati
evaṃ abhāvitaṃ cittaṃ rāgo samativijjhati ||
yathā agāraṃ succhannaṃ vuṭṭhi na samativijjhati
evaṃ subhāvitaṃ cittaṃ rāgo na samativijjhati ||

Just as rain penetrates a badly-roofed house, passion penetrates an undeveloped mind. Just as rain does not penetrate a well-roofed house, passion does not penetrate a well-developed mind.

The *Dhammapada*'s anonymous commentator, who predates Dhammapāla,[10] fills in the Nanda story that leads up to the Buddha's enunciation of these two verses. The *Dhammapada* commentary relates substantially the same events as the *Udāna* commentary, but does not share its exegetical concerns. However, the *Dhammapada* commentary inserts into the middle of the Nanda story a lengthy account of the Buddha's son Rāhula requesting the Buddha for his inheritance, and the repercussions of Rāhula's subsequent ordination. Additionally, it concludes the Nanda story with a tale of Nanda's past life. The Buddha relates that Nanda in a previous life was a donkey that carried loads of pottery for a merchant. After meeting a female donkey, the donkey refuses to work for the merchant. The merchant threatens him, rather cruelly ("I will make a goad for you, with a sixteen inch thorn; I will cut your body to shreds...)[11], but the donkey will not budge. When the merchant tempts him with the promise of a mate, however, the donkey promises to work even harder than he did before. Later the donkey loses his desire for a mate when he finds out that he would have to share his food with her. The Buddha concludes that in former times too Nanda was won to obedience by the promise of female companionship.

Two verses of the *Theragāthā* are attributed to Nanda himself:

ayoniso manasikārā, maṇḍanaṃ anuyuñjisaṃ
uddhato capalo cāsiṃ, kāma-rāgena aṭṭito ||
upāya-kusalenāhaṃ, buddhenādicca-bandhunā
yoniso paṭipajjitvā, bhave cittaṃ udabbahin ti ||
(Th 157-8)

Because of unreasoned thinking, I was addicted to ornament.
I was conceited, vain and afflicted by desire for sensual pleasures.

[10] Norman (1983:134). Burlingame (1921: Part 1:58) suggests 450 CE.
[11] trans. Burlingame (1921: Part 1:224).

> With (the aid of) the Buddha, skilled in means, kinsman of the sun,
> I, practising properly, plucked out my mind (=desire) for existence.[12]

The commentary, again by Dhammapāla, relates that the Buddha visited Nanda on his wedding day and handed him his bowl, and when Nanda followed him to the *vihāra*, had Nanda ordained against his will. The visit to heaven, the Buddha's pledge concerning the nymphs and the taunting by the other monks are entirely absent. We are merely told that the Buddha dispelled Nanda's dissatisfaction with his [skillful] means (*upāyena tassa taṃ anabhiratiṃ vinodesi*).

Jātaka 182 follows the *Udāna* in omitting the episode in which the Buddha comes to Nanda's house and leads him away. Instead, the story starts *in medias res*, with Nanda residing in the Jetavana and becoming pale and despondent when he remembers Janapada-kalyāṇī. Noticing this, the Buddha questions him and then takes him to the heaven of the Thirty-three. On the way they pass the mutilated monkey, now in an even worse condition: its fur is burnt off and it is covered in blood. In most other respects the *Jātaka* story follows that given by the versions already mentioned, though there is one small difference: no deity appears to inform the Buddha of Nanda's attainment of arahantship. Like the *Dhammapada* commentary, the *Jātaka* provides a story of Nanda's former life; this time, however, Nanda appears as a well-trained war elephant. When frightened in battle, his trainer exhorts him, whereupon the elephant screws up his courage and breaks through the opposing forces. The Buddha concludes by identifying Nanda as the elephant and himself as the elephant trainer.

Later versions of the Nanda story appear in a number of languages. They contain the elements already discussed, though there is a tendency for the stories to become longer and more elaborate. In the *Abhiniṣkramaṇa Sūtra* and in Kṣemendra's

---

[12] trans. Norman (1997:22).

verse *avadāna* Nanda does not speak of his dissatisfaction to the other monks, nor declare his intention to go home.[13] Instead, he draws a picture of his beloved on a stone. In several versions Nanda tries to escape from the monastery, only to be foiled by the Buddha. The visit to heaven occurs in all these versions, but its outcome is not always successful: Nanda still longs for a life of sensual pleasure. Evidently these later authors do not consider that the taunts of the other monks provide sufficient motivation for Nanda to apply himself rigorously to *brahmacariya*. These versions therefore follow up the visit to heaven with a visit to hell, where Nanda is given a preview of what awaits him when he has completed his stay in heaven with the nymphs.[14] It is only after this visit to hell that Nanda conscientiously applies himself to *brahmacariya* and finally achieves arhatship. The Chinese *Abhiniṣkramaṇa Sūtra* contains a highly entertaining retelling of the Nanda story, with a great deal of action and several amusing moments; for instance, we are presented with a vain Nanda who intends to go on his alms round wearing a beautifully adorned shining robe and luxurious slippers, and carrying an umbrella.[15] It also has the Buddha himself speak out against women, a topic which in the *Saundarananda* is placed in the mouth of the unnamed disciple. Some of these later stories also have the Buddha warn Nanda about the dangers of keeping bad company.[16]

---

[13] Schlingloff (1975:87) points out that this element is softened in later versions of the story, since a public declaration of his intention to leave would in itself provide sufficient grounds for the other monks to authorise his departure from the order.

[14] All the versions of the Nanda story that contain the heaven episode make it clear that Nanda can win his stay in heaven through renunciation. It appears to be taken for granted that heavenly delights can be won by adopting the renunciatory life of a recluse (*brahmacariya* in the *Udāna* and the *Dhammapada* commentary, *samaṇa-dhamma* in the *Jātaka*). Furthermore, according to the later versions, when the merit that earns Nanda his place in heaven has expired, he will be reborn in hell.

[15] Beal (1875:37). There is an echo of this incongruity in the *Saundarananda*, where the unnamed *śramaṇa* says it would be as laughable for Nanda to go home as for a richly dressed nobleman to go out begging (8:59).

[16] The Chinese *Abhiniṣkramaṇa Sūtra* and Kṣemendra's *Sundarī-nandāvadāna* both compare the influence of bad friends to the smell of rotten fish.

Having surveyed several other versions of the Nanda story, it is clear that Aśvaghoṣa's *Saundarananda* shares with them the principal elements of the story: Nanda is the Buddha's brother; he has a beautiful wife; the Buddha comes to Nanda's house; Nanda is ordained unwillingly; Nanda is unhappy with the life of a monk and considers going home to his wife; the Buddha hears of this and takes him to heaven; they see an ugly monkey and beautiful nymphs; Nanda agrees to persevere in his life as a monk if he can thereby win the nymphs; he practises diligently and achieves arahantship. This is the core Nanda story which was part of the Buddhist cultural environment from early times, and it is on this material that Aśvaghoṣa draws in his composition of the *Saundarananda*. While it is fair to say that Aśvaghoṣa makes no radical departure from the traditional plot, he is unfamiliar with the extended narrative found in the later Tibetan and Chinese versions; the *Saundarananda* has nothing about Nanda drawing a picture of his beloved on a rock, or about Nanda's attempts to escape from the monastery, or about a visit to hell, and the farcical elements favoured by the *Abhiniṣkramaṇa Sūtra* are entirely absent. Aśvaghoṣa has no use for the story of Nanda's past life attached to the *Dhammapada* commentary's version of events, and the *Jātaka*'s story of Nanda's past life as a well-trained war elephant finds a resonance in the *Saundarananda* only in so far as elephant taming provides a central metaphor for Nanda's training by the Buddha.[17]

Yet the *Saundarananda* is an original and unique work, and despite the similarities of plot, quite different from these other versions. Many of the more immediately discernible differences between the *Saundarananda* and the other versions of the story stem from the use of a different genre. Aśvaghoṣa employs the *kāvya* form; his version is therefore much longer and his pace more leisurely. He composes verse in various metres, the poem is divided into cantos (*sarga*), it contains a number of stock

[17] Chapter Three presents a detailed examination of the elephant training metaphor and its echoes in the Pali material.

descriptions, it is enriched with decorative features (*alaṃkāra*) and it strives for euphonic blend of sound. Kṣemendra's version is also in verse, but the others, except for the occasional verse, are short prose narratives in which the focus is on the action. Aśvaghoṣa is no *kāvya* slave, however. His subject matter frequently overturns *kāvya* conventions, and the *kāvya* form itself is used for the purpose of proselytism, as explained in the apologia that ends the poem (18:63-4). Aśvaghoṣa pays lip service to *kāvya*, but *kāvya* form and *kāvya* motifs are only ever the packaging of the more serious Buddhist content. The earnestness of his theme is ultimately unsuited to *kāvya*'s inherent superficiality. Occasionally, Aśvaghoṣa flouts *kāvya* niceties directly. Most memorably, Nanda's desire to return to his lovely wife, a topic that in full-blown *kāvya* would be accompanied by such stock-in-trade as peacocks calling, the monsoon arriving and other commonplaces designed to evoke the *rasa* of disappointed love (*vipralambha-śṛṅgāra*), is here stated with down-to-earth vulgarity: he is like a dog wanting to eat his own vomit (8:21). In the poem, cantos that contain a preponderance of *kāvya* material (Cantos 4, 6, 7, 10) alternate with cantos that present the Buddhist ethos (Cantos 5, 8, 9, 11), reflecting Nanda's vacillation between the two opposing forces that act on him. This alternation adds to the dramatic tension and reflects Aśvaghoṣa's interest in Nanda's internal psychological state.

One other important way in which the *Saundarananda* differs from those versions described above is Aśvaghoṣa's emphasis on his central theme of conversion. Aśvaghoṣa's concern is to present to his audience an internally coherent and psychologically plausible account of Nanda's evolution from besotted young husband to enlightened sage. All the elements of the poem are incorporated into this overall design. Information that is not immediately pertinent to this theme is omitted. For instance, Aśvaghoṣa has no interest in fitting other details of the Buddha's biography into his story of Nanda. Thus the tale of Rāhula approaching his father for his inheritance, which in the *Dhammapada* commentary is interpolated into the middle of the Nanda story, is absent in the *Saundarananda*. Also absent is any mention of which *Jātakas* were related on which occasions, information that is assiduously reported in both the *Udāna* and *Dhammapada* commentaries. Neither is Aśvaghoṣa concerned with geographical accuracy. Several accounts state that the visit to heaven is made from the Jetavana in Śrāvastī,[18] a city some distance from Nanda's home town of Kapilavāstu. Aśvaghoṣa simply leaves the location unnamed. Such details would present irrelevant distractions from the focus on Nanda's spiritual development. Furthermore, Aśvaghoṣa seeks to integrate all elements of his poem so that they mutually reinforce each other. For example, he prepares for the Canto 10 visit to heaven in Cantos 4 and 6 (4:10, 6:3, 6:35, 6:49), when Sundarī is compared to an Apsaras. While such a comparison may be a *kāvya* commonplace, the important point here is that we are forewarned that there is no essential difference between Sundarī and an Apsaras. When Nanda subsequently follows up his attachment to Sundarī with an even stronger attachment to the Apsarases, we can deduce that he is making the same mistake twice, and that his learning process is therefore incomplete. Aśvaghoṣa may have been obliged by the strictures of *kāvya* to include this kind of conventional imagery in his poem, but this did not prevent him from subjugating such similes to his main theme or from putting stock *kāvya* images to Buddhist use.

While other versions of the Nanda story concentrate on incidents of plot, the *Saundarananda* concentrates on internal events and psychological depth. Nanda's indecision is brilliantly traced; the final verses of Canto 4, for instance, have him hurrying forward and then hanging back again, torn between his wish to follow the Buddha and his desire to stay with his wife. Nanda is portrayed as passive and dependent, especially in the first half of the poem, so that the actions that he initiates in the other versions, such as his escape attempts, would be thoroughly misplaced in the *Saundarananda*. Nanda's gradually deepening insight into his own condition is subtly depicted from Canto 7

---

[18] The *Udāna* and its commentary, the *Dhammapada* commentary and the *Jātaka* agree in this.

onwards. Aśvaghoṣa is at pains to portray Nanda's spiritual reorientation as stemming from his own inner psychological motivation. In other versions, Nanda is shamed into renunciation of the Apsarases, since the taunting by his fellow monks is portrayed as the primary motivation of his change in behaviour. Aśvaghoṣa considerably softens the taunting episode, reducing it to Ānanda's gentle rebuke of Canto 11. The poet evidently did not consider the monks' unseemly teasing adequate explanation for Nanda's ongoing conversion. He also entirely leaves out the imputation that the Buddha instigates the rumour of Nanda's servitude. As outward evidence of his spiritual progress, Aśvaghoṣa has Nanda release the Buddha from his pledge *before* his enlightenment (12:13), rather than after it, as in all the other versions. Such adjustments cast Nanda in a better light and give his character greater depth. Sundarī too is granted greater psychological complexity in the *Saundarananda* than she enjoys in other versions of the story. Her sympathetic treatment in Canto 6, for example as she mentally reviews the reasons for Nanda's disappearance, is designed to inspire pity in the reader, encouraging him to identify with Nanda's difficulty in renouncing her far more than if she had been presented as a cardboard cut-out stereotype. As a final act of kindness, Aśvaghoṣa does not leave Sundarī in permanent anguish, but has the Buddha predict her reorientation to the dharma: "Following your example, your wife too will talk amongst the women at home of freedom from passion" (*vadhūr gṛhe sāpi tavānukurvatī kariṣyate strīṣu virāgiṇīḥ kathāḥ*, 18:59).

In line with the *Saundarananda*'s emphasis on internal rather than external action, the more brutal and melodramatic elements of the other versions are considerably toned down. For instance, there is no mention of Nanda's wedding taking place on the day that the Buddha comes to Nanda's house. Instead, it is a day like any other, with Nanda and Sundarī absorbed in each other and their servants tending to their needs. The other versions of the Nanda story vie with each other in inflicting horrific injuries on the unfortunate monkey sighted by Nanda and the Buddha on their way to heaven. Aśvaghoṣa merely speaks of "a monkey with one damaged eye and a red face [as though] lac had been pressed on it" (*niṣpīḍitālaktaka-rakta-vaktrāṃ śākhāmṛgīm eka-vipanna-dṛṣṭiṃ*, 10:15), sparing us the details of burnt fur and chopped-off ears, nose and tail. There is no horrific visit to hell in the *Saundarananda* to titillate the reader, and no comic moments, such as the Buddha finding Nanda hidden behind a bush. Since the poem presents Nanda's spiritual biography, such events are internalised and are depicted in Nanda's flow of thought rather than as actual events. Thus Nanda's escape attempt in the *Saundarananda* amounts to no more than a mental self-justification of his desire to return to his wife, while the incident in which Nanda paints his wife's image on a stone is internalised as Nanda's nature-inspired daydreaming about her in Canto 7. His vanity in wearing a fine robe for an alms round appears only in one simile (8:59) and in the poem's many denunciations of over-confidence in physical well-being.

A further characteristic of the *Saundarananda* is its marked didacticism. A large proportion of the poem is given over to instruction in meditation, teachings on eating and sleeping, warnings against sensual excess and so forth. This element is less pronounced in the other Nanda stories, which do not lean nearly so heavily towards proselytism. In Aśvaghoṣa's case it is not difficult to fathom authorial intention, since he tells us in the last two verses of the *Saundarananda* that "I have here expounded the truth disguised as *kāvya*" (*kāvya-vyājena tattvaṃ kathitam iha mayā*), and that this is done "for the purpose of capturing hearers whose minds are on other things [i.e. on things other than *mokṣa*, or freedom]" (*śrotṝṇāṃ grahaṇārtham anya-manasāṃ*). Several other versions[19] of the Nanda story speak of the [skillful] means (*upāya*) of the Buddha in bringing Nanda to arahantship, but only the *Saundarananda* points out that it is itself an exercise in skillful means.

A final outstanding characteristic of the poem is its great wealth of simile and metaphor, ranging from the delicately worked though standard *upamā*s of *kāvya*, such as Sundarī's

---

[19] The *Udāna* commentary, the *Theragāthā*, and the *Theragāthā* commentary, for instance.

face looking like a lotus (6:11), or her eyes like bees (4:4), to Buddhist conceptual metaphors, such as desire as thirst. Sometimes these converge, so that the heat or fever suffered by a *kāvya* lover is also the Buddhist fire of suffering[20]. Aśvaghoṣa is liberal in his use of figurative language, particularly in his portrayal of Nanda's progress towards a condition of moral and spiritual perfection, which he conceptualises as a battle against an enemy, the taming of wild animals and the cultivation of landscape, the restoration to health of a sick person, the cleansing away of dirt, or the journey of a traveller.

In contrast to the abundant imagery of the *Saundarananda*, the other versions of the Nanda story display a relative paucity of simile and metaphor. The *Dhammapada* has the simile of the ill-thatched house letting in rain, but the *Dhammapada* commentary adds little more, and this simile makes no appearance in the *Saundarananda*. The *Udāna* describes Nanda's achievement of arahantship in four metaphorical terms packed into one verse as quoted on page 59 above, which Dhammapāla analyses in the *Udāna* commentary. Dhammapāla also makes use of similes in his explanation of the events of the *Udāna*, among them an elaborate simile of a skilled man who uses one axle-pin (*āṇi*) to loosen another that is stuck, and then removes it entirely by wriggling it with his hands. Dhammapāla explains that the original stuck axle-pin is Nanda's infatuation with Janapada-kalyāṇī, the second axle-pin which drives out the first is his fascination with the Apsarases, and the wriggling with the hands is the Buddha's order to the monks to taunt Nanda. This is reminiscent of *Saundarananda* 16:72, where we find the simile of a knowledgeable man using a large pin to drive out another, smaller pin, although the context here is the choice of a correct subject of meditation and not the Buddha's skillful means. The *Abhiniṣkramaṇa Sūtra* echoes the *Saundarananda*'s prominent motif of bondage and freedom when it has the Buddha address Nanda in verse: "Does the man who wishes to escape from the wood, / When escaped, return and enter it again? / You, oh Vāgara! Seeing these things, / From the net escaped, return you

[20] 7:12, 10:49, 17:66 etc.

to the net."[21] On the whole, though, these other versions of the Nanda story lack the metaphorical power and sophistication of the *Saundarananda*.

In this chapter I have outlined the story of the *Saundarananda* and highlighted the poem's distinctive features. Secondly, I have explored the difference between the poem and several other interpretations of the same Nanda legend. Despite Aśvaghoṣa's debt to traditional material, his work is unique and compelling. The reasons for this, I have suggested, are his use of the *kāvya* form, his adherence to a central theme, his emphasis on internal psychology rather than on external drama, an abundance of didactic material and his prolific but well-organised use of figurative language. These characteristics confirm that Aśvaghoṣa wishes to do far more than simply tell a story. All the ingredients of his poem are marshalled in support of his central theme, that of conversion, or progress towards the goal of liberation. This unity of purpose is the defining feature of the *Saundarananda*.

[21] trans. Beal (1875:373-4).

CHAPTER THREE

NANDA TAMED

The inquiry into the *Saundarananda*'s conversion metaphors begins with the analysis of fifteen figures, selected on the basis that they are all inspired by the management and characteristic behaviour of elephants. This chapter consists of an initial consideration of the characteristics that elephants were assumed to possess and the status that they consequently enjoyed, as revealed by relevant secondary material. There follows a discussion of the relative agency of Nanda and the Buddha, a topic that is highly relevant to the elephant metaphor, as also to the medical metaphor in Chapter Four and to the path metaphor in Chapter Seven. Typcially, Nanda experiences the results of action that the Buddha has initiated. Thereafter follows the bulk of this chapter, which consists of a detailed investigation of the elephant metaphor. The chapter ends by drawing attention to the story of an elephant in the Pali canonical material that may have been the source for Aśvaghoṣa's elephant metaphor.

All of the *Saundarananda*'s fifteen elephant figures derive from the underlying conceptual metaphor of Nanda – or occasionally his mind – as an elephant. Naturally Aśvaghoṣa has the Asian elephant in mind, a generally docile and intelligent beast. That fact that such elephants can be domesticated is indispensable to the conceptual metaphor. I have borne in mind that according to Lakoff (1989:51), conceptual metaphors are basic and easily understood in a particular society. I have therefore attempted to establish the general understanding regarding elephants during the period under consideration. For factual information I have referred primarily to the *Mātaṅga-līlā,* which, according to its translator, is the best available Sanskrit work on elephantology or *hasti-vidyā*. Its date, however, is very uncertain (Edgerton 1931:vii). I have also referred to the *Arthaśāstra,* which has three chapters on the care and management of elephants, and which may date from roughly the same period as the *Saundarananda*.[1] To determine the connotation of "elephant" in the ancient Indian context, I have consulted more literary material, namely the *Rāmāyaṇa* and the Pali canonical works. From these sources it is possible to derive an understanding of ancient India's conception of the elephant.

It seems that elephants, due to their impressive size, strength and intelligence, and perhaps also due to the cost of their upkeep, were regarded as noble beasts, and associated with majesty, power and dignity. Hence the Buddha is traditionally held to have descended into his mother's womb in the form of an elephant (recounted in *Saundarananda* 2:50). Elephants were trained for various purposes, some ceremonial, some military, and since they were valuable animals, owned only by kings or the very wealthy, a great deal of attention was paid to their daily care and training. The *Arthaśāstra*, which contains the earliest discussion of the duties of elephant grooms, doctors, trainers, riders, cooks and so on, states that fines were to be levied for offences such as failing to clean the stables, neglecting to feed the elephants, and inappropriate striking of an elephant.[2] Elephants were not bred in captivity, since this was uneconomical. Instead, they were caught in the wild at an appropriate age and then kept in captivity and subjected to a long and difficult training program.[3] Elephants were used in war from an early date,[4] their chief military purpose being to smash through defensive structures and break up the enemies' front ranks. A final noteworthy feature of elephants is their susceptibility to the condition of must, known in Sanskrit as *mada*.[5] Male elephants will periodically go through periods of *mada*, lasting anything from a few days to several months,

---

[1] Johnston (1936:xvi) notes a similarity in the vocabulary of Aśvaghoṣa and Kauṭilya and infers that they are "not far removed" in time.

[2] KA 2:32:19

[3] Edgerton (1931:15).

[4] The Indian king Porus used elephants against Alexander the Great in 326 BCE, according to Gupta (1983:5).

[5] A detailed description of *mada* can be found in the ninth chapter of the *Mātaṅga-līlā*, where it is not negative evaluated as in the *Saundarananda*, but is instead associated with good health and vigour.

during which time they are excitable and easily enraged. Whilst in a state of *mada* the temples of the elephant become swollen and emit ichor, an oily discharge. Sanskrit literature is fond of depicting elephants in *mada*, their temples flowing with ichor as they go into battle. However, *mada* has a wide semantic range and can indicate pride, inebriation and sexual excitement as well as with bellicosity.[6] "Rut" is frequently found as a translation for *mada*. It is interesting to compare the description of the city of Ayodhyā in the first book of the *Rāmāyaṇa* to Aśvaghoṣa's description of Kapilavāstu in the *Saundarananda*. Ayodhyā is filled with "exceedingly powerful rutting elephants" (*madānvitair atibalair mātaṅgaiḥ*).[7] Rutting elephants are a stock attribute of prosperous cities in Sanskrit literature. In the *Saundarananda*, however, Aśvaghoṣa makes no mention of *mada* in his description of Kapilavāstu, merely saying "it was crowded with elephants, horses and chariots, yet it was not in confusion nor disorder" (*hasty-aśva-ratha-saṃkīrṇam asaṃkīrṇam anākulam*, 1:52). Nor does he mention *mada* when the bodhisattva leaves Kapilavāstu, when it is "thronged with multitudes of horses, elephants and chariots" (*haya-gaja-rathaughasaṃkulam*, 3:1). *Mada* in a positive context would be completely inappropriate in the *Saundarananda*, as will be discussed below.[8] To summarise the ancient Indian conception of the elephant, then, elephants signified nobility and might. Their value was enhanced when they were domesticated, and they were particularly prized for their courage and endurance in battle, for which they were carefully trained. As a medium of transformation from wild animal to highly trained fighting machine, it is clear that elephant taming provides a natural and

---

[6] MW (1899:777) lists "sexual desire or enjoyment, wantonness, lust ruttishness, rut (especially of an elephant)" among the definitions of *mada*.

[7] *Rāmāyaṇa* I:6:21

[8] Interestingly, *mada* does appear positively in Aśvaghoṣa's description of Kapilavāstu in the *Buddhacarita* 2:3 "And rut-maddened elephants from the Himalayas ... served him (King Śuddhodana), and that too without any effort on his part" (*madotkaṭā haimavatā gajās te vināpi yatnād upatasthur enam*), and at 14:108, where the bodhisattva is said to have a gait "like a rutting elephant's" (Sanskrit lost). Johnston (1936:20, 217).

appropriate conceptual metaphor for Nanda's gradual submission to the Buddha's discipline and his resulting success in attaining arhatship. The elephant metaphor therefore mirrors the *Saundarananda*'s preoccupation with the conversion process.

Nanda's spiritual progress towards the goal of liberation is not accomplished unaided. The Buddha is always present to persuade, assist, exhort and even force Nanda on his journey. The Buddha's radical intervention into Nanda's life has worried at least one modern scholar (Passi 1996:92), who writes: "I have never quite been able to come to terms with the begging-bowl incident ... the feeling that Nanda has been "unfairly coerced" remains powerful even after many readings." The commentator Dhammapāla fends off such potential criticisms on the grounds that Nanda would not have been persuaded of the dangers of sensual pleasures unless first separated from them through the Buddha's skillful means.[9] The need to exonerate the Buddha from the accusation of a coerced conversion is noticeable in Aśvaghoṣa too. His main line of defence is that Nanda's own passivity demands the Buddha's initiative. A key explanatory passage is provided at 5:15-18. Verse 5:16 distinguishes between two types of person, the superior sort who is self-dependent (*ātmāśrayaḥ*) and the second sort who is dependent on an external influence (*bāhyāśrayaḥ*). Motive (*hetu*) is strong in the self-dependent man, but trust or faith (*pratyaya*) is strong in the dependent man. Verse 5:17 argues that while the former sort of man achieves liberation easily, at a mere touch (*ghaṭṭita-mātra*), the dependent man attains liberation through dependence on others (*vimokṣam āpnoti parāśrayeṇa*). Verse 5:18 is particularly instructive:

nandaḥ sa ca pratyaya-neya-cetā
yaṃ śiśriye tan-mayatām avāpa |
yasmād imaṃ tatra cakāra yatnaṃ
taṃ sneha-paṅkān munir ujjihīrṣan || (5:18)

[9] Ud-a 3.2.170.

> And Nanda, whose mind was governed by faith, became absorbed in whomever he depended on; therefore the sage, wishing to lift him out of the mud of love, made an effort in his case.

Nanda's passivity and dependent personality are clearly brought out in this verse. The phrase *tan-mayatām avāpa* means 'became absorbed, attained identity with, became identical to'. This implies that if Nanda continued his allegiance to his wife Sundarī, he would remain dependent on her and would increasingly take on her qualities. By contrast, if he turns to the Buddha, he will gradually take on the qualities of the Buddha. Which of these two possibilities is inferior is indicated by assigning Nanda to a physical location which functions as a metaphor for his current emotional and mental state; Nanda is in the mud (*paṅka*). The mud in which he finds himself is the mud of love, affection, or attachment (*sneha*). Mud is a dirty, thick, semi-liquid viscous substance; these properties are underlined by the secondary meaning of *sneha* as viscidity or any oleaginous substance. Once stuck in the mud, it would be difficult to get out unaided, as travellers in ancient India were no doubt well aware. It is from this miry, slushy condition that the Buddha wishes to rescue Nanda. In the verse quoted, Nanda is characterised as a dependent type who becomes absorbed in whomever he happens to be with. He is a man of faith who must attain liberation through dependence on another. According to the systematisation of personality types provided by Buddhaghosa, the analysis of Nanda as a man of faith ties in neatly with his characterisation as a passionate man:

> "There are six types of persons, that is, one of greedy temperament, one of hating temperament, one of deluded temperament, one of faithful temperament, one of intelligent temperament, one of speculative temperament. Herein, one of faithful temperament is parallel to one of greedy temperament (*rāga-caritassa saddhā-carito sabhāgo*) because faith is strong when profitable [*kamma*] occurs in one of greedy

temperament, owing to its special qualities being near to those of greed. For, in an unprofitable way, greed is affectionate and not over-austere, and so, in a profitable way, is faith. Greed seeks out sense desires as objects, while faith seeks out the special qualities of virtue and so on. And greed does not give up what is harmful, while faith does not give up what is beneficial."[10]

Nanda's passivity is also subject to criticism by the unnamed *śramaṇa*, who castigates Nanda as a person who yearns for the support of someone else whilst scorning the self-reliance that offers freedom (*spṛhayet para-saṃśritāya yaḥ paribhūyātma-vaśāṃ svatantra-tām*, 8:28). Nanda cannot provide his own motivation, even after the visit to heaven, but is "propped up by the supreme teacher" (*paramācārya-viṣṭabdhaḥ*, 11:4). Nanda's lack of independence is further indicated by passive verb formations,[11] while the Buddha's corresponding agency and decisiveness are marked by a number of desideratives.[12]

The *Saundarananda*'s theme of progress, particularly assisted progress, towards the goal of liberation is embodied in some well-known Buddhist conceptual metaphors, in which Nanda features as the patient who requires healing, or the traveller who requires guidance. The characteristic behaviour of elephants is a less familiar source domain, but it furnishes Aśvaghoṣa with the material for fifteen individual figures, as indicated:

- an ordinary man who leads a life devoted to the pleasures of the senses and who is then rescued by the Buddha is like an elephant stuck in mud but then pulled out (two figures, at 8:17 and 17:72)
- an ordinary man who leads a life devoted to the pleasures of the senses and who then cultivates a more ascetic lifestyle is like an elephant in the state of *mada*

[10] Vism 102, trans. Ñāṇamoḷi (1956:102-3).
[11] 4:44, 8:53, 9:3, 17:64 etc.
[12] 3:15, 3:21, 5:5, 5:34, 5:47, 10:1, 10:43 etc.

that becomes free of *mada* (three figures, at 9:50, 12:11 and 18:61)

- a man who is encouraged to practise a more ascetic lifestyle and who eventually attains liberation is like an elephant that is captured, kept in confinement, trained, sent into battle and emerges victorious (nine figures, at 1:34, 4:40, 5:53, 7:4, 11:1, 17:24, 17:26, 17:58, 17:64, plus one indirectly related at 6:24)

These three variations on the core elephant metaphor, as well as the fifteen figures[13] that they spawn, have a direct bearing on the main theme, since they illustrate the process of change by plotting movement from one spiritual condition to another. I will now examine each of the three groups of elephant figures in turn.

3.1 The Elephant in Mud

The first variation on the elephant metaphor is that of the elephant stuck in mud. I have already noted the identification of mud with affection, or attachment. The depiction of a man who is a victim of his attachments as an elephant in the mud is a natural and easy extension of the attachment-is-mud metaphor, since it is well-known that elephants enjoy bathing in rivers. Nanda is the subject of an elephant in the mud analogy in Canto 8, where he is envisaged as a young elephant requiring the assistance of another elephant. The simile occurs during a long speech delivered by the unnamed monk to whom Nanda has revealed his longing for home. The unnamed monk endeavours to portray Nanda's longing as a fatal attraction which flies in the face of common sense. He uses a number of animal similes to demonstrate the situation; they all picture Nanda as an animal which has been saved from a danger, but which persists in a

[13] There is a 16th figure referring to elephants which I will not discuss since it is a minor simile used by way of an example to illustrate a general principle. Moreover, it is illustrative of a purification rather than the elephant training metaphor. It occurs at 15:14 and is spoken by the Buddha as a warning against backsliding. "He who has renounced bad actions but who continues to harbour ill-will is like an elephant who whips up dust over himself after bathing" (*nivṛttaṃ yasya dauḥśīlyaṃ vyāpādaś ca pravartate | hanti pāṃsubhir ātmānaṃ sa snāta iva vāraṇaḥ*).

perverse longing to again expose itself to danger. They are all variations on the underlying motif of captivity and freedom. Thus Nanda is a deer saved from a hunter but about to leap into the hunter's net (8:15), or a bird set free from a net which voluntarily flies into a cage (8:16), and so on. In 8:17 the unnamed monk says of Nanda:

> *kalabhaḥ kariṇā khalūddhṛto*
> *bahu-paṅkād viṣamān nadī-taṭāt* |
> *jala-tarṣa-vaśena tāṁ punaḥ*
> *saritaṁ grāhavatīm titīrṣati* || (8:17)

> Here is a young elephant pulled out of the thick mud at a treacherous riverbank by [another] elephant, that wants to descend into the crocodile-infested river again, impelled by its thirst for water!

A *kalabha* is a young elephant in its fifth year. Though decidedly on the young side (since an elephant is deemed worthless before the age of twelve years[14]), the *Mātaṅga-līlā* does refer to the capture of the *kalabha*[15], and it also describes a *kalabha* as controllable by a driver (*yantṛ-vaśagaḥ*[16]). The young *kalabha* elephant, then, is certainly a candidate for the training process. During the training process less experienced elephants were placed amongst fully trained elephants.[17] Here the young elephant is rescued by another, presumably wiser and better-trained elephant, who fully understands the dangerous nature of mud and crocodiles. If we identify the other elephant as the Buddha, then this second elephant is of course perfectly wise and perfectly disciplined.

The young elephant is rescued from a great mud (*bahu-paṅka*), calling to mind the mud of love (*sneha-paṅka*) from

---

[14] *Mātaṅga-līlā* 5:1

[15] *Mātaṅga-līlā* 10:11

[16] *Mātaṅga-līlā* 5:6

[17] *Mātaṅga-līlā* 10:6 explains that newly captured elephants are stabled with more trustworthy elephants.

which the Buddha desired to pull (*ujjihīrṣan*) Nanda in verse 5:18. This rescue is effected at the end of Canto 5 when Nanda is removed from his household life, so that by the time we reach 8:17 it is quite correct to describe the young elephant as "pulled out" (*uddhṛta*) of the mud. The use of the same verb *ut* + √ *hṛ*, as well as the use of mud as a metaphor for attachment, links these two verses and endorses the identification of the older elephant as the Buddha. The second half of the verse amplifies the scenario; the young elephant is tormented by thirst, a familiar Buddhist metaphor for desire. Despite the crocodiles lurking in the river, he "wants to descend into"(*titīrṣati*) it again, a translation that fits the metaphor better than Johnston's "wishes to enter". We understand that Nanda is tormented by desire and wishes to return to his home, despite its dangers - no doubt Sundarī in particular and a life devoted to sensual pleasure in general are implied.[18] This is a complex verse in which a number of conceptual metaphors overlap: Nanda is a young elephant who needs help; love is mud; home life is a river full of dangerous creatures. It indicates clearly that Nanda has made no very great progress, other than being physically moved by the Buddha. He still stands in need of correction, advice and training.

In Canto 17 Nanda achieves arhatship, and from the perspective of an enlightened sage he can now recognize the wretchedness of his former condition. In a simile strongly reminiscent of the one at 8:17 just considered, he says:

tasmāc ca vyasana-parād anartha-paṅkād
utkṛṣya kramaśithilaḥ karīva paṅkāt |
śānte 'smin virajasi vijvare viśoke
saddharme vitamasi naiṣṭhike vimuktaḥ || (17:72)

I was dragged from the worst of predicaments, the worthless slime, like a feeble-footed elephant from the mud; now I am liberated into this good dharma, which is

[18] Women are expressly compared to crocodiles which lurk in rivers in 8:37.

peaceful, without passion, without fever, without grief, without [the] darkness [of ignorance], and perfect.

The simile allows further qualification of the mud of attachment in which Nanda was trapped – it is *anartha* – worthless, useless, bad, unfortunate. In direct contrast to the bad mud (*anartha-paṅka*) is the good dharma (*sad-dharma*), which has the excellent qualities listed. Instead of being stuck in the mud, Nanda is now established in the dharma. Nanda's description of his old self as *krama-śithilaḥ,* with wobbly steps or "feeble-footed", acknowledges his former weakness and need of assistance, whilst simultaneously suggesting a second meaning of "gradually loosened"; he has been slowly prised from the mud.

3.2 The Elephant in *Mada*

The second variation on the basic elephant metaphor produces three figures that liken Nanda to an elephant either in the state of *mada* or one that is free of *mada*. As discussed at the beginning of this chapter, *mada* is a condition affecting male elephants in their prime, and in Sanskrit literature often connotes lust, intoxication or arrogance. The first of the three figures concerning elephants and *mada* occurs at the end of Canto 9, when Nanda is still tormented by desire, despite the well-intentioned homilies from the unnamed monk which make up the bulk of Cantos 8 and 9. So we hear that:

iti hitam api bahv apīdam uktaḥ
śruta-mahatā śramaṇena tena nandaḥ |
na dhṛtim upayayau na śarma lebhe
dvirada ivātimado madāndha-cetāḥ || (9:50)

Though addressed at length in this friendly fashion by the learned ascetic, Nanda did not become steadfast, he did not find peace; like an excessively ruttish elephant, his mind was blinded by lust.

The verse associates *mada* with a number of Nanda's negative characteristics – lack of peace, lack of steadfastness, and blindness. Being blind (*andha*) and so lacking sight is a common metaphor for lacking understanding. Nanda is described as *atimada*, that is, possessing *mada* to an excessive degree. He is unable to think clearly, just as an elephant with ichor[19] streaming from its temples is unable to see clearly. The compound *madāndha* also occurs at 4:8, where it is used to describe Nanda and Sundarī at the height of their physical passion for each other, and where there can be little doubt about *mada*'s equivalence to lust. Since *mada* interferes with understanding, it should be understood as an entirely negative condition.[20] Additionally, *mada* interferes with the training process, since an elephant in *mada* is uncontrollable and immune to the goad.[21] Likewise Nanda takes no heed whatsoever of the advice (that is, training) which the unnamed monk has just been giving him in Cantos 8 and 9.

After his visit to the heaven in Canto 10 and his initial longing for the Apsarases, Nanda comes to realise the foolishness of striving to win these heavenly maidens, particularly when he learns that his enjoyment of them would in any case be temporary. He therefore goes to the Buddha to tell him that he no longer experiences desire for the Apsarases:

> *khela-gāmī mahā-bāhur gajendra iva nirmadaḥ* |
> *so 'bhyagacchad gurum kāle vivakṣur bhāvam ātmanaḥ* ||
> (12:11)

---

[19] *mada* can also be used to mean ichor, or rut-fluid, as in *Mātaṅga-līlā* 9:5 and 9:14.

[20] In 3:14, *mada* is teamed with *krodha* and *bhaya* as the waves which trouble the sea of existence.

[21] *Mātaṅga-līlā* 9:16 says that an elephant in the 5th stage of *mada* is *apragṛhyo niyantuḥ*, "uncontrollable by a driver". See also *Rāmāyaṇa* II:20:15, where Lakṣmaṇa describes fate as *atyaṅkuśam ivoddāmaṃ gajaṃ mada-baloddhatam*, "like a careering elephant beyond control of the goad, in a frenzy of rut and might" (trans. Pollock 1986:127).

With stately gait and strong in arm, like a princely elephant out of rut, he came to the guru at an appropriate time, desiring to tell him of his disposition.

The simile of an elephant without rut (*nirmada*) accurately reflects Nanda's reorientation, since Nanda no longer desires the Apsarases, or indeed his wife. Since the *mada* has now abated, training can recommence. Hence Nanda goes voluntarily to his trainer, the Buddha, showing that he is now amenable to further training. This training or discipline can now begin in earnest, and takes the form of the Buddha's teachings, advice and exhortations which make up part of Canto 13 and all of Cantos 14, 15 and 16. Nanda's state of mind has clearly improved a great deal, and it is accompanied by a corresponding nobility in his physical appearance; with his large arms and stately gait[22] he seems dignified and impressive.

The third figure to incorporate both elephant and *mada* occurs right at the end of the story of Nanda, and though it is not the last simile in the poem, since there are a few in the last two verses, where Aśvaghoṣa outlines his authorial intentions, nevertheless it is in a particularly prominent position. Nanda has gone to the Buddha to formally declare to him his achievement of arhatship, whereafter the Buddha instructs Nanda to help others, just as he was helped. Nanda then takes his leave of the Buddha:

ity arhataḥ parama-kāruṇikasya śāstur
mūrdhnā vacaś ca caraṇau ca samaṃ gṛhītvā |
svasthaḥ praśānta-hṛdayo vinivṛtta-kāryaḥ
pārśvān muneḥ pratiyayau vimadaḥ karīva || (18:61)

---

[22] A slow and measured manner of walking indicated calmness and composure. Since elephants walk in this way, an elephant-like gait is a common attribute of the Buddha in Buddhist literature. In AN iii.346, the *nāga* (that is, the Buddha) is composed (*samāhito*) when walking (*gacchaṃ*), composed when standing (*ṭhito*), composed when lying (*seyyaṃ*), composed when sitting (*nisinno*). The *Lalitavistara* describes the Buddha as *nāga-vilambita-gatiḥ*, "having the slow gait of an elephant" (Lal 75.18).

So with his head he grasped the words and feet together of the worthy one, the supremely compassionate teacher; and sound in himself, his heart at ease, his task ended, he left the sage's side, like an elephant free of rut.

Nanda, now completely free from desire, is the elephant free from *mada* (*vimada*[23]). The Buddha is the trainer, or teacher (*śāstṛ*) who has effected this transformation in Nanda. Nanda has assimilated the Buddha's teachings (*vacaḥ ... gṛhītvā*), and his understanding is no longer deficient through blindness caused by lust. He is healthy and well (*svasthaḥ*) and his task is complete (*vinivṛtta-kāryaḥ*); he is fully trained and has attained the self-discipline of an arhat. So Nanda's passivity and dependence are finally overturned; he makes obeisance to the Buddha and leaves his side, to become an agent of change in his turn. The following verse (18:62) sees Nanda moving through the streets of Kapilavāstu and preaching the dharma.

3.3 Elephant Training

The final variation on the basic elephant metaphor concerns the capture and training of elephants. The comparison of Nanda's conversion to the domestication of an elephant is the most developed of the three variations, and the most productive in terms of the number of similes to which it gives rise. We first encounter this metaphor in Canto 1, which relates the history of the founding of the city of Kapilavāstu. The *Saundarananda* is the only version of the Nanda story to include the legend of Kapilavāstu's remote mythical past, and at first glance this material may appear peripheral to the central concerns, since none of the main characters even appear. Closer inspection reveals that a solid foundation is being laid for future thematic development. We hear that the sage Kapila Gautama founded an ashram at the foothills of the Himalaya mountains, and dwelt there practising austerities surrounded by numbers of ascetics.

[23] Johnston (1932:116) is surely correct to see a pun here. He takes *vimada* to mean 'freed from conceit' as well as 'freed from must'.

One day certain noble young princes come to live there, and Kapila becomes their guru. Kapila marks out a boundary on the ground, and tells the princes to build a city within this boundary once he has died. Then, at 1:34, there is the first elephant simile:

> *tataḥ kadācit te vīrās tasmin pratigate munau* |
> *babhramur yauvanoddāmā gajā iva niraṅkuśāḥ* || (1:34)

> In the course of time the sage passed away, and then those heroes wandered with youthful unrestraint, like elephants without hooks.

An *aṅkuśa* is the hook used by an elephant-driver to direct the movement of his mount. The lack of an *aṅkuśa* implies that the elephants have no driver, and that lacking direction, they wander around in an uncontrolled and impetuous manner. This interpretation is underscored by the use of the root *bhram*, which suggests mental confusion as well as physical roaming, and the adjective *uddāma*, from *dāman* 'rope, fetter', meaning 'without fetters, unrestrained, without limits'. In fact, the young princes who are the target of this simile behave so badly after Kapila's death that the resident ascetics abandon the ashram and leave for the Himalayas (1:37).

The simile of the driverless elephants indicates that without the guiding spirit of Kapila, the young princes become wild and undisciplined. It hints at the issues which the remainder of the *Saundarananda* develops more fully - the necessity of training to maintain good conduct, and the need for an outside agency to effect such training. There are a number of parallels between Nanda and the princes – they are young, nobly-born, descendents of Ikṣvāku, fond of hunting,[24] and are initially reluctant to carry out the wishes of their respective gurus. These parallels suggest that Nanda too lacks the self-restraint to moderate his own behaviour, and so stands in need of external restraint.

---

[24] Verses 5:12 and 7:3 infer that Nanda is accustomed to holding a bow.

In Canto 17 of the *Saundarananda* there is another elephant simile which mentions exactly the same instrument of elephant control, the *aṅkuśa*. By diligent practice Nanda has reached arhatship, whereupon he speaks in praise of the Buddha:

> *ahaṃ hy anāryeṇa śarīra-jena*
> *duḥkhātkmake vartmani kṛṣyamāṇaḥ* |
> *nivartitas tad-vacanāṅkuśena*
> *darpānvito nāga ivāṅkuśena* || (17:64)

> For I was being pulled down the path of suffering by ignoble physicality, but I was turned back, hooked by his words, as a proud elephant is turned back with a hook.

With the insight of an enlightened sage, Nanda can now acknowledge his indebtedness to the Buddha. He sees clearly that he himself was the elephant in need of the controlling hook, particularly since he was "filled with pride" (*darpānvitaḥ*)[25], and therefore unwilling to accept the advice of someone else. Pride is of course quite out of place in an *arhat*, and must therefore be eliminated. Whereas the young princes of Canto 1 run wild through lack of a hook, Nanda is subject to the hook wielded by the Buddha. The hook that the Buddha uses to direct Nanda is a verbal one (*tad-vacanāṅkuśena*), and indeed much of the *Saundarananda* is taken up with the Buddha's exhortations to Nanda. They make up the whole of Cantos 14, 15 and 16, and part of Cantos 5, 10, 12, 13 and 18, a total of 348 verses, amounting to a good third of the total length of the poem.

Nanda's former passivity is suggested by the use of the passive 'being dragged, pulled' (*kṛṣyamāna*); he was being impelled along a path of suffering by his physical desires. Two basic metaphors, that of the elephant and the path, have here

---

[25] Johnston appears to equate this phrase with *mada* and translates it as "must", which would fit the underlying metaphor better, but I am unsure if such a translation can be justified.

been carefully juxtaposed,[26] producing a composite picture of an elephant going astray, only to be redirected by its driver. It is no wonder that a target domain as complex as the path to enlightenment should be handled by a range of metaphors. Indeed, a third metaphor can be detected in verse 17:64; Nanda's being pulled along the wrong road by his desires suggests that his desires are conceptualised as horses pulling a chariot. Such compression of metaphors occurs frequently in the *Saundarananda*.

While Nanda is here able to acknowledge that he had been travelling down the path of suffering and that the Buddha had been the cause of his turning round, the earlier portions of the *Saundarananda* depict his reluctance to comply with the Buddha's advice. Nanda is unwilling to leave Sundarī, his ordination is more or less coerced, and he is unhappy with his life as a monk. In order to dramatise this situation, Aśvaghoṣa expands the conceptual metaphor to incorporate the preliminary to elephant training – the rounding-up and capture of the elephant. Chapter 10 of the *Mātaṅga-līlā* describes five methods of elephant capture, of which the preferred method was to construct a trap pen, place sugarcane there as a lure, chase a herd of elephants into it, and quickly block up the entrance.[27] The elephants would then be left penned up for two or three days before the elephant herdsmen went into the trap pen and tied up suitable elephants to posts. We are told that the elephants were tied up around the girth, neck and hind parts, and that iron foot bonds were placed on their two hind feet. Once the more valuable elephants had been immobilised in this way, the trap was opened and the remainder of the herd was allowed to go free.[28] A series of posts was then erected between the trap pen and the elephant stalls. When driven home to the stalls after his

---

[26] Lakoff and Turner (1989:27) point out that the richness and power of poetry stems in part from "the confluence of a number of basic metaphorical perspectives".

[27] In *Saundarananda* 5:14 the Buddha lures Nanda into a lonely side-road and blocks up the entrance to prevent him from leaving.

[28] *Mātaṅga-līlā* 10:3-5 describes this entire process.

initial capture, the elephant was always tied to one of the posts. The rope tying the elephant to one post was not untied until he had been tied to the next post. On reaching the stalls, he was lodged with elephants which had already been tamed:

> *stambhāt stambhāntaraṃ tvevaṃ yāpayitvā śanair gajān |*
> *śālāṃ praveśayed anyair āptair danti-varaiḥ saha ||*
>
> But thus having caused the elephants very gradually to proceed from one post to another, he shall bring them into the stall, together with other fine and trustworthy elephants.[29]

The first comparison of Nanda to an elephant occurs in Canto 4 of the *Saundarananda*. The Buddha has been to Nanda's house and gone away again, unnoticed. Nanda knows that he should hurry after him to remedy this slight, but he is hardly able to tear himself away from his beautiful wife. In this state of painful hesitation, we are told in 4:40 that "he went slowly, with backward gaze, like an elephant watching a playful she-elephant" (*vivṛtta-dṛṣṭiś ca śanair yayau tāṃ karīva paśyan sa laḍat-kareṇum*). Nanda is going after the Buddha, but his head is twisted round to watch Sundarī. Both Nanda and Sundarī are compared to elephants, but Nanda is obviously one under duress, since he goes slowly, and his twisted gaze indicates the direction that he would prefer to take, while Sundarī remains at liberty, since the she-elephant is described as "playful". The word *laḍat* is also suggestive of Sundarī's sportive and teasing nature, and is consistent with her mildly flirtatious attempt to ensure Nanda's return by making him promise to come back before her make-up is dry (4:36). Aśvaghoṣa does not directly refer to elephant capture, nor to the method of driving captured elephants to their new homes, but the image of the captured male elephant being led away to be tamed while the female elephant remains in the wild is so apt that it is difficult to resist drawing

[29] *Mātaṅga-līlā* 10:6, trans. Edgerton (1931:88-9).

the conclusion that there is here an intentional though indirect reference to the forced removal of an elephant.

A further two elephant similes do refer directly to elephant capture. The first occurs in Canto 5, just after Nanda has been unwillingly ordained. As a result of his ordination, he is "depressed as a newly-captured elephant" (*cintāvaśo nava-gṛhīta iva dvipendraḥ*, 5:53b). Nanda has not come willingly to his new condition but is *gṛhīta*, meaning 'seized, caught, laid hold of'.[30] Elephants that have just been captured are notoriously prone to low spirits and bad health, and may even die of grief unless tended with special care.[31] Thus Nanda's state of mind is effectively portrayed by the simile, and the comparison is given additional weight by occurring in the last verse[32] of this canto. In terms of the conceptual metaphor underlying this simile, Nanda corresponds to the elephant, the action undertaken by the Buddha in spiriting him away from his home corresponds to the rounding-up of the elephant, Nanda's ordination corresponds to the installation of the elephant in its new quarters, Nanda's subsequent life as a monk corresponds to the continuing captivity of the elephant, and his resulting unhappiness corresponds to the low spirits of an elephant in the early days of its captivity. The simile of the captured elephant not only highlights Nanda's despondency, but also suggests his passivity and the Buddha's agency.

Another figure that refers directly to elephant capture occurs at the beginning of Canto 7. Nanda is now living the life of a monk, but continues to pine for Sundarī. The trees, flowers and creatures of the lovely grove in which he finds himself serve only to remind him of his wife.

sa pītaka-kṣodam iva pratīcchan
cūta-drumebhyas tanu-puṣpa-varṣaṃ |

---

[30] Words from √*grah* are used in the *Mātaṅga-līlā* to denote capture. For instance, the 10th chapter of the *Mātaṅga-līlā* is entitled *gaja-graha*.

[31] *Mātaṅga-līlā* 11:1-4

[32] and which is therefore in a different metre, as is typical of *kāvya* poetry. Verses 5:1-52 are in *upajāti*, but 5:53 is in *vasanta-tilakā*.

dīrghaṃ niśaśvāsa vicintya bhāryāṃ
nava-graho nāga ivāvaruddhaḥ || (7:4)

Receiving from the mango trees a rain of tiny flowers like saffron powder, he thought of his wife and sighed deeply, like a newly-caught elephant in confinement.

This verse is typical of Aśvaghoṣa's style, with three *pāda*s of description followed by a short simile in the final *pāda*. As in 5:53 above, Nanda is compared to a newly-captured (*nava-grahaḥ*) elephant. However, the confinement that was merely assumed in 5:53 is here spelt out: Nanda is *avaruddhaḥ*, meaning 'kept back, shut in, imprisoned'. As described above, it was common practice to leave newly-captured elephants bound to a post within the confines of the trap pen, for quite some time, until they became compliant enough to move. Furthermore, elephants were routinely tethered whilst in their stalls; the *Arthaśāstra* includes amongst its directions for the construction of elephant stables the provision of a post in each stall.[33] It is clear that Nanda feels the constraints of his new life most keenly. We are also told the reason for his suffering; it is consequent upon thoughts of his wife (*vicintya bhāryām*). Here the mango tree[34] reminds Nanda of Sundarī. Sanskrit literature often compares women to mango trees, and Sundarī had previously been compared to a mango tree in 5:25, where she falls down with her ropes of pearls breaking, as a branch of a mango tree falls down from the weight of its fruit. Hence the mango tree is an appropriate stimulus for thoughts of Sundarī.

Nanda's experience of suffering is therefore explicitly linked to thoughts of his wife, and this suffering is likened to the suffering of a recently captured elephant in captivity. The irony here is that while Nanda interprets his suffering as arising from his enforced separation from Sundarī, from a Buddhist perspective his suffering arises from his excessive attachment for

---

[33] KA 2:31:3.

[34] specifically, a mango tree raining yellow powder. Perhaps Sundarī used saffron as an adornment which fell from her as she moved around.

her, and the separation which to him seems like bondage is actually the beginning of his liberation. This tension is reflected in the conceptual metaphor of elephant training; a well-trained elephant is considered much more valuable than one in the wild. The elephant's misery in the early phases of the training period must simply be endured, since the results are worth the initial suffering.

It seems that to some extent Sundarī can be taken as a symbol for attachment, the source of suffering. What then is one to make of the simile in 6:24, where Sundarī, hearing the news that Nanda has been ordained, "screams loudly, like a she-elephant struck in the heart with a poisoned arrow" (*virurāva coccair hṛdīva digdhābhihatā kareṇuḥ*)? There are a number of possible interpretations. The simile may imply that Nanda's attachment (personified as Sundarī) has been struck and mortally wounded, so that he will eventually achieve freedom from attachment. Alternatively, the simile may simply be comparing Sundarī to a suffering elephant as a counterpart to the simile of Nanda as a suffering elephant in 7:4. I am inclined, however, to understand this simile as outside the schema of elephant taming thus far developed, since there is no evidence or likelihood that female elephants were deliberately killed during the process of elephant capture and training. Instead, I believe that this simile draws on the source domain of hunting[35], as the mention of a poisoned arrow (*digdhaḥ*) surely indicates.[36] In any case we are left with a vivid impression of Sundarī's reaction to the news about her husband. It is an interesting exercise to link this simile to the others which draw directly on elephant training. My reading is as follows: Nanda the elephant has been removed from the wild and taken by force to a place of training and discipline. His mate the she-elephant is left behind and is still at liberty in the jungle of home-life. Home life, with its attachments and

---

[35] Elephants are hunted by the young princes in 1:36.

[36] Aśvaghoṣa may have had in mind *Rāmāyaṇa* II:27:22, where Sītā too hears unwelcome news; she is hurt by Rāma's "many words, the way poison arrows wound a cow elephant" (*sā viddhā bahubhir vākyair digdhair iva gajāṅganā*) (trans. Pollock 1986:141).

passions, is of course, dangerous. To reinforce this undercurrent, we hear what happens to the cow elephant left outside the Buddha's domain in the dangerous jungle – she is felled by a hunter's arrow. In other words, she is still prey to attacks of emotion.

There is one final set of three elephant references to consider, all occurring in Canto 17. Canto 17 contains an extended allegory of Nanda's mental conflict depicted as a battle between opposing forces, culminating in the victory of arhatship. Since many elephants were trained specifically for military purposes, and the elephant corps was an important component of the ancient Indian army, references to war elephants form a natural extension to the *Saundarananda*'s elephant training imagery. One noteworthy feature of all three references to war elephants is that it is not Nanda who is compared to an elephant. Rather, the war elephants delineate Nanda's mental state, and Nanda appears as the general or commander who marshals his forces. Nanda is no longer envisaged as an elephant, but is now in charge of the elephants, which suggests that much progress has been made along the path to enlightenment. The first war elephant comparison is at 17:24:

> *tataḥ sa bodhy-aṅga-śitāgra-śastraḥ*
> *samyak-pradhānottama-vāhana-sthaḥ* |
> *mārgāṅga-mātaṅgavatā balena*
> *śanaiḥ śanaiḥ kleśa-camūṃ jagāhe* || (17:24)

> With his weapon's blade sharpened by the constituents of enlightenment, and standing on an excellent chariot of well-directed effort, with his army which consisted of elephants of the constituents of the path, he gradually penetrated the ranks of the afflictions.

The hostile force[37] is made up of the *kleśas*, the impurities, passions or afflictions (or perhaps just lust). Nanda with his troops of elephants, which here represent the path, plunged into (*jagāhe*) their ranks. The active verb form indicates that he is actively engaged in the battle – as does the sharp weapon which he holds (*śitāgra-śastraḥ*). He can be pictured as either standing in a chariot (*vāhana-sthaḥ*) or as mounted on an elephant, since the word *vāhana* can refer to an elephant as well as a vehicle in which to travel.[38] In either case there is no longer any hint of his former passivity. His reorientation to the Buddha's teaching is so complete that he has incorporated those teachings as his front line of attack against the *kleśas*; in terms of the conceptual metaphor of elephant training, the elephant has completed its period of training[39]. It can now put to use what it has been taught, and is ready to go to war. As is appropriate to the military metaphor on which this verse is based, the long compounds are designed to communicate the quality of *ojas* (vigour or strength), thus suggesting the *vīra rasa*, the heroic 'flavour'.

Two verses later Nanda is still fighting to overcome the elephants of the opposing forces:

> *āryair balair pañcabhir eva pañca*
> *cetaḥ-khilāny apratimair babhañja |*
> *mithyāṅga-nāgāṃś ca tathāṅga-nāgair*
> *vinirdudhāvāṣṭabhir eva so 'ṣṭau ||* (17:26)

> With his five incomparable noble armies he broke up the five barren places of the mind, and with his eight

[37] The *kleśas* are envisaged as forming a *camū*, a considerable force of 129 elephants, 129 chariots, 2187 horses and 3645 infantry (see MW 1899:388), which is only broken up with difficulty (*śanaiḥ śanaiḥ*).

[38] The Pali equivalent *vāhana* is used in a similar metaphorical war context in Th 177: "Thus the wise roar, like lions in a mountain cave, heroes, victorious in battle, having conquered Māra and his elephant" (*jetvā Māraṃ savāhanaṃ*) (trans. Norman 1997:24).

[39] The whole of the preceding three cantos are made up of the Buddha's teachings to Nanda.

> elephants which were the constituents of the right path he drove off the eight elephants which were the constituents of the wrong path.

The use of active verb forms carrying very forceful meanings (*babhañja*, *vinirdudhāva*) again reveal Nanda's vigour and military effectiveness.

The military imagery continues throughout Canto 17, and in 17:58 the elephants are once more in the van of the battle:

> *bodhy-aṅga-nāgair api saptabhiḥ sa*
> *saptaiva cittānuśayān mamarda* |
> *dvīpān ivopasthita-vipraṇāśān*
> *kālo grahaiḥ saptabhir eva sapta* || (17:58)

> With his seven elephants of the constituents of enlightenment he also trampled down the seven negative predispositions of the mind, as Time with the seven planets tramples down the seven continents when their destruction is due.

Nanda uses his seven elephants, representing the constituents of enlightenment, to crush (*mamarda*) the seven evil mental tendencies. The military allegory is here reinforced with a simile likening the defeat of the seven negative predispositions to the total annihilation of the world at the end of an aeon. One could think of no more crushing defeat. This is the climax of the battle, and Nanda emerges victorious and immediately hereafter attains his goal of arhatship, as verse 17:60 testifies: "he crossed over the difficult-to-cross ocean of suffering" (*duḥkhārṇavaṃ dustaram uttatāra*).

In the foregoing three war elephant comparisons, the correspondence is no longer between Nanda and an elephant, but between the mind and an elephant. Since Nanda has taken charge of his own mental states and is actively engaged in transforming them, he is no longer seen as an elephant. Instead he can be thought of as the mahout, the elephant driver responsible for ensuring that the elephants successfully carry out their functions. He has internalised the training process. There is one other instance in the *Saundarananda* where Nanda appears as an elephant trainer and his mind as the elephant to be trained; it occurs in the first verse of Canto 11. At this point Nanda has just returned from his visit to heaven, and in return for a sojourn amongst the beautiful Apsarases in his future life, he has promised the Buddha to diligently pursue the ascetic life:

> *tatas tā yoṣito dṛṣṭvā nando nandana-cāriṇīḥ* |
> *babandha niyama-stambhe durdamaṃ capalaṃ manaḥ* ||
> (11:1)

> After seeing the women who wander in the garden of Nandana, Nanda tied his volatile mind, so difficult to tame, to the post of restraint.

Elephants are not explicitly mentioned in this verse, but since part of their training involves being tied to posts, and since elephant training is a fairly prominent conceptual metaphor in the *Saundarananda*, it seems likely that a reference to elephants is intended. *Stambha* is also the word used routinely in both the *Arthaśāstra* and the *Mātaṅga-līlā* to indicate a tying-post.[40] This metaphor and many of the elephant similes focus on the discipline, restraint and obedience to which a monk submits. In this context it is interesting to note that the *Saundarananda*'s term for "adopting the best posture" (*baddhvā paryaṅkam uttamam*, 15:1) for meditation makes use of √*bandh*, suggesting that the monk binds himself to meditation.

Having completed the analysis of the fifteen figures that feature an elephant, we can now summarise the content of the basic elephant metaphor. Firstly, an elephant is stuck in some dangerous mud at the riverside. Since he is young and his legs are wobbly, he has to be helped out by an older elephant. Still

---

[40] There are a number of Pali verses where the mind itself, rather than a monk, is compared to an elephant requiring taming. See for example Th 77 and 355-7, and Dhp 326.

thirsty, he wishes to return to the river to drink, despite the dangers of mud and crocodiles. In due course, however, he realises that staying on the solid ground is a better option. In the second scenario, an elephant is in a state of *mada*. Blinded by ichor and mad with *mada*, he is not amenable to training. Eventually the condition passes and he goes to his trainer to tell him so. He is later seen to be completely free of the condition and is entirely happy and healthy. In the third scenario, by far the most developed, some wild elephants are wandering in the jungle. Later one elephant is captured and pulled away, all the while mournfully craning his head round to watch his mate who remains at liberty. The captured elephant is kept confined and is very despondent. His mate, who had remained in the jungle, is shot by a hunter. After much coaching by his trainer, the captured elephant is ready to be used in war. He fights in several battles and emerges triumphant.

These three variations on the elephant metaphor all apply to Nanda; in each case he (or his mind) is the elephant, and each models his progression from a state of attachment to a state of liberation. Within each of the three scenarios there is at least one figure which pertains to the former state and occurs in the first half of the poem, and at least one figure which pertains to the latter state and occurs in the second half of the poem. Thus of the fifteen elephant figures, seven refer to the attached state and occur in Cantos 1, 4, 5, 6, 7, 8 and 9, while a further eight describe the unattached state and occur in Cantos 11, 12, 17 and 18. This even spread helps integrate the two halves of what sometimes seems a disparate work. We can deduce from the pattern of the figures that a key event occurs in Canto 10 which triggers Nanda's spiritual reorientation. That key event is of course the visit to heaven. It seems then that the elephant metaphor and its manifestations in various poetic figures not only embody the theme of the *Saundarananda* but also help to structure the poem.

While Aśvaghoṣa's sustained treatment of this one strand of imagery is not equalled by other versions of the Nanda story, we do find an interesting echo of the elephant motif in the Pali *Jātaka*. In *Jātaka* 182, the familiar tale of Nanda as summarised in Chapter Two constitutes the story of the present, but the story of the past describes a former birth of Nanda as an elephant. The elephant is sent by a warring king to storm the gates of Benares. The elephant is terrified by the violent defence put up by the soldiers of Benares and refuses to go near the gates. Then the elephant trainer (*hatthācariyo*) approaches and exhorts him in two canonical verses; this is enough to inspire the elephant – he is "turned by just one exhortation" (*ekovāden' eva nivattitvā*). The Buddha identifies Nanda as the elephant, and himself as the elephant trainer. The *Jātaka* is in several respects very similar to Aśvaghoṣa's conceptual metaphor of the elephant that is captured and trained for war; they both draw on the same allegorical material, they both depict a mid-point crisis which is resolved by the Buddha's intervention, and the sub-text of both stresses the importance of training and accords a vital role to the trainer. In particular, they both show the Buddha's words as instrumental in turning Nanda round.. It is possible that the author of the *Jātaka* may have been influenced by Aśvaghoṣa, or vice versa, or possibly the metaphor of a trained elephant to represent a disciplined monk was familiar to both authors from a third source.

Aśvaghoṣa may have drawn his inspiration for his elephant metaphors from early canonical material. The most sustained and best formulated example that I can find is in the *Danta-bhūmi Sutta* of the *Majjhima Nikāya*. In this *sutta*, the Buddha describes how an elephant is captured from the elephant wood, bound by the neck and forcibly led out into the open, "for the forest elephant clings to the elephant wood". The elephant is then trained, first to obey basic instructions, then in preparation for war. The tamer "ties a giant plank to his trunk; a man with a lance in his hand sits on his neck; and the elephant tamer himself stands in front of him holding a long lance pole…the elephant is being trained in the task of imperturbability… The king's elephant is able to endure blows from spears, blows from swords, blows from arrows …. Being rid of all faults and defects, purged of flaws, he is worthy of the king." The Buddha then draws an analogy with a monk, describing how a man goes forth from the home life and "comes out into the open; for gods and humans cling to the five cords of sensual pleasure." The monk is then disciplined in various ways: "Come, bhikkhu, be virtuous, restrained with the restraint of the Pātimokkha." The monk is then progressively disciplined in guarding the senses, moderation in eating, wakefulness, mindfulness, and finally, meditation. "Just as the elephant tamer plants a large post in the earth and binds the forest elephant to it by the neck in order to subdue his forest habits and to inculcate in him habits congenial to human beings, so these four foundations of mindfulness are the bindings for the mind of the noble disciple in order to subdue his habits based on the household life...in order that he may attain the true way and realise Nibbāna." When the monk attains liberation, "that bhikkhu is able to endure cold and heat, hunger and thirst... Being rid of all lust, hate, and delusion, purged of flaws, he is worthy of gifts ... an unsurpassed field of merit in the world."[41]

It is evident that elephant training as a metaphor for the discipline of the monk is worked out in a comprehensive and sustained manner within the framework of the *Danta-bhūmi Sutta*, just as it is within the *Saundarananda*. However, there is no systematic treatment of the elephant metaphor in the Pali Canon as a whole. Instead, differing elephant similes and metaphors abound in the Pali Canon, with various characteristics of the elephant being used as occasion demands. Along with similes that stress the obedience, endurance and training of the elephant[42], there are others which idealise the freedom and solitariness of the elephant, and praise him for breaking his bonds and trampling down creepers to wander at will in the jungle.[43] Some similes focus on particular aspects of the elephant, such as its size, its large footprint, or the behaviour of its young.[44] Even the *Nāga-vaggo* chapter of the *Dhammapada* mixes conflicting conceptual metaphors, so that while some

[41] Majjhima Nikāya iii.128-137 (trans. Ñāṇamoḷi and Bodhi 1995:989-996).
[42] For instance, AN ii.116; Th 31, 1141; Ud 45.
[43] Examples are MN i.386, i.450; Sn 29, 53; Th 1105, 1184; Thī 301.
[44] For instance, SN ii.217, v.43, v.231; Jā v.259.

verses (Dhp 320-322 and 326) speak approvingly of elephant training, two other verses (Dhp 329 and 330) recommend wandering alone like an elephant in the forest (*eko care mātaṅg' araññe va nāgo*).

The Pali material, just as might be expected of a voluminous and collaborative work, contains a number of diverse or even contradictory metaphors and similes; an idealised view of the lone, wild elephant counters the alternative vision of the tamed elephant integrated into social life. By contrast, as a single author exerting authorial control, Aśvaghoṣa presents a co-ordinated and integrated formulation of the elephant imagery. He has nothing about elephants breaking their bonds or roaming at will in the forest, but is more selective, choosing to develop one conceptual metaphor that supports his theme of conversion from an inferior to a superior spiritual condition. Additionally, Aśvaghoṣa's elephant imagery points to a paradox at the heart of the *Saundarananda* - that the life of the libertine, the life of attachment to sensual pleasures, is really bondage, while true liberation lies in perfect discipline. Under the tutelage of the Buddha, Nanda moves from the former to the latter, from wild elephant to noble, much-prized, fully-trained elephant, from feckless young sensualist to arhat. The figurative use of elephants is integral to this depiction and forms a coherent and sustained exposition of Aśvaghoṣa's message.

CHAPTER FOUR

NANDA HEALED

The metaphor of healing is one of the most prominent metaphors in Buddhist works, and this applies also to the *Saundarananda*. The *Saundarananda*'s medical allusions are drawn from traditional Indian medicine, Āyurveda. Any medical system, including Āyurveda, can be shown, when analysed, to consist of four elements, or 'limbs', to use the typical Indian metaphor. These four aspects are the doctor, the patient, the disease, and the treatment, and in combination they form what I call the medical model or paradigm. In the normal operation of the medical model, the doctor provides treatment to the patient who has a disease. Variations on the model are possible. The role of doctor and patient converge, for instance, when a sick person looks after himself without recourse to a medical specialist, and homeopathic medicine might serve as an example of the convergence of treatment and sickness. It might also be argued that the concept of 'patient' subsumes the concept of 'sickness', and similarly, that the concept of 'doctor' necessarily includes his curative actions. Nevertheless, I propose the four-limbed model as the basic paradigm of medical practice, and this chapter is structured accordingly.

Aśvaghoṣa adopts the medical paradigm as a vehicle to highlight certain traits of the *Saundarananda*'s two central characters, to explore issues of passivity and agency in the relationship between the two characters, to call attention to the undesirability of the pre-enlightened condition and the desirability of the enlightened condition, and above all to express movement from the pre-enlightened to the enlightened condition. Thus the primary function of the medical metaphor is to delineate the evolution from Nanda the libertine into Nanda the liberated man. These applications of the medical model to the Nanda story form the topic of this chapter. I begin the chapter with a brief survey of works I consulted in order to familiarise myself with the principles of Indian medicine, after which I discuss the emphasis placed on actual medical practice in early Buddhism. I then move on to consider the imaginative aspect of the medical model in Buddhist literature generally. This discussion functions as a preliminary to the bulk of the chapter, which consists of an exploration of some of the *Saundarananda*'s many medical allusions. This large amount of material is ordered according to the medical model defined above, using the four categories of illness, patient, doctor and treatment. I conclude with a consideration of several reasons why the medical paradigm is particularly well-suited to Aśvaghoṣa's theme of conversion.

In my investigations into early Indian medical theory and practice I have relied chiefly on four texts. Three are medical treatises, the "great threesome" (*bṛhat-trayī*) of Indian Āyurvedic medicine. These three classics are the *Caraka-saṃhitā*, dating from the early 2nd century CE, the somewhat later *Suśruta-saṃhitā* from around the 4th century CE, and Vāgbhaṭa's *Aṣṭāṅga-hṛdaya* dating from approximately 600 CE. Caraka was not the sole author of the work which now bears his name, but the editor of earlier versions, which may have been up to two or three hundred years older. The work underwent further revisions in the fourth or fifth centuries. Caraka casts his work as a teaching of the sage Ātreya, a legendary physician to whom Aśvaghoṣa refers in *Buddhacarita* 1:43. The *Caraka-Saṃhitā* is particularly noteworthy in a consideration of Aśvaghoṣa's works, since a Chinese text of the late 5th century CE[1] lists Caraka along with Aśvaghoṣa (and together with a third person, the prime minister Māṭhara) as intimate friends of the Kuṣāṇa king Kaniṣka. We are therefore presented with the interesting possibility that Aśvaghoṣa was personally acquainted with the great physician. The second of the three great early medical authorities is Suśruta. Like Caraka before him, he collated several layers of older works in compiling his treatise, and was also subject to later revisions in his turn. The third of the medical authorities is Vāgbhaṭa, author of the highly influential *Aṣṭāṅga-hṛdaya* and possibly also of a closely related prose version, the *Aṣṭāṅga-saṃgraha*. The *Aṣṭāṅga-hṛdaya* is a long,

---

[1] This document is discussed on page 2 above.

polished work that retains much of Caraka's and Suśruta's material, but presents it in a more structured and organised format.[2] Finally, the text to which I have turned most frequently is the *Mahāvagga* section from the Pali *Vinaya*. Two of the *Mahāvagga* chapters, namely chapter six, the *Bhesajja-kkhandhaka*, and chapter eight, the *Cīvara-kkhandhaka*, provide ample information testifying to the importance of medical knowledge in early Buddhism.

Contemporary discussions of the interplay between Buddhism and medicine appear to be limited to two authors, Kenneth Zysk and Raoul Birnbaum. In his book *Asceticism and Healing in Ancient India: Medicine in the Buddhist Monastery* (1991), Zysk presents a fascinating case for the primacy of early Buddhist medical practice in the subsequent development of Āyurvedic medicine, but he confines himself to factual matters and makes no mention of the impact of healing on the Buddhist imagination. Birnbaum in *The Healing Buddha* (1979) does consider the Buddhist equation of physical and spiritual disease and healing, but his discussion is short and the book is in the main devoted to translations from Chinese *sūtras* relating to Bhaiṣajyaguru and other healing figures in the Mahāyāna pantheon. Furthermore, Birnbaum does not properly engage with the medical model as a metaphor. Rather, he maintains a focus on physical illness that is cured by spiritual methods, such as meditation and the invocation of healing deities. Birnbaum is particularly alive to the potential for spiritual growth that physical illness may hold, exploring, within a specifically Mahāyānist context, the idea of illness as a catalyst for higher attainment.

Medicine was clearly considered a basic necessity in the early Buddhist world, since it is one of the four resources or requisites (*nissaya*), along with food, clothing and lodging, on

---

[2] Dominik Wujastyk (1998), in an excellent introduction to his translations from Āyurvedic literature, traces the complexities of the evolution of the *Caraka-saṃhitā* (pp. 40-2) and the *Suśruta-saṃhitā* (pp. 105-6), and summarises the debate concerning the authorship and dates of the *Aṣṭāṅga-hṛdaya* and the *Aṣṭāṅga-saṃgraha* (pp. 239-42).

which a monk could depend.[3] Although such medicine was restricted to fermented cow's urine, the fact remains that medicine was seen to be on a par with other essentials for daily living. This one medicine originally permitted by the Buddha quickly expanded into an extensive pharmacopoeia, a process described in the *Bhesajja-kkhandhaka*. The early Buddhist medical chest soon included roots, leaves, fruit, resins and salt, amongst other substances. The pattern depicted in the *Bhesajja-kkhandhaka* is that a monk falls ill, and during the course of his treatment a need arises or a lack is discovered; the carers apply to the Buddha, who then permits new substances to be used as medicines. For instance, for a group of monks who have become pale and emaciated from frequent vomiting, the Buddha allows high-calorie foods to be used as medicine - ghee, fresh butter, oil, honey and molasses (VinMV 6.1.1-5). The medicinal use of specific foods is typical of the *Bhesajja-kkhandhaka*, with dietary regulation playing a major part in the treatment of the sick. Early on in the story of the pale and emaciated monks the Buddha makes an important concession: when the monks still fail to thrive, although they are eating the high-calorie foods at the prescribed meal-times, the Buddha allows the medicines to be taken at any time, on the basis that medicines cannot be counted as substantial food (*oḷāriko āhāro*) even though they serve as nutriment (*āhārattham*).

The *Bhesajja-kkhandhaka* episodes convey a concern with the proper use of medicines, not just the times at which they are be taken, but that they should be taken only by those who really need them. Sometimes foods designated as medicines are to be used in certain strengths by the ill, but are permissible in diluted form as drinks for the healthy. So it is in the case of the "salted sour gruel" (*loṇaso-vīrakam*) at VinMV 6.16.3 given to a monk with a stomach complaint. Those who are not ill are allowed to take it as a drink mixed with water (*agilānassa udaka-sambhinnaṃ pāna-paribhogena paribhuñjitum*). Similarly in VinMV 6.27.1 sugar (*guḷam*) is allowed for the sick, sugar-water

[3] VinMV 1.30.4

(*guḷodakam*) for the well. In VinMV 6.3.1-2 the Buddha declares it an offence for a monk to make use of medicines when he is not sick (*asati paccaye paribhuñjantassa āpatti dukkaṭassa*). Medicines are to be used solely to ward off pain and to maintain health, according to a passage at MN i.10, and only after wise reflection.

As well as pointing to the growing range of medicinal substances, the *Bhesajja-kkhandhaka* also reveals the increasing sophistication of medical instruments and equipment. When a problem with existing arrangements is brought to the Buddha's attention, the Buddha sanctions a modification of the existing practice or the introduction of a new practice. An example occurs at VinMV 6.12.1-4, which begins by describing how monks used to place ointment in bowls and saucers. When dust got into the ointment, the Buddha allowed ointment boxes. The ointment boxes were uncovered, so the Buddha allowed lids. The monks put on ointment with their fingers, so the Buddha allowed an ointment stick - and so on. Often the medical modification or innovation is suggested to the Buddha, but sometimes the Buddha takes so active an interest in a medical case as to make him almost literally a physician himself. At one point the Buddha discovers that the physician Ākāsagotta has treated a monk suffering from a rectal ulcer (*bhagandalābādho*) with lancing. The Buddha is displeased, and forbids lancing in the private parts, saying the skin is too tender, the wound hard to heal and the knife hard to guide. Instead, he recommends a suppository as the proper treatment in such a case (VinMV 6.22.1-4). It is interesting to note that the Buddha has the medical knowledge to allow him to criticise an existing treatment and to suggest an alternative, in opposition to prevailing medical opinion in the form of Ākāsagotta. There is also the famous account of the Buddha caring for a sick monk, and instructing the monks to do likewise (VinMV 8.26.3).

The general impression given by the *Vinaya* literature is of a fascination with the medical process, with the Buddha personally taking an interest in medicines and treatments. Buddhist *Vinaya* literature represents the earliest extant descriptions of Indian medical practices and the earliest attempt at a codification of medicines. This close identification of the development of medical practice with the Buddhist monastic establishment has led one author, Kenneth Zysk, to argue that Āyurveda, India's traditional system of medicine, derives from the medical practices of early Buddhist monastic establishments, and not from brahminical sources, as had previously been thought.[4] Zysk rightly maintains that a proper consideration of the close connection between the medical tradition and Buddhist monasticism would deepen the understanding of Indian medical history and would also highlight this essential aspect of Buddhism, but he makes no mention, even in passing, of the considerable imaginative impact of the medical connection on Buddhist culture. In fact, the medical model of a diseased patient healed by the treatment of a skilled physician provided a fertile conceptual basis for the idea of humanity's suffering alleviated by the Buddha's teaching. The identification of the Buddha as a doctor who treats suffering humanity became so widespread that even Vāgbhaṭa, perhaps the most famed of India's medical authorities, subscribed to it. Both the *Aṣṭāṅga-hṛdaya* and the *Aṣṭāṅga-saṃgraha* commence with a nod at the Buddhist medical metaphor, contained within a verse of obeisance to the Buddha, acknowledging him as "unprecedented physician (*apūrva-vaidya*, VāgAṣṭHṛd 1.1.1) and "the one physician" (*eka-vaidya*, VāgAṣṭSam 1.1.1) who has destroyed "diseases beginning with passion" (*rāgādi-rogāḥ*, VāgAṣṭHṛd 1.1.1, VāgAṣṭSam 1.1.1).

The first and most fundamental article of the Buddhist medical metaphor is that the Buddha is the physician. A few examples will suffice to demonstrate the ubiquity of this identification. The monk Adhimutta hails the Buddha as his teacher, proclaiming him the healer of the whole world (*sabba-loka-tikicchako*, Th 722). Elsewhere the Buddha announces that he is "the unsurpassed physician and surgeon" (*anuttaro bhisakko salla-katto*, It 101) and similarly, "I am ... the

[4] Zysk (1991: Chapters 3-4) provides textual and epigraphical evidence to link medical practice to early Buddhist monasteries.

unsurpassed surgeon" (*soham ... salla-katto anuttaro*, Sn 560). In the *Mahāvastu* the Buddha is called on to cure the people of Vaiśālī, who are afflicted by a plague; he drives out the plague by his mere presence (Mvu 1.202ff.). And so on throughout Buddhist literature. Images of the Buddha as a healing figure are equally plentiful in Mahāyāna works. In the *Lalitavistara*, the Buddha is addressed as the 'king of physicians' (*vaidya-rāju*) who will 'cure' (*bheṣyasi*, Lal 206.8) the world and also as 'best of physicians' (*vaidyottama*, Lal 255.8, 265.26 etc.). One well-known appearance of the Buddha as a doctor occurs in chapter 15 of the *Lotus Sūtra*. This famous parable is provided as an explanation for why the Buddhas do not dwell constantly in the world. A father, a brilliant apothecary, is abroad while his many sons take some harmful drugs and fall ill. He returns and finds them all sick to varying degrees, and some have become deluded. He prepares an antidote, and while those that are still sane take it, the others do not. So he uses his skillful means (*upāya kauśalya*) to bring them to their senses. He goes away again, leaving the antidote behind, and while abroad, sends word of his death. The sad news shocks his sons into sanity and they take the medicine he has left them, whereupon they are all cured. The father then returns amid general rejoicing. Whatever the doctrinal significance of the parable, it is sufficient for the purposes of this chapter to notice that firstly, the physician is a master chemist with a great knowledge of substances (the Buddha is perfectly wise and skillful); secondly, his many sons are all sick (all living beings suffer); thirdly, the doctor goes away but leaves his medicine behind (the Buddha is no longer in the world but his teaching remains); and finally, the sons take the medicine and recover (people can attain liberation by following the Buddha's teachings). The process by which healing qualities are attributed to the Buddha culminates in the figure of Bhaiṣajyaguru, the Medicine Buddha popular in Tibetan and Japanese Buddhism. The *Bhaiṣajyaguru Sūtra*, a work from roughly the 4th century CE,[5] recounts Bhaiṣajyaguru's twelve great vows, one of which is to cure those who are "ugly, stupid,

[5] Birnbaum (1979:54).

deaf, blind, mute, bent and lame, hunchbacked, leprous, convulsive, insane, or who have all sorts of diseases and sufferings"; another is that those who are "ill and oppressed, who have nowhere to go and nothing to return to, who have neither doctor nor medicine, neither relatives nor immediate family", will, upon hearing his name, "be cured of all their diseases and they will be peaceful and joyous in body and mind".[6] Bhaiṣajyaguru is depicted in iconography holding a bowl of medicine in his left hand and in his right hand the stem of a myrobalan, a plant renowned for its healing properties.

The second tenet of the Buddhist medical metaphor is that the afflictions that beset mankind are analogous to physical ailments. The terms of this second proposition are by no means as stable as those just encountered in the first; the suffering that afflicts a human being and the medical condition to which it is likened both allow for some variety. Several conditions are perceived as illnesses in the Pali texts. In the *Sāmañña-phala Sutta*, the state of illness is simply the household life, while the state of well-being is the ascetic life of a monk (DN i.72). In the *Māgandiya Sutta* an extensive allegory compares a life devoted to sensual pleasure to leprosy (MN i.505-508). Vivid descriptions of the leper's efforts to alleviate his torment by tearing his open sores with his nails and by scorching his body with charcoal are set alongside the sensual man's strivings for the objects of the senses, as he vainly attempts to relieve the itching and burning of his desire. Sometimes the entire body itself is said to be diseased, likened to a wound (*vaṇa*, Mil 74), or an abscess: "'Abscess', monks, is a term for this body ..." (*gaṇḍo ti kho bhikkhave imassetaṃ ...kāyassa adhivacanam,* SN iv.83). Frequently the whole human condition, *duḥkha*, is conceived as an illness. The brahmin Piṅgiyānin uses a medical simile at AN iii.238 to testify to the effect of the Buddha's discourse on this condition:

---

[6] Birnbaum (1979:153-4).

"Sir, just as a skilled physician would systematically remove the sickness of a sick man who is suffering and extremely ill, in the same way, sir, whenever the *dhamma* of his honour Gotama is heard … then sorrow, lamentation, suffering, dejection and despair disappear."

Seyyathāpi, bho, puriso ābādhiko dukkhito bāḷha-gilāno. Tassa kusalo bhisakko ṭhānaso ābādhaṃ nīhareyya; evam evaṃ kho, bho, yato yato tassa bhoto gotamassa dhammaṃ suṇāti ... tato tato soka-parideva-dukkha-domanass-upāyāsā abbhatthaṃ gacchanti.

As well as taking the form of diseases, the sufferings which afflict mankind also very frequently present themselves as arrows, darts, splinters or any other foreign object which lodges in the body and causes pain. Sanskrit *śalya*[7] and Pali *salla* are the common terms for an object of this kind. In this context the Buddha appears as the surgeon (Sanskrit *śalya-hṛt*, Pali *salla-katto*) who removes the arrow embedded in the sufferer's body. Often the arrow indicates desire[8], sometimes grief[9] or other destructive states. In the *Theragāthā* the monk Telakāni speaks of the arrow stuck in him, and asks: "Who without a knife, without a wound, without injury to my whole body, will draw out the dart, the dart which lies inside me?" (Th 757). The dart is described as "the arrow of desire tied together with uncertainty and doubt, fastened by the strength of impetuosity, having feathers of anger, stiffened by pride, originating from the bow of craving…".[10] The *Māluṅkyaputta Sutta* contains what is undoubtedly the Pali Canon's best-known arrow-wound allegory (MN i.429-430). Māluṅkyaputta famously declares that he will renounce the robe if the Buddha doesn't answer ten questions.

---

[7] The term *śalya* has a wide semantic field and covers all manner of foreign objects from a piece of food stuck in the throat to a barbed metal arrow, as well as objects internal to the body such as tumours, teeth, nails and splinters of bone. (See Suśr 1.26).

[8] For *taṇhā-salla* see SN i.40, i.192; for *rāgasalla* see Dhp-a III.404; Pv-a 230.

[9] For *soka-salla* see Sn 985, Khp-a 153; *Mahā-niddesa* 1.5.

[10] Th 752-3, translated Norman (1997).

The Buddha responds that for Māluṅkyaputta not to wear the robe until these questions are answered would be like a man refusing to have a poisoned arrow extracted until he finds out various pieces of irrelevant information, such as the name, clan and caste of the archer, his height, what the arrow is made of, what bird provided the feathers for the arrow shaft, and so on. The man will die of his wounds before he finds out all these details, says the Buddha. Likewise Māluṅkyaputta will die before he finds answers to his questions. The arrow-wound represents the woe endured by human beings, and the wounded man's pressing need for medical attention stands here for the urgency with which the Buddha's teachings should be put into practice; a delay while one seeks to satisfy one's curiosity is irrelevant at best, life-threatening at worst.

The afflictions that beset mankind may also present themselves as poisons which enter the body from an external source, and which are fatal unless treated quickly. Sometimes poison imagery is used in conjunction with arrow imagery. Arrows smeared with poison were used in ancient India to hunt animals,[11] and the medical metaphor is expanded to include this practice. The story told by the Buddha to Māluṅkyaputta elaborates that the arrow that caused the wound was smeared with poison.[12] At other times poisoning is the result of snakebite. The opening verse of the *Sutta Nipāta* employs a snake venom simile, in which anger is likened to the venom circulating round the body: "He who subdues anger when it springs up, as spreading snake poison (*visaṭaṃ sappavisaṃ*) is subdued by antidotes (*osadhehi*), that monk leaves the lower and the higher worlds..." (Sn 1).

While the healing figure of Buddhist medical imagery is immediately recognisable as the Buddha, the suffering patient is only occasionally identified. One example is the elder Telakāni, who recognises that he has a dart embedded in his heart (Th 752-

---

[11] Aśvaghoṣa refers to this practice in 6:24.

[12] For further examples of allegories involving poisoned arrows, see MN ii.216 and MN ii.257.

7). More frequently the patient remains an anonymous representative of mankind. He is a man wounded by an arrow thickly smeared with poison (*puriso sallena viddho assa savisena gāḷhūpalepanena*, MN i.429, ii.216, ii.257), a man with leprosy (*kuṭṭhī puriso*, MN i.507), or a man who is afflicted, suffering, and gravely ill (*puriso ābādhiko asso dukkhito bāḷha-gilāno*, DN i.72; MN i.275). An interesting twist on this scenario is provided by an early Mahāyāna *sūtra*, the *Vimalakīrti-nirdeśa Sūtra*, in which a bodhisattva, appearing in the guise of the sick layman Vimalakīrti, uses his sickness as an expedient to draw visitors to his bedside. From this vantage point he preaches to them on the impermanence of the body and its susceptibility to suffering, thus dispensing the dharma while he himself remains ill. When the great bodhisattva Mañjuśrī comes to enquire after the nature of his sickness, Vimalakīrti responds:

> "As long as beings are sick, I myself will also be sick; when beings recover, I also shall recover. And why? Mañjuśrī, ... sickness rests on this round of rebirth. When all beings have escaped the pains of this sickness, then Bodhisattvas also will be free of sickness. For example, O Mañjuśrī, if the only son of a guildsman falls sick, his father and mother would also both fall sick. As long as this only son does not recover, his father and mother will also both continue suffering. Equally, O Mañjuśrī, a Bodhisattva who cherishes beings as his only son is sick when beings are sick, and is free of sickness when they are free of sickness. You asked me, O Mañjuśrī, where my sickness comes from: in a Bodhisattva sickness arises from great compassion."[13]

It is clear that Vimalakīrti's illness is a sympathetic expression of his compassion for sentient beings, who are all considered ill until they reach liberation. That all unenlightened beings are sick is the logical consequence of the point made above that the human condition, *duḥkha*, is a sickness.

---

[13] *Vimalakīrti-nirdeśa Sūtra* IV, 6-7, trans. Lamotte (1976:118).

One integral element remains outstanding in the preceding discussion of the roles played by the physician, the patient and the sickness itself in the Buddhist medical metaphor. The final constituent necessary to complete the medical model is the treatment, which is administered by the physician to the patient in order to heal his disease. In the medical metaphor, treatment stands for the exposure to any aspect of Buddhist doctrine and practice that conduces to the spiritual well-being of the practitioner. Sometimes the presence alone of the Buddha suffices to heal disease, as in the *Mahāvastu*, which relates how the Buddha three times allays an outbreak of plague by his mere presence (Mvu 1.208-225). Occasionally a teaching has an effect so profound that it extends to the physical realm, causing a disease to be eliminated. One such teaching is the seven factors of enlightenment, the recitation of which is used as an instrument of healing in SN v.79-81, curing first Mahākassapa of a painful illness, then Mahāmoggallāna, and finally the Buddha himself. In those instances when the patient is said to be suffering from a barb or arrow (*śalya* or *salla*), treatment is likened to a surgical procedure. In the *Sunakkhatta Sutta*, for instance, the Buddha illustrates the process whereby cravings are eliminated with a simile of the surgical removal of an arrow:

> "Suppose, Sunakkhatta, a man were wounded by an arrow thickly smeared with poison, and his friends and companions, his kinsmen and relatives, brought a surgeon. The surgeon would cut around the opening of the wound with a knife, then he would probe for the arrow with a probe, then he would pull out the arrow and would expel the poisonous humour without leaving a trace of it behind."

The Buddha goes on to explain his simile:

> "Sunakkhatta, I have given this simile in order to convey a meaning. This is the meaning here: 'Wound' is a term for the six internal bases. 'Poisonous humour' is a term

> for ignorance. 'Arrow' is a term for craving. 'Probe' is a term for mindfulness. 'Knife' is a term for noble wisdom. 'Surgeon' is a term for the Tathāgata, the Accomplished One, the Fully Enlightened One."[14]

The teachings of the Buddha are frequently likened to the effective treatment of a skilled physician, as they are at AN iii.238, quoted on page 106 above. The Buddha's speech is a remedy that alleviates sickness, as Nāgasena informs King Milinda:

> "The Tathāgata's words, sire, even when severe, are spoken so that beings may abandon defilements. As, sire, the drinking of foul-smelling cow's urine (*duggandham pi gomuttaṃ*) and the swallowing of distasteful medicine (*virasam pi agadaṃ*) remove illness from beings, even, so sire, the Tathāgata's words, even when severe, are purposeful and compassionate." (Mil 172).

To summarise the Buddhist medical metaphor, three conditions that require medical attention make regular appearances - disease, arrow wounds and cases of poisoning. The human afflictions for which they serve as metaphors include negative mental states such as grief, anger and desire, as well as suffering generally (*duḥkha*), and even the physical body itself. The physician who prescribes the treatment is unvaryingly representative of the Buddha (alternatively, in Mahāyāna Buddhism, an advanced bodhisattva), while the patient who receives treatment is generally an unnamed Everyman who serves as a symbol of all mankind. The treatment dispensed by the physician includes medicine, surgery and the administration of purgatives and emetics, all illustrative of the dharma, the Buddha's teaching.

The examples above typify the immense imaginative importance of the medical metaphor in many Buddhist texts.

---

[14] MN ii.259-60, trans. Ñāṇamoḷi and Bodhi (1995:866-7).

The prominence of the medical metaphor applies also to the *Saundarananda*, where it features in over fifty metaphors and similes, forming one of the cornerstones of Aśvaghoṣa's construction of the conversion theme. An analysis of the medical metaphor is therefore likely to provide a good indication of Aśvaghoṣa's conception of the conversion process. The medical metaphor appears in the *Saundarananda* as a fairly complex web of interrelated issues, which I have tried to separate out under the heads of illness, patient, doctor and treatment. The results of my analysis are presented in the remainder of this chapter.

4.1 The Illness

It is important to state at the outset that despite Aśvaghoṣa's exploitation of illness as a highly productive metaphor for human existence, he was very much aware that illness is all too frequently a literal fact of life. He routinely lists old age, sickness and death (*jarā, vyādhi, mṛtyuḥ*) as the triad that makes life unsatisfactory.[15] According to the Buddhist tradition, it was these three sights, embodied as an old man, a sick man and a corpse, which inspired the Buddha-to-be to set off on his search for the end of suffering. Aśvaghoṣa briefly mentions the event at 2:64 and recounts it at length in the *Buddhacarita*, Canto 3. The vivid description of the sick man at AśvBC 3:41 emphasises the sheer physical suffering that disease entails. In Johnston's translation, "Who is this man with swollen belly and body that heaves with his panting? His shoulders and arms are fallen in, his limbs emaciated and pale? He calls out piteously, "mother", as he leans on another for support." Sickness is one of the three great blights on human existence.

The undesirability of sickness, and its corollary, the desirability of health, together provide an obvious and potent metaphor for the unenlightened and enlightened states, for *duḥkha* and *nirvāṇa*. It is in terms of sickness and health that

---

[15] In verses 14:30, 15:15 and 15:46, for example.

Aśvaghoṣa chooses to define these states, as part of his elucidation of the Four Noble Truths:

tad vyādhi-saṃjñāṃ kuru duḥkha-satye
doṣeṣv api vyādhi-nidāna-saṃjñāṃ |
ārogya-saṃjñāṃ ca nirodha-satye
bhaiṣajya-saṃjñāṃ api mārga-satye || (16:41)

So with regard to the [first] truth, you should perceive suffering as a disease, [with regard to the second truth] faults as the cause of disease, with regard to the [third] truth the cessation [of suffering] as good health[16], and with regard to the [fourth] truth, the Path as the medicine.

Aśvaghoṣa's interpretation agrees with, but much predates, the understanding of the Four Noble Truths popularised by Buddhaghosa[17], whereby the first truth, the fact of suffering (*duḥkha*), is seen as the diagnosis of an illness, the second truth, the arising of suffering (*duḥkha-samudaya*), establishes the cause of the illness, the third truth, the cessation of suffering (*duḥkha-nirodha)*, offers a positive prognosis, and the fourth truth, the path (*mārga*), prescribes the necessary treatment to reach that condition of wellness.

Since Aśvaghoṣa explicitly relates the First Noble Truth to sickness, any negative condition which is symptomatic of *duḥkha* can be figuratively presented as an illness. However, Aśvaghoṣa also figuratively presents some specific aspects of

---

[16] I have translated *ārogya* as 'good health' although the Sanskrit word more accurately means "no sickness" since it from derives *roga* (sick) together with the negative prefix in *vṛddhi* form. For the modern Western understanding a mere absence of disease might not necessarily imply good health, but the traditional Āyurvedic approach is more holistic. Any malaise, whether physical, mental or emotional, would detract from perfect health. A description such as "freedom from sickness" should therefore be interpreted positively as excellent health.

[17] *rogo viya ca dukkha-saccaṃ, roga-nidānam iva samudaya-saccaṃ, rogavūpasamo viya nirodha-saccaṃ, bhesajjam iva magga-saccaṃ* (Vism 512).

duḥkha in terms of disease. In 15:52, the notion of immortality (*vitarkaḥ ... amaraṇāśrayaḥ*) is like a disease (*vyādhi*). In 17:9, an unskillful thought (*akuśalo vitarkaḥ*) occurring in Nanda's mind as he prepares for meditation is likened to a violent new symptom (*upadravo ghoraḥ*) in a man who is endeavouring to overcome his illness. The unskillful thought is no doubt a recurrence of his consciousness of lust (*kāma-saṃjñā*) that troubles him two verses earlier, in 17:7. According to the early medical authorities, an *upadrava* is a secondary symptom of a disease which manifests itself at a later stage in the development of that disease.[18] Attaching the label *upadrava* to Nanda's sudden unskillful thought just as he zealously sets about meditation indicates that his disease of attachment has not yet been fully eradicated, though it has at least reached another stage in its evolution. Aśvaghoṣa's understanding of metaphorical illness also includes chronic conditions, as in 16:9, where the very fact of being born is fatal (*vināśāya*), since all birth (*sarvaṃ janma*) is like food mixed with poison (*viṣa-miśram annam*). In 9:16 the body *per se* is a disease (*śarīram āturam*).

In order to comprehend Aśvaghoṣa's deployment of the medical model as a dynamic process which explains staying sick as well as getting healthy, I will try to piece together Aśvaghoṣa's understanding of the aetiology of disease, in which the constitution of the human body is crucial. The human body, the locus of disease, is the subject matter of Canto 9. Canto 9 consists of the unnamed ascetic's extended denunciation of the body, inspired by his observation that Nanda is caught up in the myth of his own physical wellness (9:4). The unnamed monk's argument is intended to persuade Nanda not to rely on his youth, good looks, health and physical prowess, but has little effect. The words *bala* occurs very frequently in this canto (27 times in a canto of just 51 verses), and indicates not strength alone, but a sense of physical well-being, fitness, health, energy and

[18] "An *upadrava* is a sickness arising at a later time which is superinduced on a sickness that had arisen previously, and which is rooted in that [prior sickness]" (*pūrvotpannaṃ vyādhiṃ jaghanya-kāla-jāto vyādhir upasṛjati sa tan-mūla evopadrava-saṃjñaḥ*, Suśr 1:35:2).

robustness generally. While Nanda feels that he has *bala* in abundance (9:2, 9:4, 9:5), the unnamed monk is at pains to emphasise the instability and weakness of the body. The body is unstable (*avyavasthitam*, 9:5), the living quarters of disease (*rogāyatanam*, 9:6), helpless before old age (*jarāvaśam*, 9:6), frail as a water-bubble (*jala-phena-durbala*, 9:6), dependent on food (*āhāra-vaśena tiṣṭhati*, 9:9), and needs to be carefully tended with good sleeping, drinking and eating habits (9:14). The human body is totally unattractive in its natural state, that is, when it is unwashed and naked (9:26). Finally, it is the vehicle of a great deal of suffering (*bahu-duḥkham*, 9:42). Aśvaghoṣa reserves some of his finest similes for the denunciation of the body: the frail yet sustenance-demanding body is like a tyrant who forcibly takes the full sum of taxes from his subjects, yet fails to protect them (9:38); or it is like sugar-cane, which, once all its juice is squeezed out, is thrown on the ground to dry it out for burning (9:31); or, in a wonderful personification of night and day as two woodsmen, a man's body is toppled by day and night wielding the saw of old age, just as a mighty tree is chopped down by two men working a saw (9:32). The extreme vulnerability of the human body to debilitating conditions is stressed throughout Canto 9.

As regards its constitution, the body is said to consist of elements (*dhātu*, 9:12, 9:13 and 9:37), a description which tallies with the traditional Buddhist view. The elements listed in 9:12 are the four primary elements of matter[19], namely water, earth, wind and fire (9:12), corresponding with the enumeration given in the Pali Canon at DN ii.293, MN i.57 and MN iii.90. The technical term for the four primary elements, *mahā-bhūta*, is used by Aśvaghoṣa in verse 15:56, again in the context of the body. The elements are mentioned in the *Buddhacarita* as a cause of sickness. When the bodhisattva asks about the unfortunate sick man whom he encounters on his second outing from the palace, his charioteer replies "the great misfortune

---

[19] There is also a larger group of six elements (*dhātu*) consisting of four primary elements plus space and mind, to which Aśvaghoṣa refers in verse 16:46.

known as sickness has developed, arisen from upsetting the elements" (*dhātu-prakopa-prabhavaḥ pravṛddhaḥ | rogābhidhānaḥ sumahān anarthaḥ*, AśvBC 3:42). On two occasions in the *Buddhacarita*, a polite enquiry after someone's health is phrased in terms of balanced elements: "He asked about the equilibrium of his elements" (*papraccha ca dhātu-sāmyam*, AśvBC 10:20) and "having asked about each other's equilibrium of elements" (*pṛṣṭvā dhātu-sāmyaṃ parasparam*, AśvBC 12:3). Balanced elements correspond to good health, but when the elements are upset, then disease ensues.

The *Saundarananda* insinuates rather than expressly declares that irritable elements are a factor in disease pathology. The elements are said to be constantly in opposition (*sadā viruddhā*, 9:12), abiding in the body only to do it harm (*anarthāya*, 9:12). The elements are defective (*duṣṭa*, 9:37). Who could be happy carrying around a body that depends on the elements (*nirvṛtaḥ ko bhavet kāyaṃ mahā-bhūtāśrayaṃ vahan*, 15:56)? Above all, it is the regular likening of the elements to snakes, surely the most dangerous creatures on the sub-continent, that gives an overwhelming impression of the aggression and virulence of the elements. The elements are like contrary snakes (*viṣamā ivoragāḥ*, 9:12), the imbalance (*viṣama*) of the elements here contrasting with the balanced elements (*dhātu-sāmyam*, AśvBC 10:20 and AśvBC 12:3 as discussed above) necessary for good health. Indeed, the elements are considerably more harmful than snakes. Snakes can be subdued by mantras, and in any case do not bite all people all the time, but the elements are not amenable to mantras, and strike everywhere at all times (*sadā ca sarvaṃ ca tudanti dhātavaḥ*, 9:13). The body is described as a hovel full of snakes (*sapannage kugṛhe*, 9:37) which one would be foolish to consider pleasurable. Bearing a body consisting of the elements is like carrying around a pot of snakes fighting each other (*paraspara-viruddhānām ahīnām iva bhājanam*, 15:56), an apt simile for illustrating the hazard posed by these reptilian elements – one small mishap and one will no longer be able to "keep a lid on it" (assuming that a *bhājanam* has a lid; if not, the danger is even more acute). Thus the portrayal of the elements in the *Saundarananda* is entirely negative, and although none of the occurrences of the word *dhātu* appears in the immediate context of disease, the elements are nothing but harmful to the human body, and so, by implication, pathogenic.[20] The elements are implacably hostile, yet intrinsic to the human body, and there is never any suggestion that they can be removed. No information is given as to why the *dhātus* are so rude, other than the Buddha's recommendation to Nanda in 16:47 that he should examine "the elements, which are full of suffering, impermanent and without self" (*duḥkhān anityāṃś ca nirātmakāṃś ca dhātūn*). It seems that, characterised as they are by these "three marks" (Sanskrit *trilakṣaṇa*, Pali *tilakkhaṇa*), this is simply their nature.

One further item is required to complete the picture of Aśvaghoṣa's presentation of disease. This is *doṣa*, the translation of which is fraught with difficulties. Aśvaghoṣa uses the word *doṣa* in three different ways: firstly, *doṣa* can mean something that is generally weak, faulty or defective. Examples are "What's wrong with that?" (*ka ivāsti doṣaḥ*, 6:48), and "seeing what was wrong with the objects of the senses" (*viṣayeṣu doṣa-darśin*, 8:25). Secondly, a more specifically Buddhist usage of *doṣa* refers to a fundamental character fault, a psychological flaw which prevents enlightenment. The *Saundarananda* does not normally specify what these faults are, and the most common reference is simply to "faults" in the plural. Verse 13:14, however, refers to "five faults, starting with hypocrisy" (*doṣāṇāṃ kuhanādīnaṃ pañcānām*) and verse 16:22, while also mentioning an unspecified "lesser fault" (*alpa-doṣaḥ*) gives what is usually considered the standard list of lust, hatred[21] and delusion. The six medical similes at 16:59-64, discussed in detail below, also give the standard listing. One character fault will tend to be dominant in one individual, and will persist

[20] This is the view of Caraka, who defines physical malfunction as an imbalance of the elements (*vikāro dhātu-vaiṣamyam*, Car 1.9.4).

[21] Providing *doṣa* in *pāda* a is interpreted as malice or hatred, like the Pali *dosa*. Verse 16:22 reads as follows:

> *doṣādhike janmani tīvra-doṣa utpadyate rāgiṇi tīvra-rāgaḥ* |
> *mohādhike moha-balādhikaś ca tad-alpa-doṣe ca tad-alpa-doṣaḥ* ||

through rebirth after rebirth, as the passage at 16:17-24 attests. Once the fault is destroyed (*doṣa-kṣayaḥ*), rebirth no longer occurs (16:24), and enlightenment is attained. One must therefore endeavour to destroy the faults, a struggle that features in numerous military similes. The *Saundarananda* insists that the faults are to be completely eradicated without leaving any trace. "Wisdom destroys faults without a remainder" (*prajñā tv aśeṣeṇa nihanti doṣān*, 16:36). Nanda accomplishes this in 17:59, where his utter destruction of the faults is compared in a burst of similes to rain extinguishing a fire, wind uprooting a tree, fire burning up ghee, and the sun evaporating water. Aśvaghoṣa's third usage of the term *doṣa* occurs in a medical context, where it refers to a substance in the body, often translated "humour", a translation which I shall adopt temporarily.

Like the elements discussed above, the humours (*doṣa*) are implicated in the pathology of disease, and like the elements, the humours are likened to snakes (14:29, 16:35). Fundamental to Āyurvedic thinking, and accepted by the *Saundarananda*, is the theory that three humours, namely wind (*vāyu*), bile or choler (*pitta*) and phlegm (*kapha*), are responsible for the onset of sickness. This is very convenient for a Buddhist author seeking to draw an analogy between spiritual debility and bodily maladies, since not only does the term *doṣa* refer to both physical humours and moral failings, but the three bodily humours which cause physical disease can be made to neatly correspond to the three main character faults of lust (*rāga*), hatred (*dveṣa*) and delusion (*moha*), which are the cause of rebirth. Aśvaghoṣa puts this happy parallel to work in the six medical similes on humoral malfunction at 16:59-64 discussed below, and also in 16:69, a verse which summarises the principle that there is a specific remedy for a specific ailment:

yathā bhiṣak pitta-kaphānilānāṁ
ya eva kopaṃ samupaiti doṣaḥ |
śamāya tasyaiva vidhiṁ vidhatte,
vyadhatta doṣeṣu tathaiva buddhaḥ || (16:69)

> Just as a doctor prescribes a treatment to pacify whichever among the humours of bile, phlegm and wind has become irritated, so too has the Buddha prescribed concerning the faults.

The effectiveness of this verse, turning on the dual meaning of *doṣa*, is further heightened by the inclusion of the word *śama*, meaning peace or calm. *Śama* is the medical tradition's standard term for the allayment of the humours, while in the Buddhist tradition it designates a desirable mental attribute in the practitioner. The correspondences set up in verse 16:69 can be charted as follows:

Source Domain	**Target Domain**
the doctor (*bhiṣaj*)	the Buddha
prescribes a treatment (*vi* + √*dhā*)	recommends a practice (*vi* + √*dhā*)
three bodily humours (*doṣa*)	psychological faults (*doṣa*)
the aim is a calm physical state (*śama*)	the aim is a calm mental state (*śama*)

This all seems logical enough until one remembers the exhortations to utterly eradicate the psychological faults (*doṣa*), without leaving any remainder. As discussed above, the *Saundarananda* over and over again urges the total destruction of the faults. If this principle is transferred from the target domain to the source domain, is one therefore to conclude that Aśvaghoṣa's model of disease requires the total elimination of the bodily humours (*doṣa*), and would such a conclusion square with Āyurvedic teachings? It appears that the medical metaphor threatens to break down when forced into too tight a fit with Buddhist doctrine.

The prevailing opinion in Āyurvedic thinking is that good health requires the humours to be in equilibrium. So for Suśruta,

sama-doṣaḥ samāgniś ca sama-dhātu-mala-kriyaḥ |
prasannātmendriya-manāḥ svastha ity abhidhīyate ||
(Suśr 1.15.41)

A person is said to be healthy when his humours are in equilibrium, his digestive fire is in equilibrium, the action of his elements and waste products is in equilibrium, and when his self, senses and mind are peaceful.

Similarly the great medical authority Vāgbhaṭa states that "illness is an imbalance of the humours, health is a balance of the humours" (*rogas tu doṣa-vaiṣamyaṃ doṣa-sāmyam arogatā*, VāgAṣṭSam 1.1.41). Indeed, Vāgbhaṭa describes the benefits of the humours, and the ill-effects that arise through their deficiency; too little wind (*vāyu*), for example, causes weariness and mental confusion, inadequate bile (*pitta*) leads to a poor digestion and colds, and a phlegm (*kapha*) deficiency brings about dizziness and heart palpitations.[22] A responsible physician will therefore seek to build up any humours that have diminished below the optimum level. Suśruta declares that "diminished humours should be strengthened, those that are irritated should be calmed" (*doṣāḥ kṣīṇā bṛṃhayitavyāḥ kupitāḥ praśamayitavyāḥ*, Suśr 4.33.3). This well-known Āyurvedic teaching has been absorbed by authors like Zysk (1991:29), who writes "The *doṣa*s are really specific waste products of digested food, occurring in quantities greater **or lesser** than needed to maintain normal health" (emphasis mine).

In attempting to reconcile the logic of Aśvaghoṣa's medical metaphor (which states that the *doṣa*s are to be eradicated) with the teaching of Āyurveda (which states that it is unhealthy if the level of the *doṣa*s sinks too low) one is faced with two equally impossible alternatives. Following the internal logic of Aśvaghoṣa's medical metaphor, the *doṣa*s would be completely eliminated, in which case, according to Āyurveda, one would be

[22] VāgAṣṭHṛd 1.11f.

considerably unwell. Or, following the Āyurvedic position, the *doṣas* would be maintained in the body and strengthened when necessary, which, when applied to Aśvaghoṣa's medical metaphor, would mean that the three psychological faults would always be present in an individual and should on occasion even be encouraged. This is clearly absurd – there is no healthy level of lust, hatred or delusion. Neither does Āyurveda accept deteriorating health as a positive outcome of therapy. It is this conundrum which forces Johnston to translate *doṣāṃś ca kāyād bhiṣag ujjihīrṣuḥ* (10:43a) as "a physician who wishes to remove diseases of the body". Johnston has no doubt accepted the standard Āyurvedic teaching that the humours (*doṣas*) are necessary for physical health, and that the desiderative *ujjihīrṣu* (intending to lift out, draw out, pull out, eradicate, remove) makes no sense in such a framework. Johnston realises that a translation such as "a physician who wishes to remove humours from the body" would be inappropriate, and therefore compromises by translating *doṣān* as 'diseases'.[23]

Fortunately, we do not have to concede that Aśvaghoṣa had a tenuous grasp on medical theory (despite his putative friendship with Caraka), nor that he forced its facts to fit his metaphor. Hartmut Scharfe (1999) has recently argued that the word *doṣa* has undergone an evolution in meaning. In the early literature (and he includes the Pali Canon, the Bower manuscript, the *Buddhacarita* and Caraka's compendium in this category), he finds that the substances in the body are only known as *doṣa* when they become inflamed. When they are not inflamed, they are not so termed. He asks "Why do we not see any "good" *doṣas* in the Pali Canon (or in *Caraka*, for that matter)?" (Scharfe 1999:614). This earlier level of literature only ever speaks of removing, destroying and pacifying the *doṣas*, never of strengthening or increasing them. It is only with Suśruta and subsequent writers that the term *doṣa* came to be used of the

[23] Other translators have made the same compromise. In a passage which speaks of a physician removing the humours by means of medicine, I. B. Horner (1963:59) translates the phrase *tehi ca dosā niggameyyum* (Mil 43) as "and if, because of them, his malady should be removed ..."

bodily substances in their natural state as well as in their inflamed state, at which point it became reasonable for medical practice to seek to strengthen the *doṣa*s. Scharfe consistently uses 'fault' for *doṣa* when translating the earlier material, and dislikes 'humour'; and he takes particular exception to Zysk's quaint rendering of *doṣa* as 'peccant humour'.[24] If one accepts Scharfe's argument that *doṣa* originally signified a purely harmful substance in the body, and that such a view was prevalent at the time of Aśvaghoṣa and Caraka, then it is entirely legitimate for the *Saundarananda* to insist on both the elimination of the psychological faults (*doṣa*s) and on the metaphorical identification of these psychological faults with the bodily humours (*doṣa*s). Verse 10:43, quoted in the paragraph above, and which on initial inspection appeared contentious, also makes perfect sense in the light of Scharfe's argument – a doctor should indeed desire to remove (*ujjihīrṣu*) the *doṣa*s from the body.

Having established the necessity of destroying both physical and psychological *doṣas*, I will move on to examine their diagnosis and treatment. Henceforward I will use the expression 'humoral fault' as a translation for the bodily *doṣa*, in order to avoid any connotation of well-being or desirable minimum level which the word 'humour' might evoke. Since disease results from a preponderance of one of the humoral faults, a treatment programme will aim initially to identify which humoral fault is responsible for the condition, and secondly to reduce that humoral fault in the affected individual. The medical correction of humoral fault figures in Canto 16, where it is set within the framework of the Buddha's instruction in meditational techniques. Aśvaghoṣa develops an extensive analogy between treatment of the three humoral faults by specific substances on the one hand, and treatment of the three character faults by specific meditational exercises on the other. The six verses from

---

[24] "Not only is the expression "humour" misleading …, but the qualification "peccant" surreptitiously affirms the negative aspect required by the context." Scharfe (1999:614).

16:59 to 16:64 describe which subject of meditation (*nimittam*) is beneficial, and which is retrograde, for each of the three character types. Thus the *rāgātmaka*, a man suffering from an excess of the fault of passion, should not meditate on loving-kindness (16:59) but on impurity (16:60), the *dveṣātmaka*, the man whose primary fault is hatred, should not meditate on impurity (16:61) but on loving-kindness (16:62), and the *mohātmaka*, the man in whom the fault of delusion predominates, should not meditate on loving-kindness or impurity (16:63), but on causality (16:64). The correct diagnosis of a person's dominant psychological fault is important, since meditating on an unsuitable subject would only exacerbate the condition, while a suitable meditation would alleviate it. The second half of each of the six verses contains a simile derived from Āyurvedic *tridoṣa* theory. Thus the *rāgātmaka* is like a man with a phlegm (*kapha*) disturbance, who should not be treated with oily substances (*sneha*, 16:59) but with astringent drugs (*rūkṣa*, 16:60). The *dveṣātmaka* is likened to a man of bile (*pitta*), who should not be treated with acids (*tīkṣṇa*, 16:61) but with cooling substances (*śīta*, 16:62). The *mohātmaka* is like a man in whom wind (*vāyu*) predominates,[25] who should not be treated with astringent remedies (*rūkṣa*, 16:63) but with oils (*snigdha*, 16:64). Thus the careful diagnosis and treatment of humoral faults becomes a metaphor for the correct choice of meditation according to character type. However, the correspondences set up between the medical and the psychological domains do not always tally, as Table 1 makes clear.

---

[25] An association of the three major types of temperament with the three humoral faults was certainly current by Buddhaghosa's time. "Some say" (*ekacce vadanti*), he reports, that "the temperaments originate in the elements and humoral faults" (*cariyā... dhātu-dosa-nidānā*, Vism 102). He presents the same scheme as Aśvaghoṣa, linking the lustful temperament (*rāga-carita*) to phlegm, the hating temperament (*dosa-carita*) to bile and the deluded temperament (*moha-carita*) to wind (Vism 103). He also mentions an alternative position whereby lust is linked to wind and delusion to phlegm. This alternative must be responsible for Birnbaum's (1979:11) equation of lust with wind and delusion with phlegm, though he provides no references to substantiate his connection.

Table 1: The doṣas and their treatment

Humoral Fault	phlegm	bile	wind
Psychological Fault	lust	hatred	delusion
Harmful Meditation	loving-kindness	impurity	loving-kindness and impurity
Harmful Treatment	oils	acids	astringents
Beneficial Meditation	impurity	loving-kindness	causality
Beneficial Treatment	astringents	cooling remedies	oils

While each humoral fault is always linked to the same character type, the prescribed treatments do not refer to the same meditation. The loving-kindness meditation, for instance, is initially equated to the oil treatment in that both are harmful for a phlegm/lust type person, yet it is subsequently equated to cooling remedies, both of which are deemed beneficial for a bile/hatred type. It is clear here that Aśvaghoṣa did not try to simplify or falsify the medical treatment of humoral faults for the sake of a tidy metaphor. The overall concept remains clear; in the source domain, disease-producing humoral faults must be diagnosed and the prescribed drugs taken, while in the target domain, *duḥkha*-producing faults must be identified and the prescribed meditation undertaken.

The *doṣas* are clearly pathogenic in both the physical and the spiritual domains. The elements (*dhātu*) are also implicated, but the *Saundarananda* does not enlarge on this topic. The physical *doṣas* are responsible for physical disease, while the psychological *doṣas* are very definitely stated to be the cause of suffering. To return to Aśvaghoṣa's medical interpretation of the Four Noble Truths at 16:41, with which this discussion started, we are told *vis-à-vis* the First Noble Truth that suffering (*duḥkha*) should be identified as disease, while its cause is provided by the explanation of the Second Noble Truth: faults should be seen as the cause of disease (*doṣeṣv api vyādhi-nidāna-saṃjñāṃ*). It is evident that (humoral) faults (*doṣa*) cause disease, and that (psychological) faults (*doṣa*) cause suffering. Other verses confirm that the *doṣa*s are the cause of suffering: "the reason for suffering is the types of faults" (*duḥkhasya ... doṣa-guṇā nimittam*, 16:17) and "one should abandon the faults, which are the cause of suffering" (*duḥkhasya hetūn prajahāti doṣān*, 16:37). Suffering is disease, and *doṣa* is its aetiology. The correspondence chart can now be extended:

Source Domain	**Target Domain**
the doctor (*bhiṣaj*)	the Buddha
prescribes a treatment (*vi* + √*dhā*)	recommends a practice (*vi* + √*dhā*)
three bodily humours (*doṣa*)	psychological faults (*doṣa*)
disease	suffering
medication	meditation
the aim is a calm physical state (*śama*)	the aim is a calm mental state (*śama*)

In the case of Nanda, *doṣa* is especially associated with life at home, complete with all the domestic pleasures for which he so yearns (5:39, 8:28), and with women generally (8:32, 8:55 and 8:62). Nanda's particular malady, his particular character flaw, is evidently lust, *rāga*, rather than hatred or delusion. Time and again we hear of Nanda's enthralment to lust and passion. From his very first appearances in the poem, Nanda is associated with passion. In 2:60 he is the embodiment of lust, *kāma*, as against the Buddha who embodies dharma. As Nanda grows up, he for ever idles away his time in pleasures (*kāmeṣv ajasraṃ pramamāda nandaḥ*, 2:63). Making love is his sole task (*madanaika-kāryaḥ*, 4:1). He is concerned chiefly with lust and passion (*kāma-rāga-pradhānaḥ*, 12:3). In 11:10 Ānanda describes Nanda as an infatuated man with a sensual nature who is in the clutches of passion (*abhiṣvaktasya kāmeṣu rāgiṇo viṣayātmanaḥ*). Nanda's illness, of course, feeds off itself, since the more he indulges in sensual pleasures, the greater his longing for such pleasures becomes. In this respect, he is like a leper:

yathā ca kuṣṭha-vyasanena duḥkhitaḥ
pratāpanān naiva śamaṃ nigacchati |
tathendriyārtheṣv ajitendriyaś caran
na kāma-bhogair upaśāntim ṛcchati || (9:44)

Just as a man afflicted with leprosy obtains no relief from heat, likewise a man of unconquered senses who is preoccupied with sensory experience finds no peace in acts of passion.

Nanda's condition of uncontrolled sensuality is likened to leprosy (*kuṣṭha*). His continual indulgence in activities pleasurable to the senses, as he attempts to assuage his sensual desires, is as futile as the leper trying to assuage his pain by burning himself. These are just some of the many examples that spell out Nanda's leaning towards sensuality; indeed, the entire story line of the *Saundarananda* hinges on Nanda's lustful nature.

The identification of passion, *rāga*, as the particular fault (*doṣa*) from which Nanda suffers is confirmed by the important medical simile at 10:43. At this point in the story Nanda has seen the Apsarases and as a result is tormented by desire. The verse reads:

doṣāṃś ca kāyād bhiṣag ujjihīrṣur

bhūyo yathā kleśayituṃ yateta |
rāgaṃ tathā tasya munir jighāṃsur
bhūyastaraṃ rāgam upānindruya || (10:43)

And just as a doctor seeks to draw out humoral faults from the body by further paining it, so the sage, intending to destroy passion in him, first brought about a far greater passion.

The verse is important because it justifies the Buddha's action in spiriting Nanda away to heaven and making him a *voyeur* of the seductive Apsarases. The Buddha is likened to a doctor, and the intended action of both the *upameya* and the *upamāna* is indicated by a desiderative. The Buddha's intention is to destroy (*jighāṃsuḥ*) Nanda's passion (*rāga*), while the doctor's intention is to draw out or remove (*ujjihīrṣuḥ*) the humours (*doṣa*). The *doṣa*s clearly correspond to *rāga* as the object of the doctor's / Buddha's desired action. The main thrust of the verse, which is that it is permissible to augment short-term suffering for a benefit in the long-term, is discussed at a later stage. For the time being it is sufficient to note that the verse sounds a note of optimism; a cure is feasible, and there is a physician on hand who has taken an interest in the case. When Nanda "shatters passion" (*rāgaṃ* ... *bibheda*, 17:38) and is thus finally cured of his disease of passion, it is in accordance with the treatment programme summarised in Table 1 above, which stipulates the practice of the impurity meditations in cases of passion. Thus Nanda's 'cure' takes place immediately after his reflection that the body is "filled with a host of impurities such as skin, sinew, marrow, blood, bone, flesh and hair" (*tvak-snāyu-medo-rudhira-asthi-māṃsa-keśādināmedhyagaṇena pūrṇam*, 17:36). One may also speculate whether the *Saundarananda*'s general emphasis on impurity (of women in Canto 8, and of the body in Canto 9) cannot be traced to the supposed therapeutic value of such an approach when an individual is diagnosed as passionate-natured.

After Nanda conquers passion (17:38), he soon reaches full arhatship (17:60), and since liberation is conceptually associated with good health, there are, as might be expected, a number of similes at this point which demonstrate Nanda's state of well-being. A simile at 17:69a, one of a cluster of nine in three consecutive verses that celebrate Nanda's achievement, likens his newly-attained state of tranquillity to wellness after a sickness of an unendurable type (*rogād ivārogyam asahya-rūpāt*[26]). The unendurable sickness of passion that caused Nanda such discomfort has now been alleviated. In a verse that equates passion to a febrile condition, we hear that without the fever (of passion), Nanda can now lie down in comfort (*sukhaṃ svapsyasi vīta-dāhaḥ*, 18:29)[27]. Similarly, 'fever-free' (*vijvara*, 17:72) is listed as one of the attributes of the enlightened state. A further simile at 18:13 makes the association between health and liberation quite clear:

> *anye 'pi santo vimumukṣavo hi*
> *śrutvā vimokṣāya nayaṃ parasya* |
> *muktasya rogād iva rogavantas*
> *tenaiva mārgeṇa sukhaṃ ghaṭante* || (18:13)
>
> For when they hear that someone has been guided to liberation, other good men hoping for liberation will also strive for happiness by the same route, just as sick people, when they hear of someone's deliverance from sickness, strive for relief by the same method.

This verse, at the beginning of Nanda's speech testifying to his enlightenment, presents one of the factors motivating him to

---

[26] I wonder if a reading of *asādhya-rūpāt* would not be preferable. Āyurvedic texts agree that illnesses are of three types, curable, incurable and those which are incurable but can be improved (Suśr 1.10, for example).

[27] The word *dāha* may simply refer to heat, but Suśruta uses it to mean fever. Aśvaghoṣa also uses *dāha* for fever at AśvBC 11:40, where a fever arising from bile (*pitta-dāha*) is treated by cooling remedies (*śīta-kriyā*). A medical interpretation of *dāha* is therefore likely, such that passion is equated to a disease, a fever, rather than to burning alone. Verse 15:3, in identifying lustful thoughts (*kāma-vitarkaḥ*) as a fever, also connects passion to a febrile condition, though using the more usual *jvara* for fever.

speak publicly of his achievement. Nanda anticipates that his example will inspire others to try the remedy that has worked successfully for him. The correspondences inherent in this simile indicate that all men, even when they are good (*santaḥ*), even when they actively desire liberation (*vimumukṣavaḥ*), are considered sick (*rogavantaḥ*). On the other hand, those lucky ones who have been guided to liberation (*vimokṣāya nayam*) are said to be free of sickness (*muktasya rogād*). Health as a metaphor for liberation is of course consistent with Aśvaghoṣa's earlier definition of the Third Noble Truth as good health (*ārogya*, 16:41). It is noteworthy that Aśvaghoṣa pays far more attention to illness as a metaphor for the unenlightened state than to good health as a metaphor for the enlightened condition; indeed, the unenlightened state features more prominently in all aspects of the *Saundarananda*. Our hero is unenlightened until close to the end of the penultimate canto, the imagery deals mainly with the unenlightened state, and even at the level of the vocabulary, the word *duḥkha* appears around 40% more frequently than the word *sukha*. This is perhaps to be expected, since only those who are sick require the ministrations of a physician. Thus Aśvaghoṣa devotes a great deal of attention to sickness, the first element of the medical paradigm.

4.2 The Patient

The second element of the medical model to consider is the patient. The word 'patient' denotes not just an ill person, but a recipient of medical care that may enable him to progress from a diseased to a healthy state. In the *Saundarananda*'s medical imagery, the patient is, of course, Nanda. Nanda is the referent of almost all the occurrences of words meaning 'sick', such as *ātura* and *roga*, whether used as substantives or adjectives, when such words are used figuratively. So, for instance, he is addressed by the unnamed monk as "you, the sick type" (*roga-vidho*, 9:12). There is never any suggestion that Nanda has any kind of physical sickness; on the contrary, as Canto 9 makes clear, he is in his prime, young, strong and healthy. But he is frequently the target of medical imagery, and one should understand all sickness ascribed to him as spiritual in nature.

There are also occasional medical similes in which the role of the sick person does not pertain to Nanda exclusively, but to mankind generally. Examples include the six similes on the treatment of humoral irritation discussed above. Additionally, the famous penultimate verse (18:63) designates me, and all other readers and auditors of the *Saundarananda*, as patients, because we have ingested the medicine (*auṣadham*) that is bottled in this poem. Primarily, though, it is Nanda who is identified as the patient.

The main point I will seek to make in connection with the depiction of Nanda as a patient is that his attitude and co-operation (or lack of it) bear heavily on the likelihood and speed of his recovery. I believe that this is evident from a number of similes, which are discussed below. If my interpretation is correct, then the medical metaphor lends much support to the *Saundarananda*'s constant appeal to the practitioner to exert himself unceasingly in following the dharma.[28] The notion that a patient can to some extent affect his own recovery is not odd, but common-sensical. It is also the opinion of the medical authorities, who hold that the patient's personal qualities, along with the severity of his disease and the skill of his doctor, strongly influence the clinical outcome of his case.

In their discussions of the patient's role in the medical process, the medical authorities are united in regarding the character of the patient as a prognostic indicator. The patient is never considered a mere passive recipient of medical intervention. For Caraka, the patient (*rogin*) is one of the four factors conducing to a positive therapeutic environment:

> *bhiṣag-dravyāṇy-upasthātā rogī pāda-catuṣṭayam* |
> *guṇavat kāraṇaṃ jñeyaṃ vikāra-vyupaśāntaye* || (Car 1.9.3)

> Physician, drug, attendant and patient – this is the foursome which, when endowed with good qualities,

[28] Examples of such calls to action occur at 5:25, 14:22 and a mini-hymn to endeavour (*vīrya*) at 16:94-8.

should be understood as the reason for the alleviation of disorders.

He goes on to specify the good qualities that a patient ought to possess:

smṛtir nirdeśa-kāritvaṃ abhīrutvam athāpi ca |
jñāpakatvaṃ ca rogāṇām āturasya guṇāḥ smṛtāḥ ||
(Car 1.9.9)

Attentiveness, obedience, fearlessness and providing information [about the illness] are considered good qualities in a sick man.

Like Caraka, Suśruta includes the patient in his list of the four essential factors of medical treatment, along with the physician, medicine and the attendant (Suśr 1.34.16). The following are the qualities in a patient that conduce to a favourable outcome:

āyuṣmān sattvavān sādhyo dravyavān ātmavān api |
āstiko vaidya-vākya-stho vyādhitaḥ pāda ucyate ||
(Suśr 1.34.21)

A sick man is considered a factor [favourable to medical treatement] when he is long-lived, courageous, curable, wealthy, self-possessed, pious and attentive to his doctor's orders.

Where the patient lacks one or more of these qualities, the conditions for successful medical treatment are less than optimum. The *Vinaya Mahāvagga* also considers the patient's character an important determinant of clinical outcome. VinMV 8.26.1-3 relates the well-known episode in which the Buddha finds a monk with dysentery lying unwashed and untended. The Buddha and Ānanda wash him and lift him onto a couch. The Buddha gathers the monks and tells them to attend to whoever amongst them should fall sick, and then proceeds to list desirable and undesirable qualities in both patients and their carers. According to the Buddha, a sick man is difficult to tend (*gilāno dupaṭṭhāko*) when he has five qualities:

> *asappāyakārī hoti, sappāye mattaṃ na jānāti, bhesajjaṃ na paṭisevitā hoti, atthakāmassa gilānupaṭṭhākassa yathābhūtaṃ ābādhaṃ nāvikattā hoti abhikkamantaṃ vā abhikkamatīti paṭikkamantaṃ vā paṭikkamatīti ṭhitaṃ vā ṭhito 'ti, uppannānaṃ sārīrikānaṃ vedanānaṃ dukkhānaṃ tibbānaṃ kharānaṃ kaṭukānaṃ asātānaṃ amanāpānaṃ pāṇaharānaṃ anadhivāsakajātiko hoti.* (VinMV 8.26.5)

> He does not do what is beneficial; he knows no moderation in what is beneficial; he does not take his medicine; he does not describe his disease accurately to a sympathetic attendant by saying as it advances, 'It is advancing', or as it retreats, 'It is retreating', or as it stays the same, 'It is stable'; he is not the type to endure painful, sharp, piercing, fierce, unpleasant, awful, life-threatening physical feelings which arise.

A sick man is easy to tend (*gilāno supaṭṭhāko*), on the other hand, when he has the opposite five qualities: "he does what is beneficial; he knows moderation in what is beneficial; he takes his medicine; he describes his disease accurately …" (VinMV 8.26.6).

Finally, the medical authority Vāgbhaṭa joins his predecessors in seeing the patient's character as a factor contributing to outcome of his illness. He enumerates the following attributes as desirable in a patient:

> *āḍhyo rogī bhiṣag-vaśyo jñāpakaḥ sattvavān api* (VāgAṣṭHṛd 1.1.29)

> The [ideal] patient is wealthy, obedient to the physician, provides information [about his illness], and is courageous too.

Thus the medical authorities are united in their opinion that the patient can affect the progress of his disease for better or worse. Compiling the evidence from the four texts quoted above, a composite picture of the ideal patient emerges as someone who is attentive to his doctor's instructions and carries them out obediently (all four of the texts include obedience in their lists), is sufficiently *compos mentis* to provide an accurate account of his illness (included in three lists), is brave in submitting to treatment (included in three lists), is attentive, pious, and takes medicine in appropriate quantities without overdosing (each included in one list). Additionally, Vāgbhaṭa and Suśruta stipulate that the patient should be wealthy. A wealthy patient is better-nourished and better-housed, and better able to afford expensive medications – and better able to reward his doctor financially! Actually, I assume the doctor's disinterest, so that when the medical authorities describe a quality that they consider desirable in a patient, they do so not because it makes the doctor's life easier, but because it improves the patient's condition.

In the earlier sections of the *Saundarananda*, Nanda does not measure up to the picture of the ideal patient as portrayed in the medical texts, which, as has just been noted, all stress obedience as a key quality. Clearly it is important that the patient should acknowledge the doctor's superior expertise and carefully carry out his instructions with regard to treatment and remedies. Midway through the *Saundarananda*, in Canto 9, Nanda is still unwilling to conform to the principle of obedience in a patient:

> *yathā hi vaidyasya cikīrṣataḥ śivaṃ*
> *vaco na gṛhṇāti mumūrṣur āturaḥ* |
> *tathaiva matto bala-rūpa-yauvanair*
> *hitaṃ na jagrāha sa tasya tad vacaḥ* || (9:2)

> Just as a sick and dying man takes no notice of the beneficent words of the doctor who wishes to treat him, so Nanda, intoxicated with his physical fitness, good looks and youthfulness, took no notice of his well-intentioned words.

The "well-intentioned words" form the bulk of Canto 8 and are spoken by the unnamed monk in his attempt to dissuade Nanda from returning to his wife. Nanda pays no attention (*na jagrāha*); in fact, he hasn't listened to a word the monk has said (*na tasya śuśrāva ... vacaḥ*, 9:1). This is calamitous for him, as the medical simile illustrates. Nanda is sick (*āturaḥ*) and going to die (*mumūrṣuḥ*). He is in need of treatment, and there is someone on hand who wishes to cure him (*cikīrṣataḥ*), but Nanda is as yet unwilling to submit to the superior wisdom of a higher authority.

Nanda's unco-operativeness betrays his unwillingness to work towards enlightenment. When Aśvaghoṣa likens this recalcitrant attitude to a desperately sick patient ignoring a physician's advice, he is appealing to the universal desire for good health, using the easily-understood terms of the medical metaphor to illustrate the absurdity of Nanda's position. It is irrational to want to stay sick when a cure is on offer. In ignoring medical advice, Nanda demonstrates his wish to stay sick. Ānanda detects this inclination in Nanda, comparing him to "a man who would like to be ill" (*ākāṅkṣet ... rogam*, 11:28). Nanda's counterintuitive attitude is best summed up by the adjective *mumūrṣu*, 'on the point of death', 'intending to die', 'desiring to die'. The Buddha tells Nanda that "your wish not to leave your home is like the wish of a death-desiring man not to leave an area of plague" (*naivāsti moktuṃ matir ālayaṃ te deśaṃ mumūrṣor iva sopasargam*, 5:39). Medical similes such as this one reveal the paradox that what is normally considered 'a full life' (home, family, many activities) actually makes for death, while the monastic who withdraws from life can win liberation and conquer death. Nanda's wish to stay at home is therefore a death wish, akin to the death wish of the plague-courting man.

Nanda's perversity is further illustrated by his tendency to overindulge in medicine. The logic of Aśvaghoṣa's medical metaphor dictates that medicine is generally equated to the Buddha's teachings. However, there is a somewhat different conception of medicine behind two similes, at 9:45 and 11:28, which draws on the known tendency of some people to overdoctor themselves. The Pali Canon is aware of this attraction to medicine, which is something in the way of an addiction, and therefore places a number of restrictions on the use of medicines, some of which were mentioned at the beginning of this chapter. Some medicines are only permitted to those who are sick (VinMV 6.3.1-2), some can be taken in a diluted form by the well (VinMV 6.16.3 and 6.27.1). In any case, medicines should always be used carefully and thoughtfully (MN i.10). Nanda's pleasure-addicted personality is exposed by a medical simile in verse 9:45:

> *yathā hi bhaiṣajya-sukhābhikāṅkṣayā*
> *bhajeta rogān na bhajeta tat-kṣayam |*
> *tathā śarīre bahu-duḥkha-bhājane*
> *rameta mohād viṣayābhikāṅkṣayā ||* (9:45)

> For as one might cultivate diseases rather than their disappearance through a desire for the pleasures of medication, so through a befuddled desire for the objects of the senses one might find pleasure in the body, that recipient of many pains.

This verse is spoken by the unnamed monk as he attempts to convince Nanda that it is foolish to derive pleasure from anything as unstable and prone to suffering as one's body. Here the objects of the senses (*viṣaya*) are equated to medication or medical treatment (*bhaiṣajya*). Since medical treatment is usually feared and avoided if at all possible, such an equation demonstrates the foolishness in striving to maximise sensual experience. Cultivating physical pleasure is like cultivating illness, something no rational person would do. Verse 11:28 makes the same point:

> *ākāṅkṣec ca yathā rogaṃ pratīkāra-sukhepsayā* |
> *duḥkham anvicchati bhavāṃs tathā viṣaya-tṛṣṇayā* ||
> (11:28)
>
> You are seeking out suffering with your thirst for sensory experience, as though someone would wish for illness in order to enjoy the pleasure of a remedy.

Once again the objects of the senses (*viṣaya*) are the medicinal countermeasure (*pratīkāra*), while suffering (*duḥkham*) is aligned with sickness (*rogam*). This simile sheds light on Nanda's motivation. He does not wish to be well, but prefers to remain ill, because he so enjoys taking medicine. In other words, Nanda wants to stay unenlightened so that his pleasant sensual experience can continue. Nanda's predilection for medicine is easily recognised as folly, and the reader is encouraged by the structure of the simile to recognise Nanda's enthusiasm for worldly pleasures likewise as a madness[29].

Nanda proves a recalcitrant patient in other ways. He does not bear his 'treatment' bravely. He initially refuses ordination (5:35), and when he is eventually ordained his eyes stream with tears (5:51). He spends much of Canto 7 feeding his pain at leaving his wife by dwelling on memories of her. At last, however, Nanda's visit to heaven initiates a profound change in his attitude. The turning point comes when Nanda, who has previously refused to listen to advice, now begs the Buddha for help:

> *prasīda sīdāmi vimuñca mā mune*

---

[29] It also fits Aśvaghoṣa's conception of any worldly pleasure (*sukha*) as not pleasurable in itself, but only seeming so in contrast to suffering (*duḥkha*). *Sukha* is merely an antidote, or counteragent (*pratīkāra*), against *duḥkha*. Thus *duḥkha-pratīkāra* appears as an epithet for *sukha*, for example at 17:19 and 18:37, and at AśvBC 11:36, 39 and 40.

vasundharā-dhairya na dhairyam asti me |
asūn vimokṣyāmi vimukta-mānasa
prayaccha vā vāg-amṛtaṃ mumūrṣave || (10:54)

Please, O sage firm as the earth, I am sinking, save me who am without firmness. I will give up my life, O man of liberated mind, unless you grant me in my dying moment the ambrosia of your words.

Nanda makes the crucial realisation that the condition from which he is suffering is life-threatening, and he acknowledges that he is in imminent danger of death (*mumūrṣu*). Equally crucially, he realises that the speech of the Buddha can grant deathlessness (*vāg-amṛta*). Nanda repeats his request for the Buddha's life-saving assistance in a medical simile at the end of the next verse:

ahaṃ hi daṣṭo hṛdi manmathāhinā
vidhatsva tasmād agadaṃ mahā-bhiṣak || (10:55cd)

I have been bitten in the heart by the snake of love; therefore prescribe an antidote for me, O great physician!

In addressing the Buddha as *mahā-bhiṣak*, Nanda nominates the Buddha as his doctor. He asks the Buddha to arrange, prepare or concoct (*vidhatsva*, which I have translated 'prescribe') a medication for him. Remembering the recommendations of the medical treatises that the ideal patient should be able to provide information about his condition, it is noteworthy that Nanda can here verbalise his illness. He identifies his illness as lust, and he uses a violent image, that of a snake biting him in the heart, to describe the seriousness of his condition. The snake, greatly feared since its bite brings death, is a token of the loathsome and fatal nature of lust. And when Nanda locates the site of the injury as his heart, one is aware that Nanda's illness is internal rather than external. Real snakes cannot bite as far as the heart, but the snake of love can. One is reminded of the snake-like faults (*doṣa*) and elements (*dhātu*) discussed earlier. In his metaphor of love as a snake, Nanda uses the word *manmatha* for 'love' a word more typical of *kāvya* than Buddhism. As well as its meaning of 'amorous passion', *Manmatha* is also a name of the god of love, who strikes people with his flower-arrows. This connotation has the effect of softening the violent image. So while the medical metaphor indicates that Nanda has made much progress, in that he is able to identify his disease, gauge its seriousness, describe his condition to his doctor and ask for treatment to begin, it would seem that he is still partially entrenched in the *kāvya* world-view – a reflection of the fact that at this stage Nanda has not entirely given up his longing for sensual pleasures, but merely exchanged earthly pleasures for heavenly ones.

In the two verses at the end of the heaven episode in Canto 10 just discussed, Nanda for the first time appeals to the Buddha for help. He has, as it were, made an appointment with the doctor. This is an important milestone in Nanda's conversion, and he becomes a more compliant patient from this point onwards. At the beginning of the following canto, Ānanda sees an improvement in Nanda, and congratulates him:

> *durharo mānaso vyādhir balavāṃś ca tavābhavat* |
> *vinivṛtto yadi sa te sarvathā dhṛtimān asi* || (11:12)

> Your illness was mental; it was intense and difficult to remove. If it has been reversed, you are resolute in every way!

Ānanda's appreciation of Nanda's firmness (*dhṛti*) is of course premature; but the point is that an improvement in Nanda's condition is ascribed to his own efforts, not to any external event. Nanda cannot get well without wanting to get well and without trying to get well. When Nanda subsequently learns from Ānanda that a sojourn in heaven with the Apsarases would in any case be temporary, he finally renounces his desire for them. This renunciation has an immediate effect on his health:

> *svarga-tarṣān nivṛttaś ca sadyaḥ svastha ivābhavat |*
> *mṛṣṭād apathyād virato jijīviṣur ivāturaḥ ||* (12:6)

> When he had turned away from his thirst for heaven, he suddenly seemed to become well, like a sick man who gives up tasty but unhealthy food in his determination to live.

Previously Nanda had been death-desiring (*mumūrṣu*). Now he is described as desiring to live (*jijīviṣu*). The change in his motivation is due to relinquishing his desire for heaven (*svarga-tarṣa*) and the lovely Apsarases who live there. The desire for the Apsarases is likened to food that is tasty (*mṛṣṭa*) but not good for one (*apathya*). Since Āyurvedic treatment very frequently involves dietary regulation, with some foodstuffs being avoided and others recommended according to the patient's constitution,[30] it is quite clear that a treatment regime has begun. The turnabout in Nanda's attitude has an immediate beneficial effect on him, so that he now seems well (*svastha*). The 'seems' (*iva*) is important though - Nanda will not be truly well until he reaches enlightenment in Canto 17.

After Nanda renounces the Apsarases, he goes to the Buddha and asks to be taught (12:17). The Buddha includes a metaphor of poisoning in his reply:

> *sarva-duḥkhāpahaṃ tat tu hasta-sthaṃ amṛtaṃ tava |*
> *viṣaṃ pītvā yad agadaṃ samaye pātum icchasi ||* (12:25)

> Having drunk poison, you wish to drink an antidote in time; that cup of deathlessness is within your reach, and it destroys all suffering.

---

[30] See for instance Caraka's chapter 1.7, in which he mentions that there are "appropriate diets for particular constitutions"; and his description of someone who ignores the advice not to eat curds at night, and so develops "a fever, blood-bile, spreading rashes ... or even serious jaundice", trans. Wujastyk (1998:59)

Here, Nanda has ingested something worse than tasty but unwholesome food; he has consumed poison (*viṣaṃ pītvā*). He has been poisoned by his sensual desires (the previous verse refers to lust, *kāma*, as an enemy). However, Nanda is no longer content to continue being poisoned. His will-power has been triggered. Just as Nanda's volition is stressed by the desiderative adjective *jijīviṣu* in verse 12:6 above, so it is marked here by the verb 'you wish' (*icchasi*). Nanda's motivation has been successfully redirected, and his complete healing can now be predicted with some confidence. By the beginning of Canto 17, Nanda determination to win liberation has matured to the extent that he can be described as 'well' (*svastha*, 17:6d).

An interesting and important feature arises through a consideration of the role of the patient in the *Saundarananda*'s medical metaphor, which I shall designate by means of the oxymoron 'active patient'. After the heaven episode, which represents a turning point in Nanda's conversion, Nanda's passivity diminishes as he increasingly directs his volition towards the goal of enlightenment. It has previously been noted that much of the *Saundarananda*'s imagery, and even its grammar, reinforce the portrayal of the Buddha as the agent, and Nanda as the passive recipient of action, in the earlier cantos at least. Within the terms of the medical metaphor too, I have shown how the patient's awareness of his condition and his willingness to strive against his sickness are crucial if he is to make a recovery. Thus the Buddha advises Nanda that notions of immortality "are to be strenuously fought off, just as a sickness in one's self [should be strenuously fought off]" (*yatnena sa vihantavyo vyādhir ātma-gato yathā*, 15:52cd).

In verse 16:40 Aśvaghoṣa is adamant that the patient's awareness and understanding of his disease are indispensable to his attainment of health:

yo vyādhito vyādhim avaiti samyag
vyādher nidānaṃ ca tad-auṣadhaṃ ca |
ārogyam āpnoti hi so 'cireṇa
mitrair abhijñair upacaryamāṇaḥ ||. (16:40)

> The sick man who understands his disease correctly, and its cause and its remedy, will, when tended by knowledgeable friends, soon attain good health.

Verse 16:40 stresses that the patient must know (*avaiti*) not just his disease, but also how it came about and how it can be treated. While Aśvaghoṣa may have exaggerated the extent to which a patient is required to analyse and understand his illness, the principle of a well-informed and informative patient appears regularly in the medical authorities. It was noted earlier that the qualities of an ideal patient listed in medical texts invariably include the ability to provide an accurate and detailed description of the sickness. So for Caraka, informativeness (*jñāpakatva*) is desirable in a patient; the *Vinaya Mahāvagga* says that an easy patient is someone who explains or makes clear (*āvi-kattā*) his illness as it really is (*yathā-bhūtaṃ ābādham)*. Suśruta and Vāgbhaṭa agree. Caraka adds that attentiveness or mindfulness (*smṛti*) is recommended in a patient.[31] It is no surprise that the medical authorities stress the skill of the patient in observing and accurately reporting the symptoms and stages of his disease, since this information would have been one of the few diagnostic devices available to the physician.[32]

Verse 16:40 is a preamble to the medical interpretation of the Four Noble Truths in verse 16:41, which states, as was discussed previously, that suffering is to be understood as a sickness (*vyādhi*), the faults as the cause of sickness (*vyādhi-nidāna*), enlightenment as good health (*ārogya*), and the path to enlightenment as the medicine (*auṣadha*). Verse 16:40 employs the same medical vocabulary as 16:41 - *vyādhi*, *nidāna*, *auṣadha*, *ārogya* – and the two verses are obviously a pair. Taking the values assigned to the medical terms in 16:41 and inserting them

---

[31] For all references, see page 130 above.

[32] In Chinese versions of the biography of the famed doctor Jīvaka, he is said to have discovered a jewel which permitted him to see the insides of people's bodies, thus providing him with a diagnostic tool other than his own examination of a patient and the patient's description of his symptoms (Zysk 1991:56).

into the metaphor in 16:40, it becomes evident that Aśvaghoṣa places a considerable emphasis on the practitioner's personal responsibility for his attainment of liberation. The practitioner must have a perfect understanding of suffering, its cause and the path, that is, the First, Second and Fourth Noble Truths. The Third Noble Truth, deliverance from suffering (*nirvāṇa*), will then soon (*acireṇa*) follow.

When a patient has been healed, the natural response is gratitude to one's doctor. Hence when the famous doctor Jīvaka performs cranial surgery on a rich merchant and cures him of a long-standing head disease, the merchant offers Jīvaka all his property and himself as a slave (VinMV 8.1.20).[33] Nanda too, now that he is healthy, adopts the correct attitude of gratitude towards his physician. So Nanda is likened to a healthy man saved from illness by auspicious treatment grateful (*kṛtajñaḥ*) to the physician (*yathopadeśena śivena mukto rogād arogo bhiṣajaṃ kṛtajñaḥ*, 17:33). The Buddha commends Nanda's attitude, telling him "this gratitude is worthy of you" (*tavaiva ceyaṃ sadṛśī kṛtajñatā*, 18:52).

Nanda also wishes to bear testimony to the efficacy of his cure. Thus he approaches the Buddha in the final canto and tells him that he wishes to speak personally of his course of treatment (*svaṃ tūpacāraṃ pravivakṣur asmi*, 18:12). The word *upacāraḥ* is used several times in the *Saundarananda* – at 8:3, 16:61, 16:62, 16:64 and 18:63 - to mean medical attendance, medical practice, doctoring. In bearing witness to his cure, Nanda is motivated not just by gratitude to his physician, but also by a wish to benefit those who may still be sick, as his next verse attests:

anye 'pi santo vimumukṣavo hi
śrutvā vimokṣāya nayaṃ parasya |
muktasya rogād iva rogavantas

[33] See also the simile at Mil 139, where Nāgasena proffers the picture of a recovered patient grateful to his doctor as an image for the Buddha's three months of solitary meditation following his enlightenment.

> *tenaiva mārgeṇa sukhaṃ ghaṭante* || (18:13)
>
> For when they hear that someone has been guided to liberation, other good men hoping for liberation will also strive for happiness by the same route, just as sick people, when they hear of someone's deliverance from sickness, strive for relief by the same method.

Nanda then spends the next six verses (18:14-19) summarising his achievement, speaking of his understanding of the absence of self and his lack of attachment. In this he resembles a grateful patient who recommends his doctor and his course of treatment, so that other patients will wish to be treated in the same way. Thus the reputation of the doctor and his methods spread by word of mouth, just as early Buddhism adopted proselytism to spread its message. Since Nanda was previously entrenched in the habits of a libertine, but has now achieved liberation, he will be a shining example to others that he encounters. The Buddha, commenting that people will be amazed when they see Nanda teaching dharma in the city (18:58), encourages him to dedicate himself to other people (18:57).

The foregoing discussion of the patient, the second element of the medical model, has shown that the patient's acknowledgement of his diseased state and his willing participation in the course of treatment are pre-requisites for his recovery. The *Saundarananda*, through its medical similes, effectively portrays the change in Nanda as he gradually conforms to the portrait of the ideal patient, and his progression from a deadly illness to good health. The change in Nanda's attitude, so crucial to his cure (despite a wholesome environment, despite the attention of his doctor), is very aptly depicted through the medical metaphor.

4.3 The Doctor

Nanda's eventual attainment of the Buddhist *summum bonum* is an enormous achievement on his part. Nevertheless, such an achievement could not occur unassisted; had the Buddha not dramatically intervened in his personal life, Nanda would very likely have continued to live pleasurably at home, and thus remained condemned to the cycle of birth and death.[34] The important passage at 5:15-18 distinguishes two types of person on the basis of their capacity to attain liberation: the man who is dependent on something external to himself (*bāhyāśrayaḥ*, 5:16), who attains liberation through dependence on someone else (*vimokṣam āpnoti parāśrayeṇa*, 5:17), and secondly, and in sharp contrast to the first type, that rare individual who is self-dependent (*ātmāśrayaḥ*, 5:16) and who effortlessly (*ayatnataḥ*) attains liberation with just the merest nudge (*nirmucyate ghaṭṭita-mātra eva*). Since Nanda's dependent personality places him firmly in the first category, some forceful action on the Buddha's part was necessary to enable Nanda to achieve enlightenment. To restate this principle in terms of the medical metaphor, while it is necessary for the patient to willingly participate in and actively contribute to his own recovery, as the foregoing discussion has shown, the experience, knowledge and instructions of the physician are indispensable to the whole process of healing. The physician, then, is the third element in the medical model of the conversion process.

The qualities of a good doctor are naturally the subject of some discussion in the medical treatises. For Caraka, a good doctor is so important that self-immolation is preferable to being treated by an ignoramus (*varam ātmā huto 'jñena na cikitsā pravartitā*, Car 1.9.15). He describes a good doctor's qualities in these words:

> *śrute paryavadātatvaṃ bahuśo dṛṣṭa-karmatā* |
> *dākṣyaṃ śaucam iti jñeyaṃ vaidye guṇa-catuṣṭayam* ||
> (Car 1.9.6)

[34] Nanda admits as much in 18:41.

The fourfold virtues of a doctor are considered to be great erudition, considerable practical experience, dexterity and cleanliness.

Caraka also defines the best doctor (*bhiṣaktamaḥ*):

hetau liṅge praśamane rogāṇām apunar-bhave |
jñānaṃ catur-vidhaṃ yasya sa rājarho bhiṣaktamaḥ ||
(Car 1.9.19)

The best doctor, one fit for a king, is one who is knowledgeable with respect to four areas – the cause, symptoms, pacification and non-recurrence of diseases.

Additionally, the ideal doctor should also display kindness and compassion to those who are suffering (*maitrī kāruṇyam ārteṣu*, Car 1.9.26).

Like Caraka, Suśruta believes that a good doctor is of utmost importance in curing illness. In the absence of a physician, the three remaining factors of medical treatment (that is, the patient, medicine and attendant) are useless (*apārthakāḥ*, Suśr 1.34.17). Only a physician of quality can always save a sick person (*vaidyas tu guṇavān ekas tārayed āturaṃ sadā*, Suśr 1.34.18). Suśruta's list of qualities desirable in a doctor runs as follows:

adhigata-tantreṇopāsita-tantrārthena dṛṣṭa-karmaṇā kṛta-yogyena śāstraṃ nigadatā rājānujñātena nīca-nakha-romṇā śucinā śukla-vastra-parihitena chatravatā daṇḍa-hastena sopānatkenānuddhata-veśena sumanasā kalyāṇābhivyāhāreṇākuhakena bandhu-bhūtena bhūtānāṃ susahāyavatā vaidyena viśikhā 'nupraveṣṭavyā || (Suśr 1.10.3)

A doctor who has understood the science of medicine and has practised its goals, who has observed treatment and has himself carried out such practices, who can recite the treatises, is authorised by the king, keeps his nails and hair short, is clothed in white garments, has an umbrella, holds a stick, wears shoes, dresses modestly, who is benevolent, kindly spoken and honest, who is a brother to all beings and has good assistants – he may embark on medical practice.

Vāgbhaṭa is more concise; he states that a doctor should be dextrous, should have been trained in the meaning of the treatises by a skilled person, should have practical experience and be pure (*dakṣa-tīrthāttaśāstrārtho dṛṣṭa-karmā śucir bhiṣak*, VāgAṣṭHṛd 1.1.28).

According to the *Vinaya Mahāvagga*, one who tends the sick is fit to do so (*alaṃ gilānaṃ upaṭṭhātum*) when he has five qualities:

> *paṭibalo hoti bhesajjaṃ vidhātuṃ, sappāyāsappāyaṃ jānāti, asappāyaṃ apanāmeti sappāyaṃ upanāmeti, metta-citto gilānaṃ upaṭṭhāti no āmisantaro, ajegucchī hoti uccāraṃ vā passāvaṃ vā kheḷaṃ vā vantaṃ vā nīhātuṃ, paṭibalo hoti gilānaṃ kālena kālaṃ dhammiyā kathāya sandassetuṃ samādapetuṃ samuttejetuṃ sampahaṃsetuṃ . imehi kho bhikkhave pañcah' aṅgehi samannāgato gilānupaṭṭhāko alaṃ gilānaṃ upaṭṭhātuṃ.* (VinMV 8.26.8)
>
> He is competent to prepare medicine; he knows what is beneficial and what is not beneficial; he removes what is not beneficial and presents what is beneficial; he tends to the sick out of the kindness of his heart, not out of greed; he does not find it disgusting to remove excrement or urine or phlegm or vomit; he is able to instruct, rouse, delight and gladden the sick from time to time with *dhamma*-talk. Monks, one who tends the sick is fit to tend the sick when he is endowed with these five qualities.

The four texts quoted above point to the desirability of several features in a doctor. Appearing most regularly in the lists is the doctor's knowledge. It is vital that the doctor should be well-trained, learned and thoroughly acquainted with his subject. Additionally, his knowledge should extend beyond the merely theoretical; three of the texts refer to the importance of observation and practical experience (*dṛṣṭa-karman*). The doctor's benevolence is listed by three of the texts; Caraka mentions *maitrī*, the *Vinaya Mahāvagga* stipulates *metta-citta*, while Suśruta's ideal doctor is a brother to all creatures. Caraka and Vāgbhaṭa mention the cleanliness or moral purity (*śaucam, śuci*) of the doctor, while Suśruta likes hygienic short fingernails and hair. Caraka and Vāgbhaṭa include dexterity in their lists, a particularly important attribute for surgeons. The *Mahāvagga*, the oldest of the four texts, focuses on the practical aspect of caring for the sick, stating that carers should not be squeamish about cleaning up their patients.[35]

As has been previously stated, the identification of the Buddha as the doctor who treats suffering humanity is so widespread as to be a Buddhist commonplace. The *Saundarananda* is no exception, and in its deployment of the medical model as a metaphor for the conversion process, the Buddha frequently appears in the guise of the doctor figure. It is therefore easy to overlook the appearance of two other characters who also take on the guise of a doctor.

The unnamed monk who seeks to deter Nanda from returning home is one such figure. He adopts the standard terms of the medical metaphor at the beginning of Canto 8:

> *dvi-vidhā samudeti vedanā*
> *niyataṃ cetasi deha eva ca* |
> *śruta-vidhy-upacāra-kovidā*
> *dvi-vidhā eva tayoś cikitsakāḥ* || (8:3)

Pain is of two kinds, arising in the mind or in the body.
So for the two kinds of pain there are two kinds of

---

[35] The later texts sub-divide the role of the carer into physician and attendant / nurse.

physician, those learned in the prescriptions of scripture and those skilled in medical practice.

While the unnamed monk draws a distinction between those who treat physical pain, and those who treat mental pain, he refers to both as 'physicians' (*cikitsakāḥ*). He then invites Nanda to reveal his thoughts to him:

atha duḥkam idaṃ mano-mayaṃ
vada vakṣyāmi yad atra bheṣajaṃ |
manaso hi rajas-tamasvino
bhiṣajo 'dhyātmavidaḥ parīkṣakāḥ || (8:5)

So tell me about your mental suffering, and I will prescribe a remedy for it; for careful examiners who understand the psyche are doctors for minds filled with passion and dark ignorance.

Here the unnamed monk rather ambitiously counts himself amongst the careful examiners (*parīkṣakāḥ*) who understand human psychology, casting them (and himself) as doctors (*bhiṣajaḥ*) of the mind (*manasaḥ*). Nanda responds to his invitation, saying that he cannot enjoy anything without his wife, and that he wishes to give up the monkhood and go home (8:12-13). The unnamed monk's 'medication' (*bheṣajam*) follows - a virulent denunciation of the pleasures of domestic life in general and of women in particular. His attempt at negative conditioning falls on deaf ears; Nanda pays not the slightest attention (*na tasya śuśrāva ... vacaḥ*, 9:1). Verse 9:2, which has already been quoted as an illustration of Nanda's refusal to comply with medical advice, is worth quoting again, since it reinforces the identification of the unnamed monk as a doctor:

yathā hi vaidyasya cikīrṣataḥ śivaṃ
vaco na gṛhṇāti mumūrṣur āturaḥ |
tathaiva matto bala-rūpa-yauvanair
hitaṃ na jagrāha sa tasya tad vacaḥ || (9:2)

> Just as a sick and dying man takes no notice of the beneficent words of the doctor who wishes to treat him, so Nanda, intoxicated with his physical fitness, good looks and youthfulness, took no notice of his well-intentioned words.

The structure of the metaphor indicates that the unnamed monk is identifiable as a doctor (*vaidya*) who is hoping to cure (*cikīrṣa aḥ*) his patient. The unnamed monk renews his efforts in Canto 9, in which he tries to persuade Nanda to forsake his trust in his own physical prowess. However, as has been noted, his attempts are unsuccessful. At the end of Canto 9, therefore, the unnamed monk goes to the Buddha to report that Nanda remains obdurate (9:51).

Ānanda's description of the transience of rebirth in the heavenly realms, which he delivers in Canto 11 in an effort to dissuade Nanda from his plan to earn the Apsarases through asceticism, is also seen in a medical light. First of all, Ānanda places Nanda in the patient role, recognising that Nanda suffered from a serious (*balavān*) illness (*vyādhi*, 11:12). Nanda is to be congratulated if it is in remission (*vinivṛtta*, 11:12). However, Ānanda has heard rumours that Nanda is practising restraint solely to win the Apsarases, and he asks him if this is true (11:19). He then offers to help:

> *yadi tāvad idaṃ satyaṃ vakṣyāmi atra yad auṣadham* |
> (11:20ab)
>
> If it is true, I will prescribe a medication for it.

Ānanda's offer of help is made in a phrase almost identical to the unnamed monk's similar offer of help made earlier (*vakṣyāmi yad atra bheṣajaṃ*, 8:5). Ānanda, like the unnamed monk, presents himself as physician capable of giving salutary medicine (*auṣadham*) to Nanda, the patient. Nanda says nothing in response to Ānanda's questioning, but Ānanda can tell from his face that the rumours are true (11:22). Ānanda therefore proceeds to dole out his medicine – an extended attack on the aspiration for heaven and on sensuality generally (11:23-62), which, even when it is of a refined heavenly sort, brings neither tranquillity nor permanent satisfaction.

Ānanda's medicine is clearly more efficacious than the unnamed monk's. Instead of simply ignoring Ānanda's unwelcome words, Nanda is profoundly shocked (*bhṛśaṃ saṃvegam eyivān*, 12:4) and he at last turns away from the enticements of heaven (*svargān nivavṛte*,12:5). There is an immediate and noticeable improvement in his health (*sadyaḥ svasthaḥ*) as a result of this new-found determination to live (*jijīviṣu*, 12:6, quoted on page 139 above). Nanda's decision to work for his survival, as has already been noted, indicates the increased likelihood of his recovery. As such, Ānanda's results demonstrate that he is a superior physician to the unnamed monk. It is only fitting that Aśvaghoṣa presents Ānanda, one of the chief disciples and the Buddha's personal attendant, in a more favourable light than the unnamed monk.

Apart from Ānanda's greater eminence, there is another reason why the unnamed monk's medicine of Cantos 8 and 9 fails, while Ānanda's medicine delivered in Canto 11 succeeds. It is because Nanda has, in the meantime, in Canto 10, been seen by the best doctor of all. At the end of Canto 9 the unnamed monk abandons his efforts to stiffen Nanda's resolve, and instead makes his way to the Buddha to report the matter:

> *sattvāśayānuśaya-bhāva-parīkṣakāya*
> *buddhāya tattva-viduṣe kathayāṃcakāra* | (9:51cd)

> He related it to the Buddha, the truth-knower, the examiner of the mental dispositions, latent tendencies and emotional dispositions of all beings.

Ironically, the unnamed monk had previously labelled himself as a psychologist, one of the "examiners who understand the psyche" (*adhyātmavidaḥ parīkṣakāḥ*, 8:5). But in that instance we had only his own word for it. When the Buddha is said to be the "examiner of the mental dispositions, latent tendencies and emotional dispositions of all beings (*sattvāśayānuśaya-bhāva-parīkṣaka*, 9:51), it is the authorial voice that tells us so. It is the Buddha, and not the unnamed monk, who is the supreme examiner and careful observer of the dispositions of human beings, just as a good doctor carefully examines his patient and observes his symptoms. Nanda's seemingly hopeless case has, one might say, been referred to a specialist. The situation is reminiscent of the accounts of Jīvaka's cures, in which a desperately ill person is seen by a succession of doctors to no avail, until Jīvaka takes control of the treatment, at which point the patient is cured.[36]

The Buddha is the great doctor (*mahā-bhiṣak*, 10:55), the best of physicians (*bhiṣak-pradhānam*, 17:73) who, in his compassion, operates in the world with the object of healing (*cikitsārtham*, 13:7). His mere presence has a curative effect, so that as long as he dwells in Kapilavāstu, the city remains free from illness (*anāmaya*, 3:42). The Buddha is a skillful healer who knows what to do in complex cases, as is evident from the similes likening meditation to medicine, where treatment varies according to which humoral fault preponderates in an individual (16:59-64 and 16:69, as discussed earlier). Furthermore, the Buddha is presented as a doctor capable of carrying out surgical procedures (5:47 and 17:65, to be discussed in the next section). And when Nanda gives thanks to his guru in the final canto, he compares him to a surgeon, stating that the barb of wrong views (*dṛṣṭi-śalya*, 18:7) that afflicted him was removed by the Buddha "like an arrow drawn out by a surgeon" (*samuddhṛtaḥ śalyahṛteva śalyaḥ*, 18:7).

When Nanda achieves the stage of stream-entry in 17:27, he experiences profound gratitude to the Buddha. The passage describing his gratitude includes a striking parallel between the attributes of the Buddha and those of a good physician:

yathopadeśena śivena mukto

[36] Examples are Jīvaka's cures of a merchant's wife at VinMV 8.1.8-13 and a rich merchant at VinMV 8.1.20.

rogād arogo bhiṣajaṃ kṛtajñaḥ |
anusmaran paśyati citta-dṛṣṭyā
maitryā ca śāstra-jñatayā ca tuṣṭaḥ ||
āryeṇa mārgeṇa tathaiva muktas
tathāgataṃ tattvavid ārya-sattvaḥ |
anusmaran paśyati kāyasākṣī
maitryā ca sarva-jñatayā ca tuṣṭaḥ || (17:33-4)

Just as a healthy man who was delivered from illness by successful treatment in his gratitude forms a mental picture of his doctor, and in remembering him, is delighted by his kindness and specialist knowledge, likewise a man liberated by the noble path, who knows reality and possesses the noble truth, is witness to the Tathāgata, and in remembering him, is delighted by his kindness and omniscience.

It seems that the liberated man (*muktaḥ*) engages in the practice of the recollection of the Buddha (*buddhānusmṛti*), just as the grateful patient, after his cure, calls to mind the good qualities of his doctor. This pair of verses serves as a fine example of the Buddhist medical metaphor, with the man in good health corresponding to the liberated man (and *ipso facto* the sick man is a man not yet liberated), and the doctor corresponding to the Buddha, the Tathāgata. The Buddha's omniscience (*sarva-jñatā*) is likened to a doctor's knowledge of the medical treatises (*śāstra-jñatā*), while the Buddha's benevolence (*maitrī*) is likened to the kindness (*maitrī*) of a doctor. We saw earlier that the medical authorities are unanimous in proclaiming these two virtues as essential qualities in a doctor; and the Buddha has them in abundance. The *Saundarananda* bears frequent testimony to the Buddha's wisdom, particularly to his ability to discern the hearts and minds of Nanda and other human beings. Thus the Buddha is an expert in paths (*mārga-kovida*, 3:3); he knows reality (9:51); he knows all decisions that people make (*niścaya-kovida*, 10:2); he knows that Nanda is immersed in thoughts of his wife (10:3); he is free of ignorance (*tamaḥ-prahīṇa*, 10:58); he knows when Nanda has become a fitting recipient of the dharma (13:9); he knows the gradual path (*kramajña*, 13:9); he understands the nature, qualities and disposition of all beings (17:73); he is free of doubt (*niḥsaṃśaya*, 18:8); and he is the all-knowing one (*sarvajña*) who already knows what Nanda is about to tell him (18:12). The Buddha's compassion is stressed to perhaps an even greater extent. For example, the Buddha is supremely compassionate (*parama-kāruṇika*, 3:15), the greatly compassionate one (*mahā-kāruṇika*) who notices Nanda's distress and comforts him by placing his hand on the latter's head (5:21); he speaks with compassion for all creatures (*sarveṣu bhuteṣu anukampakena*, 5:33); in his kindness (*maitrī-manas*) he asks Ānanda to ordain Nanda (5:34); he even took on human birth out of his great compassion (*saṃdadhe kāyaṃ mahā-karuṇayā*, 13:8); his speech is a cow which has udders of loving-kindness (*maitrī-stanī*, 18:11); and he is wonderfully kind in his intentions (*atimaitra-cetas*, 18:47).

I began this section with a summary of how the various medical treatises present the medical practitioner. They demonstrate a lofty idealism by assigning to him numerous desirable qualities. When Aśvaghoṣa shows us the Buddha through the lens of the medical metaphor, he allows us to view the Buddha as an ideal doctor, imbued with all the qualities of care, compassion, skill and specialist knowledge that such an ideal implies. Two other characters also take a hand in Nanda's conversion by preaching to him at length, and their efforts too are portrayed in a medical light. The first, the unnamed monk, makes no impact at all, and the second, Ānanda, while making a considerable impression on Nanda, does so only because in the meantime Nanda has been rendered more pliable by his Buddha-engineered visit to heaven. It is only the Buddha, finally, who is consistently equated to a physician; he is the doctor par excellence, the physician who is finally able to heal Nanda's illness.

4.4 The Treatment

This section will examine the final aspect of the medical model, the treatment that the doctor delivers to his patient in order to heal his disease. Thus far, this chapter has demonstrated the regularity with which Aśvaghoṣa presents the Buddha as a skilled and compassionate physician, and Nanda as a sick man, initially intractable, but increasingly amenable to treatment and responsive to his doctor. I have also shown that the lustful state of attachment from which Nanda suffers is likened to an illness, an illness severe enough to be considered life-threatening. In this section I will explore the methods employed by the Buddha to save Nanda's life and grant him perfect health.

It is no easy matter to cure an illness as severe and long-standing as Nanda's case of lustful attachment. Ānanda comments that Nanda's illness was intense and difficult to remove (*durharo ... vyādhir balavān*, 11:12). Moreover, a resistant case such as his calls for forceful action:

> *vyādhir alpena yatnena mṛduḥ pratinivāryate |*
> *prabalaḥ prabalair eva yatnair naśyati vā na vā ||*
> (11:11)
>
> A mild illness can be checked with little effort, but a violent illness is destroyed only with great effort, if at all.

What is in Buddhist terms a happy ending, and in medical terms a successful clinical outcome, finally prevails only because both the Buddha and, eventually, Nanda make strenuous efforts (*prabalair ... yatnair*) to overcome Nanda's illness. Although the quoted verse (11:11) is spoken by Ānanda in the context of his mistaken assumption that Nanda has cured himself, it has a wider application. The maxim that Aśvaghoṣa puts into Ānanda's mouth also functions as a defence of the Buddha's robust action. Ānanda states that therapy must needs be aggressive in order to eliminate (*naśyati*) a particularly virulent disease (*vyādhir ... prabalaḥ*). Passing this maxim through the medical metaphor translator, we arrive at the understanding that the Buddha's invasive techniques are essential for the elimination of Nanda's attachment syndrome. The principle that the end justifies the means underlies much of the *Saundarananda*'s imagery of medical treatment.

There is no doubt as to the severity of Nanda's illness; several times, he is said to be at death's door (*mumūrṣu* 5:39, 9:2, 10:54). After he has seen the entrancing Apsarases at the end of Canto 10, Nanda's illness reaches its climax, and correspondingly his suffering reaches its moment of maximum intensity. Furthermore, Nanda's disease is long-standing and deeply entrenched, since his condition of attachment dates from the moment of his birth. He is associated with fire, a familiar symbol of desire, and is born to his mother "like fire [appearing] in firesticks" (*araṇyām iva pāvakaḥ*, 2:57). He is like the god of love in human form (2:59), he is the embodiment of lust (2:60), and he forever spends his time in pleasurable pursuits (2:63). On the other hand, the depiction of Nanda's relationship with Sundarī is evocative of a new and passionate love affair. Other versions of the Nanda story (Dhammapāla's commentaries on the *Theragāthā* and the *Udāna*, and the commentary on the *Dhammapada*) have it that Nanda is taken from his home and ordained on the very day of his wedding. Dhammapāla adds that the events occurred when Nanda came of age (*vaya-ppatta-kāle*, Th-a 2.32). Despite Nanda's evident youth, there is little doubt that his is a chronic condition. Nanda has long suffered from his attachment-sickness, but at the point of the Buddha's intervention it has flared up in a particularly acute form. The medical authorities recommend that physicians should not embark on the treatment of long-standing diseases; Suśruta, for example, advises the physician to keep away from diseases which started more than a year earlier.[37] According to the Buddhist perspective, however, all beings are ill and suffering from the time of their birth.

Though Nanda's disease is severe and entrenched and he is in a critical condition, we have seen that he resists attempts to

---

[37] *parisaṃvatsarotthitāṃś ca vikārān prāyaśo varjayet*, Suśr 1.10.7

heal him. In such circumstances, the physician is justified in using force to treat the patient against his will:

> *aniṣṭam apy auṣadham āturāya*
> *dadāti vaidyaś ca yathā nigṛhya |*
> *tadvan mayoktaṃ pratikūlam etat*
> *tubhyaṃ hitodarkam anugrahāya ||* (5:48)

> Just as a doctor holds down a sick man while he gives him unwanted medicine, so also have I done you a kindness in saying something that will benefit you, though it is contrary [to what you wish to hear].

This verse is spoken by the Buddha to Nanda as part of his effort to persuade Nanda to leave Sundarī. The Buddha, likening himself to a doctor, equates Nanda ("you", *tubhyam*) with a sick man *(āturāya)*, the equation being emphasised by the dative case of both *tubhyam* and *āturāya*. The medicine (*auṣadham*) is qualified by the adjective *aniṣṭam*. *Aniṣṭam* is derived from the negative prefix *an* and the past participle of √*iṣ*, 'to wish, want', together producing a meaning of 'not wanted', 'unwished', 'undesired'. Since the doctor is giving (*dadāti*) the medicine, it is clear that he does not consider the medicine undesirable; it is the patient who considers the medicine undesirable. Evidently the medicine, which correlates to the Buddha's advice, is being administered to the patient against his will. The patient does not want to take the medicine, nor does Nanda want to carry out the Buddha's instructions – and small wonder. The Buddha has just been speaking of the illusoriness of sensual pleasures (5:23), outlining how they hamper the attainment of true happiness (5:28). The Buddha decrees that separation from one's loved ones is therefore necessary (*avaśyabhāvī priya-viprayogaḥ*, 5:29), and so he instructs Nanda to "give up the net of delusion labelled 'lover'" (*priyābhidhānaṃ tyaja moha-jālam*, 5:45). Nanda finds such advice *pratikūla*, from *kūla* 'bank', 'slope', meaning 'against the bank', 'against the slope', and therefore with a connotation of 'uphill' or 'contrary to the natural course'.

The Buddha's proposition, that Nanda leave his home and ordain as a monk, goes against Nanda's inclinations. From Nanda's perspective, such advice is all very unpalatable, and separation from Sundarī is practically unbearable. It is, for Nanda, the bitterest pill to swallow.

This particularly rich simile lends itself to further extrapolation. The Buddha likens himself to a doctor who gives medicine to a patient **after holding him down** (*nigṛhya*). This suggests that a similar restraining action can be attributed to the Buddha himself. In reading Canto 5, one notices that Nanda's physical movements have indeed been hindered by the Buddha. The Buddha manages to shake off the large number of people following him (5:5) and leads Nanda into a quiet lane (5:6). Then he hands Nanda his begging bowl (5:11), an action that in itself would surely make it virtually impossible for Nanda to leave, since the options of either going home with the bowl, or placing it on the ground, would both imply enormous disrespect. When Nanda tries to leave though he still has the bowl in his hands (5:13), the Buddha bodily blocks his exit route (5:14) before leading him to the monastery (5:20). Finally, despite Nanda's stated objection (5:35), he is ordained by Ānanda (5:51). The degree to which the Buddha engineers the entire situation must inevitably raise a question concerning coerced conversion. It is interesting to note that though other versions of the Nanda legend show the Buddha pressurising Nanda to some extent, none of them contains the detail of the quiet lane and the obstruction of its exit. Aśvaghoṣa has added these episodes to maintain narrative momentum and dramatic tension. However, this does leave him with a problem of how to justify the Buddha's very forceful actions. He therefore turns to the medical metaphor to counter any imputation of unethical action on the Buddha's part.

The medical metaphor provides a highly suitable justification for the purposeful causing of pain, since there can be no doubt as to either the motives of the doctor or the future benefit to the patient. The medical simile under discussion directs attention to both these aspects. The Buddha says that he speaks out of kindness, or as a favour (*anugrahāya*); and I have already shown, in the discussion of the attributes of the ideal doctor, that compassion is of great importance. The Buddha also mentions that his speech is for Nanda's benefit (*hitodarkam)*, though Nanda may not yet realise it. Other Buddhist texts also summon the medical metaphor to the defence of a dubious action. The *Milinda-pañha* exploits the medical metaphor in the context of the dilemma concerning Devadatta (Mil 108-10). Why, King Milinda wants to know, did the Buddha allow Devadatta to join the order of monks, when he knew in advance that Devadatta would cause a split in the order, thus bringing on himself an infinity of rebirths in hell? The dilemma, as King Milinda sees it, is that either the Buddha was not truly compassionate, or he was not omniscient. Nāgasena asserts both the compassion and the omniscience of the Buddha, since the good consequences of Devadatta's going forth as a monk provide some limit to the otherwise endlessly bad consequences brought about by causing a schism. Nāgasena adduces the medical metaphor to bolster his argument:

> "Supposing, sire, that a wound, full of old blood, had been perforated by an going inside and is suddenly attacked by the union of acute wind, bile, phlegm, change of season and the stress of circumstances, and that in assuaging it a clever physician and surgeon smears the opening of the wound with a harsh, pungent, caustic, bitter medicament so as to heal it. When he has healed it and when what had become soft has been cut away with a knife, he cauterises it with a stick. After cauterising it, he administers a caustic lotion for accomplishing the cure of the person who was afflicted by the disease by closing his wound. Now, sire, when the physician and surgeon smeared on the medicament, cut away with the knife, cauterised with the stick and administered the caustic lotion, did he have an ill-disposed mind?" "No, revered sir, he did those things that had to be done with a well-disposed mind, desiring a cure." "But were those painful feelings that arose while

the physician and surgeon was doing what had to be done with the medicaments a source from which he might produce any demerit?" "Revered sir, the physician and surgeon did those things that had to be done with a well-disposed mind, desiring a cure. So how could he produce any demerit from such a source? That physician and surgeon, revered sir, is one who will go to heaven."[38]

The doctor's good intentions are, it seems, never at issue. Nanda is the patient who is 'held down', specifically in the quiet lane of Canto 5, but also in the mendicant order generally, so that medicine may be administered to him. Since the treatment, unpleasant though it may be, is ultimately for his own good, Nanda is told to simply accept it:

varaṃ hitodarkam aniṣṭam annaṃ
na svādu yat syād ahitānubaddham |
yasmād ahaṃ tvā viniyojayāmi
śive śucau vartmani vipriye 'pi || (5:46)

Unpleasant food which results in your welfare is better than food that might taste good but has harmful consequences. Therefore I commit you to a benign and pure path, though it doesn't please you.

Āyurvedic medicine traditionally included nutrition within its remit and frequently made recommendations concerning food. On the grounds of health, certain foods were to be avoided, others ingested. In this verse, Nanda is encouraged to adopt a healthy eating policy, since the things he enjoys are not necessarily good for him.[39] Verse 5:46 is a companion to 5:48 just discussed, sharing with it the theme of present suffering for

---

[38] Mil 112, trans. Horner (1963:156-7).

[39] Ānanda makes a similar point later on when he says "It is as difficult to find beneficial advice that is pleasing as it is to find a medicine that is both palatable and effective" (*durlabhaṃ tu priya-hitaṃ svādu pathyam ivauṣadham*, 11:16).

the sake of future benefit. Further, both verses 5:46 and 5:48 attribute a benign paternalism to the Buddha, to whose superior insight Nanda is enjoined to resign himself. The two verses also share some vocabulary; the treatment proposed by the Buddha – medicine in the case of 5:48, dietary regulation in the case of 5:46 - is 'unwanted' (*aniṣṭam*) by Nanda, but the Buddha presses him to accept it on the basis of its long-term benefit (*hitodarkam*). The intervening verse 5:47 reinforces the message of its neighbours via the medical metaphor in combination with a simile of childcare:

> *bālasya dhātrī vinigṛhya loṣṭam*
> *yathoddharaty āsya-puṭa-praviṣṭam* |
> *tathojjihīrṣuḥ khalu rāga-śalyaṃ*
> *tat tvām avocaṃ paruṣaṃ hitāya* || (5:47)

> I truly wish to draw out the dart of passion [from you] and [so] have spoken severely to you for your own good, just as a nurse keeps a firm hold on a child while she takes out the clod of earth that has got into its mouth.

Here the image of a child-minder (*dhātrī*) holding fast a child in order to take a lump of earth out of its mouth expresses the same essential relationship between the Buddha as a care-giver and Nanda as a recipient of care. The Buddha's paternalism is strongly suggested, while Nanda is reduced to a toddler who stuffs dirt into his mouth. I shall have more to say later about the medical metaphor of arrow-extraction. For the moment it suffices to note that the medical metaphor, in tandem with the simile of the nanny, once again provides a justification for restraining Nanda so that he may be acted on against his will. The general thrust of the three verses at 5:46-8 is that firstly, the Buddha, with his superior insight, knows what is ultimately best for Nanda. Secondly, Nanda finds the Buddha's recommended course of action painful and unpleasant. Finally, the Buddha is exempt from any criticism for restraining Nanda and acting on him against his will. One is reminded of the contemporary aphorism "no pain, no gain".

Nanda is not provided with any immediate pain-relief. On the contrary, his suffering intensifies. Nanda's face may stream with tears while his head is shaved at the end of Canto 5, but this is just the beginning of his woe. By Canto 7 Nanda is depressed (*dīna*, 7:3a), tearful (*sabāṣpa*, 7:6c), suffering (*duḥkhita*, 7:9c), and burning in his heart with the fire of passion (*kāmāgnināntar-hṛdi dahyamāna*, 7:12c). In Canto 8 he is still weeping (8:2), and looks so miserable that the unnamed monk approaches to offer assistance, casting his advice, as we have seen, in a medical light (8:5). Nanda's suffering reaches its peak in Canto 10, in which the Buddha takes Nanda to heaven to show him the winsome Apsarases. Several lovely verses using many *kāvya* conventions prepare for the sighting of the Apsarases by describing the trees and birds of heaven (10:19-31). Verses 10:35-39 celebrate the sensuousness and beauty of the Apsarases. The effect of these celestial maidens on Nanda is immediate and catastrophic. His body shivers with passion (*nandasya rāgeṇa tanur vivepe*, 10:39c) and he suffers agitation and torment (*viklavārtaḥ*, 10:41b). It is only by the power of the Buddha that he endures what would be unbearable for others (*soḍhum asahyam anyaiḥ*, 10:46c). Nanda's affliction is presented as a fire, *kāvya*'s usual symbol of passion. Thus he says, for example, that he is scorched by the fire of lust (*rāgāgninā ... abhidahye*, 10:52d), and that the fire of lust threatens to burn him up right now (*rāgāgnir adyaiva hi māṃ didhakṣuḥ*, 10:53c). Eventually Nanda admits that he is dying, and begs the Buddha to save his life: "I will give up my life, O man of liberated mind, unless you grant me in my dying moment the ambrosia of your words" (*asūn vimokṣyāmi vimukta-mānasa prayaccha vā vāg-amṛtaṃ mumūrṣave*, 10:54). Nanda's health has deteriorated to the extent that he is at death's door. There can be no doubt that the visit to heaven has stimulated his suffering. Comparing the carefree and contented Nanda of Canto 4 to the violently agitated human torch of Canto 10, it is obvious that Nanda has got worse rather than better. The long-term benefit (*hitodarkam*, 5:46 and 5:48) promised in Canto 5 has not yet materialised.

The responsibility for Nanda's increased sufferings lies with the Buddha. The Buddha initially takes Nanda by the hand (*pāṇau gṛhītvā*, 10:3) to bear him up to the Himalayas, where he shows Nanda the ugly one-eyed monkey (10:16) and receives his assurance that his wife is incomparably more attractive than the monkey (10:17). Then, "with a view to a further motivating factor"(*hetv-antaraṃ kiṃcid avekṣamāṇaḥ*, 10:18b), the Buddha again holds Nanda (*ālambya nandam*, 10:18) and transports him to heaven. In heaven Nanda encounters the nymphs, with the calamitous effect that we have seen. The Buddha's agency lies behind this entire chain of events. We have every reason to ask why the compassionate Buddha purposefully plans Nanda's increased suffering. Dhammapāla, in his commentary on the *Udāna*'s version of the Nanda story, asks this very question: "But why did the Lord cause the venerable Nanda with his [already] lustful mind to see the Apsarases?" (*kasmā pana bhagavā avassuta-cittaṃ āyasmantaṃ nandaṃ accharāyo olokāpesi*, Ud-a 3.2.172).

One possible answer to Dhammapāla's question is that the Buddha is attempting to drive Nanda to the point at which his suffering becomes so intolerable that he is forced to do something about it. According to Caraka, a person, particularly a foolish person, is apt to ignore an illness when its symptoms are relatively mild. The likelihood of his seeking assistance grows in proportion to the increasing discomfort that he experiences:

> But the simpleton, whether from stupidity or negligence, does not notice a disease when it first appears, like a fool not noticing an enemy. For a disease starts out tiny, but later it grows. Once it has taken root, it robs a fool of both strength and life. As long as nothing hurts, a fool pays no attention to real knowledge. But once he is in pain, he finally begins to give thought to getting rid of the disease. Then he summons his children, his wife and

family, and says, "Call a doctor, it doesn't matter who, even if it costs me everything I have!"[40]

Caraka here makes the point that the sick man's foolishness and neglect can endanger his life. The *Saundarananda*'s unnamed monk makes a similar point when he urges Nanda to reveal the nature of his distress:

tad iyaṃ yadi kāyikī rujā
bhiṣaje tūrṇam anūnam ucyatām |
viniguhya hi rogam āturo
nacirāt tīvram anartham ṛcchati || (8:4)

So if your illness is physical, tell the whole matter to a doctor straightaway, for greater woe soon befalls a sick man who fails to disclose his illness.

The unnamed monk's advice echoes Caraka's warning that failure to seek medical advice promptly will result in a worsening of the disease. For reasons such as these, the Buddha may have intentionally inflicted further pain on Nanda in order to force him to pay attention to his illness.

There is a further possible explanation of the Buddha's seemingly heartless act of exposing Nanda to the achingly desirable Apsarases. It could be that this exposure is itself part of Nanda's treatment. Aśvaghoṣa puts forward such an explanation in a verse already quoted once:

doṣāṃś ca kāyād bhiṣag ujjihīrṣur
bhūyo yathā kleśayituṃ yateta |
rāgaṃ tathā tasya munir jighāṃsur
bhūyastaraṃ rāgam upānindruya || (10:43)

And just as a doctor seeks to draw out humoral faults from the body by further paining it, so the sage,

[40] Car 1.11.57-61, trans. Wujastyk (2001:74).

intending to destroy passion in him, brought about a far greater passion.

At this most critical moment in Nanda's conversion, with his suffering at its peak, one notes that the medical metaphor is again pressed into service to exonerate the Buddha. In this case, the doctor actively strives (*yateta*) to cause greater physical pain, but this is not gratuitous pain. The doctor's intention, as expressed by the desiderative adjective *ujjihīrṣu*, is to take the underlying cause of the disease, the humoral faults (*doṣān*), out of body. The increased pain is somehow or other a necessary part of the patient's treatment, and corrrespondingly, the suffering endured by Nanda is a necessary preliminary to his spiritual progress. The 'greater passion' (*bhūyastaraṃ rāgam*) is, it seems, part of Nanda's treatment. The medical simile in verse 10:43 implies that aggravating an illness before it can begin to improve is a recognised therapeutic principle.

Two verses after 10:43, there is further mention of the therapeutic principle of treating like with like. We are told that "a severe sickness destroys a small sickness" (*gurvī rujā hanti rujām ca mṛdvīm*, 10:45c), while the Buddha who instigates the treatment is described as "wishing to beat back passion with passion" (*rāgeṇa rāgaṃ pratihantu-kāma*, 10:47c). But how does such treatment work? Is it as basic as, say, crushing my hand in a car door makes me forget the small paper cut I had on my finger? This is possible, and Nanda does indeed forget about his beloved wife the moment he sets eyes on the Apsarases (10:47). I believe, however, that Nanda's pain-inducing treatment is rather more sophisticated and more in tune with Āyurvedic thinking. Nanda is subjected to a purge.

Several centuries after the composition of the *Saundarananda*, Dhammapāla reflected on the Nanda story, and in much the manner of Aśvaghoṣa before him, felt that the Buddha's seeming callousness called for an explanation. In his commentary on the *Udāna*'s version of the Nanda story, he poses the question that I have already cited: "But why did the Lord cause the venerable Nanda with his [already] lustful mind to see the Apsarases?" In answer to his own question, Dhammapāla, like Aśvaghoṣa, resorts to the medical metaphor, and comes up with a very similar justification:

> *yathā hi kusalo vejjo ussanna-dosaṃ puggalaṃ tikicchanto sineha-pānādinā paṭhamaṃ dose ukkiledetvā pacchā vamana-virecanehi sammadeva nīharāpeti, evaṃ vineyya-damana-kusalo bhagavā ussanna-rāgaṃ āyasmantaṃ nandaṃ devaccharāyo dassetvā ukkiledesi ariya-magga-bhesajjena anavasesato nīharitukāmoti veditabbaṃ* (Ud-a 3.2.172)
>
> For it should be understood that an expert doctor, in curing a person of an accumulated humoral fault, first makes the humoral faults worse with drinks of oil and so on, and then causes them to be completely ejected by vomiting and purging. Likewise the Lord, expert in taming those to be trained, [first] showed the celestial Apsarases to the venerable Nanda who had an accumulation of passion, making him worse, and [then] wished to eject them, with nothing left over, with the medicine of the noble path.[41]

The key word in Dhammapāla's explanation is *ukkiledetvā* (and similarly *ukkiledesi*), from the causative of *ut* + √*klid*, which according to PED means to take dirt out, to clean out, or to disinfect. Under *kilijjati*, though, PED suggests an alternative meaning: "to become heated, to get into a state of inflammation, to fester", linking this discrepancy to a confusion between √*klid* and √*kliś*. Under *ut* + √*kliś*, MW lists "to excite, stir up" as meanings of the causative form. Suśruta regularly uses *utkleśa*

---

[41] Th-a 2.33 likewise compares the Apsarases to a drink of oil by which a doctor prepares a patient for purging. Mil 169 also likens Nanda's exposure to the Apsarases to medical treatment, though without suggesting that he has to be made worse before he can be made better.

to signify humoral aggravation.[42] This is a more attractive translation of *ukkiledetvā*. Were *ukkiledetvā* to mean cleaned out or disinfected, it would be redundant, since it would merely duplicate *nīharāpeti* (caused to be ejected, caused to be thrown out). The sequence of actions too (***paṭhamaṃ*** ... *ukkiledetvā* ... ***pacchā*** ... *nīharāpeti*) seems to support an interpretation of *ukkiledetvā* as inflamed, stirred up, exacerbated, made worse, and I therefore adopt this as the more likely meaning of Dhammapāla's comment.

Dhammapāla's medical simile, then, compares the Buddha to a physician who treats excessive humoral faults by first exacerbating his patient's illness with oily drinks (*sineha-pānādinā*) before going on to eliminate it with substances that induce vomiting and diarrhoea (*vamana-virecanehi*). I believe that Aśvaghoṣa too had evacuative therapy in mind when he says in 10:43, in exculpation of the Buddha, that the Buddha is like a doctor who initiates a deterioration in his patient so that the humoral faults can then be drawn out. The authorities testify that such evacuative or cleansing therapy (*saṃśodhana*) is sound medical practice. Caraka is convinced of its effectiveness:

> *malāpahaṃ roga-haraṃ bala-varṇa-prasādanam |*
> *pītvā saṃśodhanaṃ samyag āyuṣā yujyate ciram ||*
> (Car 1.15.22)

> When [the patient] has drunk evacuative substances, waste matter is removed, disease is eliminated, and his strength and complexion are improved; he is endowed with perfect health for a long time.

For Caraka, this cleansing therapy (*saṃśodhana*) is of two kinds, consisting of the administration of either emetics (*vamana*), which induce vomiting, or purgatives (*virecana*),

---

[42] At Suśr 4:33:6 for instance, where Suśruta comments that an emetic works best when it is given to someone whose humoral faults have been stirred up (*utkleśya*) by the preparatory stages of oiling, sweating, and a diet of soft foods.

which induce diarrhoea. He discusses both of these procedures in Chapter 15 of the first section of his *saṃhitā*, in the verses which precede the quote given above. A patient treated by these procedures will find that his humoral fault never flares up again: "there is no recurrence of [humoral faults] that are subdued with evacuative procedures" (*jitāḥ saṃśodhanair ye [doṣāḥ] tu na teṣāṃ punar udbhavaḥ*, Car 1.16.20). Suśruta agrees that evacuative treatments combat humoral faults: "emetics and purgatives are used to remove faults" (*vamana-virecane vartete nirharaṇe doṣāṇām*, Suśr 4.33.3). Vāgbhaṭa is equally certain that cleansing therapy expels the *doṣas* from the body: "cleansing therapy is that which causes the humoral faults to go out [of the body], and is of five kinds" (*yad īrayed bahir doṣān pañcadhā śodhanam*, 1.14.5). Vāgbhaṭa lists enemas (*nirūha*), emesis (*vamana*), purging of the body (*kāya-reka*), purging of the head (*śiro-reka*) and blood-letting (*asra-visruti*) (1.14.5). A set of five cleansing therapies, known as *pañca-karma*, became standard Āyurvedic practice, though the treatments included in the list of five varies. The *pañca-karma* is still very much in evidence today and is gaining worldwide popularity.

It is difficult to prove that in taking Nanda to heaven, the Buddha administers evacuative therapy, since no word conclusively indicating evacuative therapy, such as *saṃśodhana*, *virecana* or *vamana*, appears in the *Saundarananda*, but there is some circumstantial evidence. I take as my starting point the diagnosis of Nanda's illness as passion. As verse 10:43 states, it is passion (*rāga*) that the Buddha wishes to expel from Nanda. According to Aśvaghoṣa's six similes on the treatment of humoral faults at 16:59-64, a man of passionate nature, a *rāgātmaka*, corresponds to a man with a phlegm condition (*kaphātmaka*, 16:60). So in terms of the medical metaphor, Nanda can be identified as a phlegm patient. The medical authorities assert that though an over-abundance of phlegm can strike at any time due to factors such as one's diet and the climate in which one lives, it is associated particularly with young people and springtime.[43] Vāgbhaṭa (VāgAH 1.1.6) lists

[43] Suśr 1.6.12, 1.21.24

the three humoral faults as wind (*vāyu*), bile (*pitta*) and phlegm (*kapha*), and says of them that "they occur in the last, middle and first [stages of life] respectively" (*te 'ntamadhyādigāḥ kramāt*, VāgAH 1.1.7). It was previously noted that certain versions of the Nanda story have him taken from his home on his wedding day, so it is is hardly feasible that he is an old or even a middle-aged man; besides, his youth, physical strength and sexual appetite are a frequent refrain in the *Saundarananda*. In fact, an excessive desire for sex is symptomatic of a phlegm condition.[44] Phlegm is characterised by oiliness[45], hence Aśvaghoṣa is quite correct when he warns in 16:59 that treatment with oils will make a phlegm patient worse. Phlegm people are already saturated with oil. The dual meaning of *sneha* ('love' and 'oil') permits the inference that since oil (*sneha*) is bad for a man with a phlegm (*kapha*) condition, then love (*sneha*) is bad for a man suffering from passion (*rāga*). Nevertheless, the *Saundarananda* does not exploit the potential afforded by this dual meaning, referring only once to love as a viscous substance.[46]

Caraka explains the treatment for excessive phlegm (*kapha*) in some detail. First the patient is subjected to two preparatory procedures, oiling (*sneha*) and sweating (*sveda*), which Caraka describes in chapters 13 and 14 of his first section, the *Sūtrasthāna*. The patient then receives the evacuative therapy (*saṃśodhana*) proper, which is described in chapter 15. Caraka describes two types of evacuative therapy, one causing vomiting (*vamana*), and one causing diarrhoea (*virecana*). The first type, *vamana*, is recommended in patients with excessive *kapha*, while the second type is more appropriate for bile (*pitta*) patients. After the patient has completed the initial course of oiling and sweating, the physician administers an emetic drug (Car 1.15.9).

---

[44] Excess phlegm acts as an aphrodisiac to stimulate the sex drive, as well as being responsible for a number of other symptoms such as colds, hypersalivation and expectoration, and an aversion to cool things (Obeyesekere 1977:163-4).

[45] VāgAH 1.1.12 describes phlegm as unctuous (*snigdha*).

[46] The Buddha desires to extricate Nanda from "the mud of love" (*sneha-paṅkāt*, 5:18).

The patient is then encouraged to vomit (Car 1.15.12). The physician carefully observes the bouts of vomiting to judge whether the correct dosage has been administered (Car 1.15.12). After vomiting well, the patient should inhale medicated smoke and bathe (Car 1.15.14). The patient is then advised on measures to secure his future well-being (Car 1.15.16). He is also instructed to eat very light meals for the next few days before gradually returning to his normal diet (Car 1.15.16). In the *Cikitsā-sthāna*, the fourth section of the *Suśruta-saṃhitā*, Suśruta gives a similar though less detailed description of the procedure. First the patient is oiled and sweated (Suśr 4.33.2). The next day he is given an emetic and made to vomit (Suśr 4.33.5). He then inhales medicated smoke (Suśr 4.33.7) and is given advice on his meals (Suśr 4.33.9-10).

Cleansing therapies such as those mentioned by Caraka and Suśruta were undoubtedly an entirely standard treatment, considered suitable even for the Buddha himself, as related in VinMV 8.1.30-33. We hear that the Buddha became sick and wished to drink a purgative (*icchati tathāgato virecanaṃ pātuṃ*). Ānanda goes for help to the famed physician Jīvaka, who orders him to lubricate the Tathāgata's body for a few days (*bhagavato kāyaṃ katipāhaṃ sinehetha*). Jīvaka, deciding that it would not be suitable to give the Buddha a strong purgative, offers three handfuls of lotuses to the Buddha to smell. Jīvaka returns later and asks the Buddha "Lord, is the Lord purged?" (*viritto bhante bhagavā*). Jīvaka then orders a bath, which brings on the 30th and last purge. Finally, Jīvaka prescribes a liquid diet until the Buddha's health returns to normal. This account of the Buddha's purge agrees, more or less, with Caraka's and Suśruta's description of the process. The cleansing treatment appears to consist of the following stages:

- preparatory procedures (oiling and sweating)
- the drinking (or in the Buddha's case, smelling) of an evacuative substance
- the occurrence of vomiting or diarrhoea
- concluding procedures (smoke inhalation, bathing, advice on future well-being or dietary advice)

The *Vinaya Mahāvagga* names neither the illness nor the humoral fault for the treatment of which Jīvaka prescribes the purge by lotuses. It merely states that "there was an accumulation of humoral faults in the Lord's body" (*bhagavato kāyo dosābhisanno hoti*). The medical authorities, however, all link the two main types of evacuative therapy to specific humoral faults. Caraka states that emetics are the best amongst phlegm-removing drugs (*vamanaṃ śleṣma-harāṇām*, Car 1.25.40), whilst purgatives are the best amongst bile-removing drugs (*virecanaṃ pitta-harāṇām*, Car 1.25.40). Suśruta recommends emesis for all phlegm-born illnesses (Suśr 4:33:13). Vāgbhaṭa lists the *doṣas* as *vāyu*, *pitta* and *kapha* (VāgAH 1.1.6) and, following the same order, says of them:

> *śarīra-jānāṃ doṣāṇāṃ krameṇa param auṣadhaṃ |*
> *bastir vireko vamanaṃ tathā tailaṃ ghṛtaṃ madhu ||*
> (VāgAH 1.1.25-6)
>
> The best medicine for humoral faults arising in the body is enema, purging and emetics respectively, likewise oil, ghee and honey.

Vāgbhaṭa[47] therefore agrees with Caraka and Suśruta that emetics (*vamanam*) are the best treatment for cases of phlegm. Nanda, then, as a phlegm patient, is a likely candidate for emetic therapy.

A large number of substances are known by the Āyurvedic tradition to have emetic properties, the most effective of which is the *madana* fruit. During the course of his description of emetic treatment, Caraka states that the physician "makes him [the patient] drink an astringent drink of *madana* fruit to which is added honey, liquorice, rock salt and sugar-cane treacle" (*madhu-madhuka-saindhava-phāṇitopahitāṃ madana-phala-kaṣāya-mātrāṃ pāyayet*, Car 1.15.9). Suśruta lists 23 trees,

---

[47] See also VāgAS 1.47, which agrees that emesis is the best cure for increased phlegm.

starting with *madana*, the fruit or roots of which have emetic properties (Suśr 1.39.3). In the case of *madana* it is the fruit that is used, since the root is extremely poisonous. Suśruta adds that "*madana* fruit is the very best of all fruit etc. that have emetic properties" (*vamana-dravyāṇāṃ phalādīnāṃ madana-phalāni śreṣṭhatamāni bhavanti*, Suśr 1.43.3). The fruit of the *madana* should be dried, powdered and given to the patient with honey and *saindhava* salt (Suśr 1.43.3). Indeed, *madana* is so effective an emetic that it is used to rapidly induce vomiting in a king who has been poisoned (Suśr 5.1.14).

While *madana* in the technical vocabulary of the medical treatises refers to the fruit of the *Vanguiera Spinosa* or thorn-apple tree, in broader contexts the primary referent of the word is 'passion' or 'lust'. It is, for example, an appellation for the god of love. The word *madana* appears three times in the context of Nanda's Apsarases experience, at 10:36, 10:56 and 11:5. *Madana* qualifies the Apsarases as they first surround Nanda: passion, one hears, is their sole activity (*madanaika-kāryāḥ* , 10:36). Then, as Nanda begins to suffer a violent reaction to the sight of the Apsarases – when the drug, as it were, 'begins to bite' - he describes himself as "bitten by the snake of passion" (*daṣṭo madanāhinā*, 10:56). The beginning of the following canto finds Nanda practising self-restraint and celibacy, albeit with little enthusiasm, as he attempts to win the Apsarases for himself. The after-effects on Nanda of his experience is described as follows:

saṃvṛtena ca śāntena tīvreṇa madanena ca |
jalāgner iva saṃsargāc chaśāma ca śuśoṣa ca || (11:5)

He was pacified by calming restraint, and drained by violent passion, just as [one is both calmed and dried up] from the combination of water and fire.

Nanda has become dry, withered, or parched (*śuśoṣa*) because he has been treated with a strong dose of *madana* (*tīvreṇa madanena*), just as a patient would be drained by fits of vomiting brought on by strong emetic drugs.

If my assumption - that Aśvaghoṣa conceived of Nanda's Apsarases experience as an emetic procedure - is correct, then one would expect the experience to draw out his passion (*rāga*), just as emesis draws out excessive phlegm (*kapha*). Caraka describes how the physician, after administering the emetic drug *madana*, carefully observes the ensuing bouts of vomiting to judge whether the appropriate amount of the drug has been administered (Car 1.15.12). This is important, since too large a dosage is dangerous and calls for remedial measures, while too small a dosage would not bring the desired result. Similarly, the Buddha watches the effect of the Apsarases on Nanda, and asks him the question about his preference for his wife or the Apsarases after "judging that Nanda's passion had risen" (*matvā tato nandam udīrṇa-rāgam*, 10:47a). *Udīrṇa*, literally meaning "gone upwards", indicates not just the intensification of Nanda's passion, but its upward movement prior to expulsion. Following his experience in heaven, Nanda seems to be free of passion (*vīta-rāga iva*, 11:7c) and has turned away from his passion for his wife (*bhāryā-rāgāt parāṅmukhaḥ*, 11:8b). Nanda does seem improved, as Ānanda remarks (11:12), but until he achieves liberation, any cure must necessarily be considered partial.

I have demonstrated above that the Buddha's actions in taking Nanda to heaven and showing him the Apsarases is justified by Aśvaghoṣa on the basis of a medical analogy. Furthermore, I have suggested that Aśvaghoṣa has in mind a specific medical procedure. This procedure I take to be emesis. Emesis is the standard treatment for phlegm conditions (*kapha*). The procedure is initiated by the administration of *madana*, the emetic drug *par excellence*. The aim of the procedure is to cleanse the system by expelling accumulated phlegm. The patient is left weak and dehydrated, but calmer, and thereafter progresses to good health. The discomfort of the procedure is short-lived, and justifiable on the grounds of its efficacy in securing improved health. This detoxifying therapy provides a model for Nanda's experience. Nanda suffers from passion (*rāga*), the psychological fault which is equated by Aśvaghoṣa to the humoral fault of phlegm. In order to expel accumulated passion from Nanda, the Buddha subjects him to a painful experience. The painful experience is triggered by the vision of the Apsarases, who epitomise passion (*madana*). Afterwards Nanda feels drained but calmer, and begins to make spiritual progress. The long-term benefit to Nanda of his visit to heaven is soon seen to outweigh the short-term suffering that it induces in him.

In my argument for an underlying metaphor of emesis I have not considered the preliminary stages of oiling and sweating, nor the concluding stages of smoke inhalation, bathing and dietary advice, as I do not believe the analogy can be pushed so far. However, it is worth noting that the Buddha does go on to give Nanda a great deal of advice on food (14:1-19). It is always possible, of course, that there is no underlying metaphor of emesis. The evidence for the emesis metaphor is largely circumstantial, and not incontrovertible. *Madana* makes perfect sense at 10:36, 10:56 and 11:5 taken in its primary sense of 'passion', without any need to superimpose on it a connotation of 'emetic drug'. And when Aśvaghoṣa seeks to exonerate the Buddha from the suspicion of gratuitous cruelty by comparing him, in 10:43, to a doctor who seeks to draw out humoral faults from the body by causing it further pain, he may have been thinking of an entirely different procedure.

Nevertheless, the conceptualisation of passion and desire as unwholesome bodily waste-matter is not unknown elsewhere in Aśvaghoṣa's poetry, nor in Buddhist literature generally. For example, the Buddha tries to bolster Nanda's resolve by telling him of previous king-seers who smilingly set off for the forest "after spitting out desires" (*niṣṭhīvya kāmān*, 5:38). The unnamed monk likens Nanda, in his desire to return home to his lover, to "a wretched dog that wants to eat the food it has itself vomited" (*aśanaṃ khalu vāntam ātmanā kṛpaṇaḥ śvā punar attum icchati*, 8:21). In a similar context, in Canto 9 of the *Buddhacarita* a deputation from king Śuddhodana tries to persuade the bodhisattva to return to the palace. The bodhisattva rejects their pleas, saying that taking up desires once they have been renounced (*saṃtyajya kāmān punar ādadīta*, AśvBC 9:46d) would be like eating vomited food (*vāntam annaṃ punar ādadīta*, AśvBC 9:46b). These two similes are particulary disgusting since they focus on re-ingestion of waste-matter that has already been rejected by the body. The Buddhist poet Mātṛceṭa, writing shortly after Aśvaghoṣa, describes the Buddha as "spewing out the operation of desires" (*vāntecchopavicāra*, *Śatapañcāśatka* 63). Similarly in the *Lalitavistara* the Buddha says he has expelled desire "like a ball of mucus"(*yathā pakva-kheṭa-piṇḍam*, Lal 177.32). In all these cases, the waste that has been expelled from the body is a metaphor for desire. The power of these images derives from the cultural taboo surrounding the re-ingestion of such waste.

Since unwholesome actions and thoughts (such as those involving desire) can be portrayed as bodily waste-matter, it follows that any action which combats such thoughts and actions can be portrayed as an aid to the expulsion of waste-matter from the body. Āyurvedic medicine commonly incorporates such procedures into its treatment programs, so it is not surprising that metaphors of internal cleansing or evacuative treatment arose in the Buddhist imagination. Richard Gombrich (1991) has argued that a metaphor of purging lies behind the term *pātimokkha*, the name of the set of rules observed by Buddhist monks and nuns. The observation and the recitation of the rules therefore functions as the purgation of any offence a monk or nun may have committed. A metaphor of evacuative treatment appears in the *Aṅguttara Nikāya* in two *suttas*, one devoted to each of the two major types of evacuative therapy. In the *Vamana Sutta* (AN v.219), the Buddha addresses a group of monks: "'Monks, physicians adminster an emetic (*vamanam*) for countering sickness arising from bile (*pitta*), phlegm (*semha*), for countering sickness arising from wind (*vāta*). Monks, I say that this is emesis (*vamanam*), but it is not an annhilation. Emesis may succeed, or it may fail. Monks, I will teach you the noble emesis (*ariyaṃ vamanam*) which succeeds and does not fail." The noble emesis which the Buddha outlines consists in this instance of the Noble Eightfold Path, which causes false view and so on to be vomited (*micchādiṭṭhi vantā hoti*). The accompanying *Tikicchaka Sutta* (AN v.218) has nearly identical wording, except that purge (*virecanam*) appears in the place of emesis (*vamanam*). So if Aśvaghoṣa did indeed turn to the principles of Āyurvedic evacuative therapy for assistance in presenting his understanding of the Apsarases episode, his would not be the only instance of such therapies being put to figurative use in a Buddhist context.

The *Saundarananda* presents Nanda's passion (*rāga*) as a defect which must be taken out of him in order that he may reach the goal of liberation. I have described at length how one medical procedure, emesis, functions as a metaphor for the removal of passion. There is one other procedure that operates in the same way - the surgical extraction of a poisoned arrow from a patient's body. As a metaphor for the expulsion of unhelpful thoughts and actions from the practitioner, arrow extraction appears more regularly in Buddhist literature than does evacuative therapy. Aśvaghoṣa refers to arrow extraction three times. It first occurs in Canto 5, when the Buddha seeks to persuade Nanda to leave home. The Buddha speaks of a nurse holding down a child to remove dirt from its mouth, and then tells Nanda that "wishing to draw out the dart of passion, I likewise spoke severely to you for your own good" (*tathojjihīrṣuḥ khalu rāga-śalyaṃ tat tvām avocaṃ paruṣaṃ hitāya*, 5:47cd). As has already been noted more than once, the medical metaphor provides a justification for acting on Nanda against his will. Passion is portrayed as a foreign object (*rāga-śalyam*) buried in the body, where it is likely to cause pain and inflammation. The Buddha's harsh speech (*paruṣam*) is the instrument whereby the arrow of passion is to be removed, and he announces his definite intention to do so (*ujjihīrṣuḥ khalu*). When Nanda reaches liberation in 17:60, he utters a paean of praise to the Buddha, testifying to the successful completion of the operation and the skill and compassion of its overseer: "the arrow of lust that was lodged in my heart was pulled out under the direction of the compassionate teacher" (*tasyājñayā kāruṇikasya śāstur hṛdi-stham utpāṭya hi rāga-śalyam*, 17:65ab). Notice that the arrow was extracted from the vicinity of the vital organ of the heart, a reminder of the life-threatening nature of Nanda's former condition of passion. Whether or not *ājñā* carries the meaning of the special knowledge of a person who has reached enlightment, which Johnston (1932:108) feels may apply here, it is clear that all the credit for Nanda's perfect health belongs to the Buddha.

In a final surgical simile, the arrow or splinter stands for false views (*dṛṣṭi*) rather than for passion:

> *yā dṛṣṭi-śalyo hṛdayāvagāḍhaḥ*
> *prabho bhṛśaṃ mām atudat sutīkṣṇaḥ* |
> *tvad-vākya-saṃdaṃśa-mukhena me sa*
> *samuddhṛtaḥ śalya-hṛteva śalyaḥ* || (18:7)

> The arrow of wrong views that was plunged into my heart, O Lord, had struck me forcibly and was extremely sharp. It was extracted by the forceps of your words, like an arrow removed by a surgeon.

Again, the arrow is located in the vital region of the heart. The forceful 'plunged' (*avagāḍha*) stresses how deeply rooted was this particular arrow, as does its sharpness (*sutīkṣṇaḥ*) and the fact that it had struck Nanda very forcibly (*bhṛśaṃ mām atudat*). Since the arrow was firmly and deeply embedded in Nanda's heart, it would have caused a great deal of pain as well as being particularly difficult to remove. The instrument of extraction is the speech of the Buddha, likened here to the jaws of a pair of surgical forceps (*tvad-vākya-saṃdaṃśa-mukhena*) which, one imagines, grip the arrow and yank it free.

When Nanda's suffering is depicted as an arrow lodged in his body, then the Buddha's speech, with its capacity to excise unwholesome thoughts and behaviours, is portrayed as a surgical instrument. However, when Nanda's illness is presented as a case of poisoning, then the words of the Buddha are more appropriately seen as a remedy or antidote, a potent potion that is imbibed by the patient to counteract his malady. Thus Nanda, formerly ruled by his senses, ascribes his new-found freedom from his senses to the curative power of the words of the Buddha:

yat pītam āsvāda-vaśendriyeṇa
darpeṇa kandarpa-viṣaṃ mayāsīt |
tan me hataṃ tvad-vacanāgadena
viṣaṃ vināśīva mahāgadena || (18:9)

That love-poison that I drunk in my pride when my senses were ruled by relish was eradicated by the antidote of your words, like a deadly poison eradicated by a powerful antidote.

In this verse Nanda presents love metaphorically as a poison (*kandarpa-viṣam*) that he has consumed. The words of the Buddha are the remedy (*tvad-vacanāgadena*) which effectively destroyed (*hatam*) the poison. A simile in the last *pāda* further emphasises the metaphor: "like a deadly poison [eradicated] by a powerful antidote". Thus the Buddha's words, already described as a remedy (*tvad-vacanāgadena*), are further qualified as a potent remedy (*mahāgadena*).

In my consideration of this fourth and final element of the medical paradigm, I have shown that Nanda is subjected to several kinds of treatment. Each treatment type is appropriate for a particular condition. When Nanda is viewed as suffering from an excess of phlegm, he receives emetic therapy. When a foreign object is embedded in his heart, it is removed with a surgical instrument, in the form of the Buddha's speech. When he is poisoned, then he receives an antidote, again in the form of the *buddha-vacana*. I have shown, too, that more than once in the *Saundarananda* the medical metaphor functions as a justification both for actions perpetrated on Nanda against his will and for augmenting his suffering. It is clear that Aśvaghoṣa had some qualms about the incidents that constitute the Nanda story. Unable to tamper with a plot structure that was fixed in traditional lore, Aśvaghoṣa resorts to the medical metaphor to exonerate the Buddha from any suspicion of unethical action, just as the commentator Dhammapāla was to do several centuries later when he found himself in similar circumstances. Thus we are led to think of the beautiful Apsarases as rather like a good dose of castor oil, administered to Nanda to help him clear passion out of his system. Evacuative treatment was from ancient times a standard procedure, widely accepted as an effective treatment for humoral complaints. By suggesting, however faintly, that the Apsarases function as an emetic stimulant, Aśvaghoṣa wins for the Buddha's actions in Canto 10 the same ready acceptance that was granted by his contemporaries to evacuative therapy.

4.5 Summary of the Medical Metaphor

At the beginning of this chapter I pointed out that the four-limbed model of medical practice – a doctor providing treatment to a patient who has an illness – was widely adopted by the Buddhist tradition as an appropriate and powerful metaphor for the Buddha providing succour to mankind afflicted by *duḥkha*. Aśvaghoṣa frequently resorts to the medical metaphor in his retelling of the Nanda story, and the bulk of the chapter investigates Aśvaghoṣa's application of the medical metaphor to the Nanda material. It does so by considering in four separate sections the four elements of the medical paradigm, that is, disease, patient, doctor and treatment. The first section, on disease, notes Aśvaghoṣa's equation of the unenlightened and enlightened states to illness and health respectively. It examines the *Saundarananda*'s presentation of the body, which is made up of elements (*dhātu*) and humoral faults (*doṣa*), as the locus of disease. Much of the first section is taken up by drawing out Aśvaghoṣa's intertwining of psychological faults (*doṣa*) and the Āyurvedic concept of humoral faults (*doṣa*). I demonstrated that the three *doṣas* as humoral faults preventing good health are a good parallel to the three *doṣas* as character faults preventing liberation, providing that the three humoral substances are considered as faults (*doṣa*) only once they reach excessive, pathogenic levels. Aśvaghoṣa uses the medical metaphor to show that the three faults must be carefully distinguished from each other so that the correct remedial action can be undertaken. The psychological fault with which the *Saundarananda* most concerns itself, since it is the one which afflicts Nanda, is passion (*rāga*). Passion is deeply entrenched in Nanda and causes him a great deal of suffering. Its cure coincides with Nanda's attainment of enlightenment, and the first section concludes with some remarks on the *Saundarananda*'s characterisation of liberation as a disease-free state.

The second and third sections of this chapter analyse the roles played by Nanda and the Buddha as patient and doctor. Both sections look to the luminaries of the Āyurvedic tradition, namely Caraka, Suśruta and Vāgbhaṭa, and to the Pali *Vinaya Mahāvagga*, for idealised representations of these two roles. In the second section, the ideal patient emerges as somebody who is primarily obedient to his physician and, to a somewhat lesser extent, informative about his own condition. The medical authorities are agreed that these and various other positive characteristics have a high correlation with the good clinical outcome of a case. At first Nanda does not meet these criteria. However, as the Buddha's teachings begin to have an effect on him, Nanda increasingly conforms to the portrait of the ideal patient, one who recognises his illness and actively participates in his own recovery. Nanda's evolution into an active patient is, as the second section demonstrates, an indispensable factor in his cure. Āyurveda's insistence that recovery is dependent on a patient's personal qualities provides a highly suitable metaphor for Aśvaghoṣa's portrayal of Nanda's liberation as dependent on his obedience, volition and energy. In the third section, the focus switches to the doctor. The idealised doctor appears as highly learned, experienced, dextrous and caring. In line with the traditional Buddhist conception of the Buddha as a healing figure, the Buddha appears in the *Saundarananda* as the physician *par excellence*, though it was noted that because both the unnamed monk and Ānanda try to help Nanda, they too are partially represented in medical guise. The Buddha, though, remains Nanda's primary care-giver, and in this role it is his compassion and kindness that are repeatedly stressed, and find a natural expression in his depiction as a doctor benevolently dispensing life-saving treatment. The emphasis on the doctor's good intentions is crucial in mitigating the impression that the Buddha may be toying with Nanda.

In the final section of this chapter, I demonstrated that in two key episodes in the *Saundarananda* (the coerced ordination in Canto 5 and the exposure to the Apsarases in Canto 10), the Buddha's potentially controversial manipulation of Nanda is justified by an appeal to the medical metaphor. When Nanda is subjected to a restraint that verges on the physical, it is because he resembles a tiresome patient who won't take his medicine; and when his sufferings are purposefully intensified by the sight of the Apsarases, it is because a short-term exacerbation of pain is a customary form of treatment. I have argued that such customary treatment should be understood as something akin to traditional Āyurvedic evacuative therapy. Emesis is the regular Āyurvedic treatement for excess phlegm, the medical metaphor as espoused by Aśvaghoṣa equates phlegm to passion, and Nanda's sickness is easily diagnosed as passion. Regardless, however, of the specifics of the treatment meted out to Nanda, it is beyond doubt that the medical metaphor proves remarkably fruitful in circumventing potentially contentious issues. Aśvaghoṣa on several occasions provides a medical interpretation for the more questionable aspects of the traditional story. Any painful experience, so long as it can understood as a treatment or medicine, is acceptable on the grounds of its long-term benefit to the patient, the good intentions of the doctor, and its eventual approval by the patient himself. The medical metaphor provides a robust riposte to the question that readers through the ages are likely to have asked: "Why couldn't the Buddha just leave Nanda alone?"

Aśvaghoṣa uses the medical allusions as he does much of his figurative material, to bolster his theme of conversion or spiritual turn-around. In general, the medical scenario of a patient cured of his disease by the medicine dispensed by a doctor provides an excellent conceptual model for Nanda relieved of *duḥkha* by the teachings of the Buddha. However, the medical model cannot cope with the full scope of the Buddhist conception of *duḥkha* and *nirvāṇa*. It cannot fully express the congenital and universal nature of *duḥkha*, nor the supreme unprecedented death-defying health of *nirvāṇa*. In the medical scenario, the patient, if things go well, recovers the state of health he previously enjoyed. In the Buddhist adaptation of this model, people are born sick, and continue in sickness until they reach liberation, which is a state they have never previously attained. Liberation is not a recovery of a lost state, but the winning of a new one. Medical practice provides a good metaphor for the spiritual progress of the Buddhist practitioner, but it remains a metaphor; Buddhists are quite aware that physical illness is one thing and spiritual illness another, and that curing the latter does not necessarily imply a cure for the former. Thus the commentary on the *Theragāthā* relates that the leprous monk Samitigutta achieved enlightenment but not a cure for leprosy (Th-a 1.185-6).

Despite these constraints on metaphorical fit, the medical metaphor remains particularly well suited to Aśvaghoṣa's purposes. There are several reasons why the medical model proves such a fertile source of figurative language for Buddhism generally, and for Aśvaghoṣa in particular. Firstly, sickness and good health are emotive and highly persuasive concepts. The strong response elicted from an audience with regard to medical matters can be redirected via the medical metaphor to Buddhist matters. For instance, all human beings prize good health, so by equating liberation with health, the enlightened state can be seen as similarly advantageous, blissful and universally desirable. Conversely, nobody wants to be sick, so in labelling *duḥkha*, the human condition, as a sickness, all the negative connotations normally associated with sickness can be brought to bear on *duḥkha*. The lengths to which people are prepared to go to remove ill health and to achieve good health - the merchant's son at VinMV 8.1.22 who endures abdominal surgery to untwist his bowels serves as a good example – should be similarly applied to the practitioner's strivings for enlightenment. Secondly, since disease is a physical phenomenon, the medical metaphor suits Buddhism's generally low opinion of the body.[48] The body is

[48] Occasionally the body itself is said to be a disease, as at MN i.500 and SN iii.189. Aśvaghoṣa also exploits the association between a swelling and the body, on several occasions using the word *samucchraya* – a swelling or a tumour – as a synonym for the human body.

simply a vehicle for disease, as Aśvaghoṣa reveals in Canto 9 of the *Saundarananda*. Thirdly, some vocabulary is shared by Āyurvedic medicine and Buddhist dogma; *doṣa* is both a humoral fault and a psychological fault (and it is neat that there are three of each), while *śama* means both relief from illness and a state of spiritual peace. Aśvaghoṣa trades on this vocabulary in order to portray passion as a humoral fault engendering disease. Fourthly, the medical metaphor allows the Buddha to be seen as healer, and therefore possessed of all the caring and compassionate qualities and the specialist knowledge normally associated with such a figure. A further reason for frequent recourse to the medical metaphor is to share in the optimistic spirit of the medical system whose whole business is the reduction of suffering. The stories concerning the famous physician Jīvaka in the *Vinaya Mahāvagga* bear testimony to the possibility of last-minute miracle cures in seemingly hopeless cases. The very idea of medicine suggests that illness is not a hopeless state, and that something can be done. Lastly, treatment by surgery and evacuative procedures can readily reflect the concept of enlightenment as a state attainable when negative factors are removed or 'taken out' of the practitioner, while conversely, treatment by the imbibing of medicine reflects the wholesome effect of Buddhist doctrines on the practitioner.

The penultimate verse of the *Saundarananda* is a good point at which to conclude a discussion of the medical metaphor. The verse reads:

ity eṣā vyupaśāntaye na rataye mokṣārtha-garbhā kṛtiḥ
śrotṝṇāṃ grahaṇārtham anya-manasāṃ kāvyopacārāt kṛtā |
yan mokṣāt kṛtam anyad atra hi mayā tat kāvya-dharmāt kṛtaṃ
pātuṃ tiktam ivauṣadhaṃ madhu-yutaṃ hṛdyaṃ kathaṃ syād iti || (18:63)

This composition on the subject of liberation is for calming [the reader], not for his pleasure. It is fashioned

> out of *kāvya*-medicine with the intention of capturing an audience whose minds are on other things. Thinking how it could be made pleasant, I have handled in it things other than liberation, things created due to the character of *kāvya*, as bitter medicine is mixed with honey when it is drunk.[49]

Here we have Aśvaghoṣa's *apologia* for his use of the *kāvya* form, perhaps to counter the criticism that a *kavi-bhikṣu* must inevitably have attracted. Aśvaghoṣa makes one final appeal to the medical metaphor, this time in order to sanction his own belletristic activity. This poem is made out of that medical attendance (*upacāra*, Aśvaghoṣa's standard term for medical treatment or doctoring) which consists of *kāvya*. The compound *kāvyopacāra* I take as a *karmadhāraya* compound meaning 'poetry-medicine'. The poem has as its subject the Buddhist goal of liberation (*mokṣārtha*), but since this may prove somewhat indigestible or hard to swallow for some readers, the poem also includes other more superficially delightful (*hṛdyam*) things. A medical simile spells out Aśvaghoṣa's method: the poem is rendered palatable by the addition of *kāvya* elements, just as honey (*madhu*) is put into bitter medicine (*tiktam...auṣadham*) so that it might be pleasant to drink (*pātum...hṛdyaṃ...syāt*). Thus we, the *Saundarananda*'s readers or audience, are invited to put ourselves in Nanda's place, and to receive Aśvaghoṣa's spoonful of sugar along with the medicine it masks, in the hope that in imbibing it we too will derive some measure of tranquillity (*vyupaśānti*).

---

[49] The poetician Bhāmaha makes a remarkably similar statement: "Even instruction is acceptable when it is mixed with the sweet taste of *kāvya*; they who first sip honey [also] drink sharp medicine" (*svādu-kāvya-rasonmiśraṃ śāstram apy upayuñjate | prathamālīḍha-madhavaḥ pibanti kaṭu bheṣajam ||* BhāKA 5:3).

CHAPTER FIVE

NANDA REFINED

In the *Jātaka* collection there is a story of a junior monk who is receiving instruction from Sāriputta. Sāriputta sets him an impurity meditation, but four months pass by and though the monk tries hard he makes absolutely no progress. Sāriputta is obliged to ask for the Buddha's help in this difficult case, and it is then explained that because the monk spent 500 successive births as a goldsmith, the cumulative effect of seeing pure gold for such a long time has made impurity a useless subject of meditation for him.[1] This charming tale illustrates the connotation of purity that gold has traditionally carried. The world's most prized metal is a natural symbol for purity because unlike other metals, it does not rust, tarnish or corrode. This chapter examines how gold functions in the *Saundarananda* as a general indicator of spiritual achievement, and more specifically, how the process of gold refining is adopted as a metaphor for mental development. The gold metaphor does not feature as prominently in the *Saundarananda* as either the medical or the elephant training metaphors discussed in the preceding chapters, yet it is worthy of note because gold refining so neatly models an abstract mental process. Additionally, two of the poem's references to gold closely parallel the Pali *Aṅguttara Nikāya*, and in any case the ancient technology described holds an inherent curiosity value. The chapter opens with a brief survey of the four stages of gold production in ancient India – mining, washing, smelting and making a gold article – since this background knowledge is useful for the full appreciation of the gold refining metaphor. Next the chapter moves to a discussion of the figurative value of gold, showing that gold is associated at various times with both the Buddha and Nanda as betokening estimable qualities. Thereafter, the chapter will focus on the metaphor of gold refining as it appears in Cantos 15 and 16 and its parallels with the Pali material. From this comparison with the Pali material follows the proposition that Aśvaghoṣa noticed,

---

[1] *Jātaka* no. 25.

and emended, an anomaly in the *Aṅguttara Nikāya* version of the metaphor. Finally, this chapter considers why gold is a peculiarly apt symbol for the enlightened mind.

5.1 Gold Production in Ancient India

Gold has been highly valued in India for thousands of years. Evidence from carbon dating indicates that surface deposits of gold-bearing sand and gravel have been worked since the Indus valley civilisations. Such gold-bearing deposits, known as placers, are generally found in the sediment of rivers that have flowed over rocks containing gold ore. Most of ancient India's gold seems to have been taken from placer deposits in the northern parts of the country; the rivers in the Panjab, Madhya Pradesh, Bihar, Kashmir and Nepal have yielded gold particles up to recent times. The earliest evidence for the more technically demanding bedrock mining comes from the Hatti mine in Karnataka, which has been dated to the eighth century BCE (Agrawal and Margabandhu 1975-6:138). Indian miners at Hatti achieved the remarkable feat of sinking shafts which, at almost 200 metres, were the deepest in the ancient world. Several other goldfields in the Deccan were worked in the pre-Common Era, while Kolar, modern India's best-known gold reef, has produced gold since the fourth century CE. After gold-bearing rocks had been retrieved from the earth, they were crushed in order to free the gold from other minerals, usually quartz, in which it was embedded. Gold-rich sand retrieved from a river was the product of erosion and would not need to be crushed. Perhaps due to the geographical separation of the two types of mining, surface mining occurring in northern areas and deep mining further south, the Sanskrit and Pali literature gives little indication of familiarity with the latter type. On the other hand mountains, particularly the Himalayas, are frequently associated with gold. The *Saundarananda* has the Buddha and Nanda arrive at "the Himalayan mountains endowed with gold ore" (*kāñcana-dhātumantaṃ ... himavantam*, 10:5).

Both gold-rich sediment from placer deposits and crushed gold ore from mines consisted of a mixture of variously-sized mineral particles. In the second stage of gold production, these particles were separated out by either a dry or a wet technique, both of which depended on gold's characteristic heaviness for their effectiveness. The dry technique involved winnowing, in which air served as the medium of separation. The second technique used water to separate lighter particles of dross from the heavier gold particles. 19th century accounts of the procedure for washing gold[2] agree with each other in all essential elements, and the procedure adopted by ancient gold-washers cannot have differed greatly. The gold-washers select a suitable site next to a river that had been previously inspected for traces of gold, and set up a wooden trough with a narrow slit at one end. A rough sieve made of grass is placed over the trough. After discarding the larger stones, the gold-washers scrape up the sand from the riverbank and pile it onto the sieve. Water is then poured over the pile of sand. The finer particles and the water pass through into the trough, while coarser particles remain on the sieve and are thrown away. More water is poured into the trough and is simultaneously agitated with the hand. Being heavy, the gold particles sink to the bottom of the trough, while the lighter particles of dross run out of the trough through the slit at its end. Eventually only a small amount of very fine, sparkling sand – gold dust - is left in the trough. 19th century observers relate how the gold particles were then amalgamated with mercury, though such a technique appears to have been unknown at the time of the *Saundarananda*.

The gold dust obtained from the washing process still contained a variety of other minerals, including zinc, copper, silver and iron. In particular, native gold virtually always contains traces of silver. In order to remove such impurities, the gold particles were placed in a crucible, together with certain other ingredients, notably salt,[3] that acted as a flux to facilitate melting and separating, and heated in a furnace. In time, and with repetitive treatments, the silver was converted into silver chloride and absorbed into molten slag which could then be

---

[2] See for instance Cautley (1835); Jenkins (1838); Abbott (1847).

[3] *Chāndogya Upaniṣad* 4.17.7, *Jaiminīya Upaniṣad* 3.17.3 and KA 2.14.23 all refer to the property of salt to act as a flux in joining separate pieces of gold.

skimmed off the surface. Exposing the native gold to a high temperature also had the effect of burning off any organic matter and of encouraging the separate particles of gold to fuse together. Since gold melts at 1063° centigrade, the act of blowing on the fire, presumably with either bellows or blowpipe, was a crucial part of the procedure; the *Ṛg Veda* names the artisan who smelts metal as a "blower" (*dhmātṛ*, RV 5.9.5). The molten, refined gold would then be poured into moulds or simple casts and left to solidify. The success of the entire process was dependent on constant supervision and repeated treatment.

In the final stage of the manufacturing process, the refined gold was worked into ornaments or coins by a goldsmith (*suvarṇa-kāra*). He could also brighten old ornaments by heating them just once, or he could melt and re-shape them. This must have been a major part of his trade, since jewellery, handed down as family heirlooms and dowries, would presumably be re-sized for new owners. The *Arthaśāstra* testifies to the great skill of the goldsmiths. Their range of expertise included encrusting gold with gems, making golden beads, forming solid or hollow golden objects, gold-plating silver or copper articles, and beating out gold leaf in various colours (KA 2.13.37-47). Aśvaghoṣa must have had an intricately worked piece of jewellery in mind when he compares a lion to an arm ornament in a simile very typical of *kāvya* in its close observation and detailed visual texture. Unfortunately the verse is partially corrupt, but the contrast of the yellow gold against the paler silver is not in doubt:

> *manaḥśilā-dhātu-śilāśrayeṇa*
> *pītākṛtāṃso virarāja siṃhaḥ* |
> *saṃtapta-cāmīkara-bhakti-citraṃ*
> *rūpyāṅgadaṃ śīrṇam ivāmbikasya*[4] || (10:9)

---

[4] The last word is corrupt and the name is Johnston's (1932:55) conjecture.

> A lion with his shoulder yellowed from reclining on a rock of red arsenic appeared like Ambika's broken silver armlet variously etched with refined gold.

Gold was aesthetically pleasing, though its buying power was more valued by rulers, who considered large reserves of gold a prerequisite for the efficient functioning of the state. Kauṭilya makes it clear that gold mines were the property of the state (KA 2.12.22), and additional revenue was generated by nine different taxes that were levied on the gold manufacturing process (KA 2.12.35-6). A well-stocked treasury was important for the economic welfare of the state and the maintenance of an army, which in turn provided security against aggressors:

> *ākara-prabhavaḥ kośaḥ kośād daṇḍaḥ prajāyate |*
> *pṛthivī kośa-daṇḍābhyāṃ prāpyate kośa-bhūṣaṇā ||*
> (KA 2.12.37)

> The treasury has its source in the mines; from the treasury the army comes into being. With the treasury and the army, the earth is obtained with the treasury as its ornament.[5]

In the *Saundarananda*, the attainment of wealth allows the Ikṣvāku princes to build Kapilavāstu (1:39-41). Gold indicates wealth, and establishes that Nanda is a rich man: the mirror that Nanda holds for Sundarī has a golden handle (6:29), and Sundarī's couch has golden feet (6:31). Golden ornaments are listed along with other luxury items as things that make women attractive (8:50)[6]. Gold also features in the description of Sundarī's curvaceous figure in a lovely line embellished with *yamaka* on 'd' and 'r', and the repetition of *darīm*. Nanda is trying to tear himself away from his wife, but as he hurries after the Buddha he turns round to take one last look at her:

---

[5] Trans. Kangle.

[6] The word *tapanīya* is used here, indicating gold refined in the fire.

chātodarīṃ pīna-payodharoruṃ
sa sundarīṃ rukma-darīm ivādreḥ | (4:41ab)

[seeing] Sundarī, with her waist compacted [between] her swelling breasts and thighs like a golden fissure in a mountain ...

Sundarī's midriff, doubtless exposed in the traditional manner, takes on a golden sheen, and seems narrow in contrast to the bulk of her breasts and hips. The line successfully evokes Sundarī's shapeliness and gives substance to Nanda's desire for her, while the rendering of her physical appearance in terms of geomorphological features is suggestive of the vertical theme explored in Chapter Six. However, while gold is occasionally associated with Sundarī, most of the poem's gold is found not on earth but in heaven. The pleasure-garden of Indra, described in Canto 10 as having trees producing gold-threaded garments as fruit (10:22), golden lotuses (10:24), other trees of gold and jewels (10:25) and golden birds (10:29-30), is typical of the ancient Indian conception of heaven as a bejewelled and gold filled treasure-house.

5.2 The Figurative Value of Gold

The beauty, rarity and high economic worth of gold ensured that it soon acquired a correspondingly high figurative value. Since gold tops the hierarchy of metals, anything said to be golden implies the possession of a host of excellent and praiseworthy features and is considered the best of its type. The Buddha is therefore frequently associated with gold, even while still in his mother's womb. The Pali texts relate that the bodhisatta's mother can see him in her womb as clearly as one can see a thread strung through fine beryl (MN iii.122), but the *Mahāvastu*, which is more exuberant in tone than the Pali texts in its presentation of the same episode, adds that the embryo is a body of pure gold (Mvu 1.213). Gold is suggestive of purity, and the *Mahāvastu* is at pains to point out that while the bodhisattva is in his mother's womb, he is not polluted by bile, phlegm or blood, and has his body rubbed with perfumes and washed clean. The *Lalitavistara*, a text which particularly exaggerates the miraculous elements surrounding the conception and birth of the bodhisattva, even provides a gold sanctum for the baby to sit in whilst in his mother's womb, hence avoiding contact with the womb altogether: "The chamber shone like gold that has been refined twice by a skilled smith, perfect and unflawed by quartz" (*tad yathāpi nāma dvi-nirdhāntaṃ suvarṇaṃ kuśalena karmakāreṇa suparinisṭhitam apagata-kāca-doṣam evaṃ sa kūṭāgāro virājate*, Lal 48.27-8). The association with gold continues after his birth. The *Sutta Nipāta*, describing how the Sakyans showed the baby bodhisatta to the sage Asita, compares the baby to "radiant gold wrought by a highly skilled [smith] in a furnace" (*kumāraṃ jalitam iva suvaṇṇaṃ ukkā-mukhe va sukusula-sampahaṭṭham*, Sn 686). The classic example of the positive connotion of gold is the inclusion of golden skin as one of the 32 marks of the great man.[7]

Aśvaghoṣa taps into these traditions when he describes the Buddha as having "golden arms as thick as a yoke" (*suvarṇa-pīna-yuga-bāhu*, 3:6), and, whilst performing the series of miracles in Canto 3, as shining "with light like refined gold" (*tapta-kanaka-sadṛśa-prabhayā*, 3:24). I will return to the particular significance of this comparison a little later. Watching the miracles, the king venerates him as though he were a raised banner encircled with gold and jewels (3:25). The origin of gold within the earth inspires a simile at 13:4-6 that explains the Buddha's relationship to the world:

> *pāṃsubhyaḥ kāñcanaṃ jātaṃ viśuddhaṃ nirmalaṃ śuci |*
> *sthitaṃ pāṃsuṣv api yathā pāṃsu-doṣair na lipyate ||*
> (13:4)
> ...
> *tadvad loke munir jāto lokasyānugrahaṃ caran |*
> *kṛtitvān nirmalatvāc ca loka-dharmair na lipyate ||*
> (13:6)

[7] See DN ii.17, iii.143; MN ii.136 etc.

> Just as gold originates in dust, but is pure, flawless and clean, and though it remains in the dust it is not soiled by dust-spots ... likewise the sage is born in the world and operates as a favour to the world, but because of his perfectedness and spotlessness he is not soiled by any worldly thing.

The intervening verse 13:5 makes the same point with the standard comparison of a lotus unstained by water. In the gold simile, gold is taken to be quite distinct from and unaffected by the dirt or dust (*pāṃsu*) in which it is embedded, and does not itself become dirty or dusty. Similarly, the Buddha is unaffected by the world though in close contact with it. Gold, signifying purity, is the antitype of dirt and hence, by extension, of moral defects.

The principle of unsulliable purity that is embodied in the image of gold lying in the earth reappears in the final verse of the poem, though on this occasion it is applied to the teachings of the Buddha rather than to the Buddha himself. In the last verse Aśvaghoṣa tells his readers that he has described "truth in the guise of poetry" (*kāvyā-vyājena tattvaṃ*, 18:64b), and so:

> *tad buddhvā śāmikaṃ yat tad avahitam ito grāhyaṃ na lalitaṃ*
> *pāṃsubhyo dhātu-jebhyo niyatam upakaraṃ cāmīkaram iti* ||
> (18:64cd)

> Knowing this, that which relates to peace should be carefully extracted from it, not the entertaining part. Serviceable gold inevitably comes from ore-born dust.

The word for 'gold', *cāmīkara*, is the poem's final word, and forms part of the concluding figure of corroboration (*arthāntara-nyāsa*) that serves to substantiate the point just made. Aśvaghoṣa is inviting his reader to extract the nugget of truth from the dross of *kāvya* through the mechanism of the gold refining metaphor. At the same time the metaphor allows the poet to express his opinion of the ultimate worthlessness of the conventions and style of *kāvya* poetry as opposed to the absolute value of Buddhist doctrine.

Since gold represents that which Aśvaghoṣa most highly values, including the dharma and the Buddha himself, it is telling that for the first nine cantos of the poem Nanda is not associated with gold at all. Instead, Nanda presents a paradox in that though he is a rich man he does not share the golden purity of the Buddha, a mendicant without possessions. The logic of the gold metaphor dictates that any figurative connection between Nanda and gold would indicate progress towards the Buddhist goal of liberation. If Nanda were golden than his conversion would be complete. The first occasion in the poem on which Nanda is associated with gold is when the Buddha takes him by the hand to fly to Indra's heaven at the beginning of Canto 10. Nanda and the Buddha flying through the clear sky are compared to a pair of *cakravāka* birds:

> *kāṣāya-vastrau kanakāvadātau*
> *virejatus tau nabhasi prasanne |*
> *anyonya-saṁśliṣṭa-vikīrṇa-pakṣau*
> *saraḥ-prakīrṇāv iva cakravākau ||* (10:4)

> With their ochre garments they shone like refined gold in the clear sky, like a pair of *cakravākas* rising from a lake, their wings outstretched to clasp one another.

In this verse the compound *kanakāvadātau* (from *kanaka*, gold, and *ava* + √*dai*, to purify or cleanse) applies to both Nanda and the Buddha, with the dual form indicating that Nanda partakes of the Buddha's gold-associated qualities of purity. *Avadāta* can also mean white or dazzling. Hence the colour of the ochre robes in the sky, perhaps as the sun catches them, suggests the colour and sparkle of purified gold, and is also pertinent to the simile in the last *pāda*, since the *cakravāka* bird has reddish-brown wings. While in Canto 10 Nanda is temporarily golden due to his association with the Buddha, on his own he is not said to be golden until the last canto, after his attainment of liberation. At this point Nanda approaches the Buddha and bows to him:

> *kāṣāya-vāsāḥ kanakāvadātas*
> *tataḥ sa mūrdhnā gurave praṇeme* | (18:5ab)
>
> Shining like refined gold in his ochre garments, he bowed his head to the guru.

The first *pāda* is virtually identical to the first *pāda* of verse 10:4 just quoted, with the key difference that this time the compound *kanakāvadātaḥ* is in the singular and applies solely to Nanda, indicating that he now possesses excellence and purity independently of the Buddha. Perhaps there is also a hint that the attainment of enlightenment, as represented by gold, is connected to monastic discipline, as represented by the monk's robe. The association with refined (*avadāta*) gold also indicates a mastery of meditation, as the rest of this chapter will illustrate. Finally, to complete his identification with the noble metal, Nanda is compared to a great gold pillar (*haimo mahāstambha iva*, 18:20) as he prostrates himself on the earth before the Buddha. *Haima*, as the *vṛddhi* form of *heman*, underscores the notion of development.

5.3 The Gradual Removal of Dirt (Verses 15:66-9)

So far I have demonstrated that gold has a figurative function in the *Saundarananda* in a very general way in that it indicates an exalted state. However, the correspondence between gold and excellence is worked out in rather greater detail in Cantos 15 and 16 as part of the Buddha's instruction in meditation. Cantos 15 and 16 each contain a short series of verses in which Aśvaghoṣa engages with the conceptual metaphor of mental development as the refining of gold. He draws a number of details from the activity of gold refining (which functions as the source domain) and applies them to the procedure for refining the mind (the target domain). He does this at 15:66-69, a passage at the end of Canto 15 that bears a close resemblance to the first part of the

Pali text at AN i.253-6, and also at 16:65-7, a passage that relates to the remainder of the same text, at AN i.256-8. The PTS edition of the Pali Canon recognises no break in the passage, but the Burmese edition names the portion of text at AN i.253-6 the *Paṃsu-dhovaka Sutta*, and the following portion of text at AN i.256-8 the *Nimitta Sutta*. These names will be used in the remainder of this chapter to refer to the two *Aṅguttara* passages. To begin with, I quote and translate the last four verses of *Saundarananda* Canto 15 in their entirety:

suvarṇa-hetor api pāṃsu-dhāvako
vihāya pāṃsūn bṛhato yathāditaḥ |
jahāti sūkṣmān api tad-viśuddhaye
viśodhya hemāvayavān niyacchati || (15:66)

vimokṣa-hetor api yukta-mānaso
vihāya doṣān bṛhatas tathāditaḥ |
jahāti sūkṣmān api tad-viśuddhaye
viśodhya dharmāvayavān niyacchati || (15:67)

krameṇādbhiḥ śuddhaṃ kanakam iha pāṃsu-vyavahitaṃ
yathāgnau karmāraḥ pacati bhṛśam āvartayati ca |
tathā yogācāro nipuṇam iha doṣa-vyavahitam
viśodhya kleśebhyaḥ śamayati manaḥ saṃkṣipati ca ||
(15:68)

yathā ca svacchandād upanayati karmāśraya-sukhaṃ
suvarṇaṃ karmāro bahu-vidham alaṃkāra-vidhiṣu |
manaḥ-śuddho bhikṣur vaśagatam abhijñāsv api tathā
yatheccham yatreccham śamayati manaḥ prerayati ca ||
(15:69)

15:66 To obtain gold, a dirt-washer discards first the large bits of grit, and then, to refine it further, he discards also the tiny bits of grit. After this cleansing, he retains the particles of gold.

15:67 To obtain liberation, a man with a focused mind will likewise abandon first gross faults, and then, to further refine [his mind], he abandons also subtle faults. After this cleansing, he retains the constituents of dharma.

15:68 Just as in this world a goldsmith [takes] gold that has been washed with water and separated from the dirt in gradual stages, and heats it in the fire and turns it frequently, so does the practitioner of yoga, having first cleansed his mind of defilements so that it is completely separated from faults in this world, then makes it calm and concentrated.

15:69 And as the goldsmith brings gold to a good state for working at will into various ornaments of many kinds, so too the monk of cleansed mind pacifies his mind, so that it is under his control, and then directs it as he wishes, wherever he wishes amongst the five supernatural faculties.

These four verses are placed in a fairly prominent postion at the end of the canto. *Kāvya* convention demands a change in metre as the end of a canto approaches, and Aśvaghoṣa, after 65 simple *anuṣṭubh*s, has chosen to mark the end of Canto 15 with two rather more complex metres, the 12-syllable *vaṃśastha* for verses 66 and 67, and the 17-syllable *śikhariṇī* for verses 68 and 69. The four verses construct a parallel between the refining of the Buddhist practitioner's state of mind on the one hand, and on the other, the method of gold production outlined at the beginning of this chapter. While there is no reference to the activities of mining and crushing the ore that constitute the first stage of the manufacturing process, the remaining three stages - washing, smelting, and fabricating a gold article - are clearly identifiable in verses 15:66, 15:68 and and 15:69 respectively. The process of washing the gold-bearing sediment, in which impurites are discarded in descending order of size, is the subject of 15:66, while its application to Buddhist practice is given in

15:67.[8] In fact, verses 66 and 67 mirror each other very closely, differing in only a few words. The man undertaking the washing process is the dirt-washer (*pāṃsu-dhāvaka*), who corresponds to the man whose mind is disciplined (*yukta-mānasa*). The unwanted gravel (*pāṃsu*) appears here in two sizes, large (*bṛhat*) and small (*sūkṣma*), corresponding to major and minor faults (*doṣa*) from which the practitioner seeks to free himself. In the *Paṃsu-dhovaka Sutta*, the dirt-washer (*paṃsu-dhovaka*) washes away grit and gravel impurities (*upakkilesā*) of three different grades, coarse (*oḷārika*), medium (*majjhima*) and fine (*sukhuma*). More important than numerically categorising the impurities, though, is the principle that they are to be discarded in order of size. The *Paṃsu-dhovaka Sutta* also supplies some additional information inessential to the structure of the metaphor, and better suited to its prose medium. It mentions that the dirt-washer washes the sand in a trough (*doṇi*), and it expands on the nature of the impurities in both the source and the target domains.

Once the impurities have been discarded as far as they can be by washing, the dirt-washer is left with residual particles of gold (*hemāvayavān*), and the practitioner likewise is left with the constituents of dharma (*dharmāvayavān*). Presumably these constituents of the dharma refer to a mental state. This is certainly the case in the *Paṃsu-dhovaka Sutta*, which has, corresponding to the gold dust (*suvaṇṇa-sikatā*) left to the dirt-washer, "the thought of the dharma" (*dhamma-vitakka*)[9] left to the practitioner. Neither the constituents of the dharma nor the gold dust to which it is likened represent the pinnacle of achievement, since we know that gold dust prior to being heated

[8] Aśvaghoṣa briefly revisits this parallel in 16:80cd, when we hear that "they [mental imperfections] are to be abandoned, like the impurities in gold, by removing them according to their coarseness" (*tato yathā-sthūla-nibarhaṇena suvarṇa-doṣā iva te praheyāḥ*).

[9] The commentary on the *Aṅguttara Nikāya* specifies *dhamma-vitakkā nāma dasa-vipassanupakkilesa-vitakkā*, referring to the ten extremely subtle imperfections, such as seeing colours, that hinder meditation. These subtle impurities have yet to be eliminated.

in the fire still contains traces of a number of other metals. Aśvaghoṣa pays little attention to the fact that the crude gold is not yet in its perfected state, merely implying that such is the case by admitting another stage in the process, which is that the goldsmith heats and turns the gold and eventually brings it to a "good state for working" (*karmāśraya-sukham*, 15:69a). The *Paṃsu-dhovaka Sutta*, however, expands on the imperfections of crude gold – it is not soft (*na mudu*), nor workable (*na kammaniya*), nor radiant (*na pabhassara*), but brittle (*pabhaṅgu*) and imperfect for working (*na sammā upeti kammāya*). Several other Pali passages associate all or some of these attributes with crude gold, and their opposites with refined gold.[10] The same attributes can equally well be associated with the mind when it is imperfectly trained, and their opposites when it is fully trained.[11] Indeed, adjectives such as *mudu* and *kammaniya* are used of the Buddha's mind upon his attainment of liberation (MN i.247). The *Paṃsu-dhovaka Sutta* provides a different set of descriptions of the imperfectly trained mind. The concentration (*samādhi*) of such a mind is not peaceful (*na santa*), not exalted (*na paṇīta*), has not reached tranquillity (*na paṭippassaddha-laddha*), is not one-pointed (*na ekodi-bhāvādhigata*) and, in an unusual compound, its defilements are suppressed by will-power (*sa-saṅkhāra-niggayha-vārita-gata*). The point is that just as unrefined gold still contains impurities though it has been washed clean of dross, so is the mind of the practitioner still defective after it has been cleansed of major and minor faults.

While verses 15:66-7 present the gradual washing away of dross as a model for mental and moral improvement, verse 15:68 moves the analogy on to the next logical step in the gold manufacturing process, that of smelting. Thus we hear no more of the dirt-washer; instead, the smith (*karmāraḥ*) continues the process of gold refining. This must certainly have reflected actual practice, since dirt-washing required diligence but no great

---

[10] MN iii.243; AN i.256-8, iii.16-19; SN v.92.

[11] MN iii.243; AN i.256-9, iii.16-19; SN v.92. The conceptualisation of the well-developed mind as well-refined gold must have been generally understood, since on occasion (AN i.9, iv.421) these attributes are applied to the mind alone without mention of gold.

skill and probably took place next to rivers, while goldsmithing was a skilled craft undertaken in workshops.[12] The change of personnel in the source domain is inconvenient for the metaphor, since in the target domain the practitioner remains the same. Aśvaghoṣa notes the change with slightly different nomenclature – the man of controlled mind is now a practitioner of yoga (*yogācāraḥ*). In verse 15:68 two finite present tense verbs refer to the actions of the smith, who 'cooks' (*pacati*) and turns (*āvartayati*) the gold, balanced by a further two finite present tense verbs that refer to the actions of the practitioner, who calms (*śamayati*) and concentrates (*saṃkṣipati*) his mind. The equation of mind (*manas*) to gold (*kanaka*) is evident. The persistence required of the practitioner in order to fully develop his mind is stressed by the repetitive nature (*bhṛśam*) of the goldsmith's task.

When the goldsmith persists in his efforts, the gold finally becomes a suitable material with which to work (*karmāśraya-sukhaṃ*). He can now complete the final stage in the gold manufacturing process, that of making a gold article. Verse 15:69 therefore states that the goldsmith turns the gold into different ornaments (*alaṃkāra-vidhiṣu*), and more importantly, that he does so as he pleases (*svacchandāt*). The goldsmith has the necessary skill to create whatever article he chooses to create. Likewise the practitioner, who is now said to be a monk (*bhikṣu*), has made his mind supple and refined enough to put it to use. In the case of the monk, it is not the state of liberation that corresponds to the finished gold articles, as might perhaps be expected, but the supernormal powers or faculties (*abhijñāsu*). The same declension – the locative plural - is used for both the supernormal powers and the various gold ornaments, which serves to underscore the mapping between these two products of their makers' skill and training.

One might pause at this point and consider the context within which Aśvaghoṣa sets this reference to the supernormal powers.

---

[12] KA 2.13.1 describes a workshop (*akṣa-śālā*) for the manufacture of gold and silver.

The reference occurs at the very end of Canto 15, a canto that consists of the Buddha's advice to Nanda on mental development. The canto commences with straightforward instructions on how Nanda should position his body for meditation – he should sit up straight with his legs crossed (15:1) and concentrate on the tip of his nose (15:2). Thereafter Nanda should cultivate thoughts inimical to passion and malevolence, and throw off all attachment to family and country by reminding himself that death awaits. All unskillful notions should be countered by concentration on the in- and out-breath (15:64). The gold refining allegory follows hard upon this specific instruction. Turning to Canto 16, we find in the very first verse the only other mention of the supernormal powers in the *Saundarananda*:

> *evaṃ mano-dhāraṇayā krameṇa*
> *vyapohya kiṃcit samupohya kiṃcit |*
> *dhyānāni catvāry adhigamya yogī*
> *prāpnoty abhijñā niyamena pañca ||* (16:1)

> Thus by using mental concentration to gradually take a little away and to add a little, the yogin attains the four meditative states, and then inevitably acquires the five supernormal faculties.

Thus the poem's two references to the supernormal powers occur in two consecutive verses, though in different cantos.

Aśvaghoṣa is clear that the supernormal powers are attained after the four meditative states (Sanskrit *dhyāna,* Pali *jhāna*). This point is in accord with the Buddhist tradition, which sees the supernormal powers as products of the extraordinarily powerful degree of mental concentration achieved in the 4th *dhyāna*. Buddhaghosa states in his *Visuddhimagga*, Theravāda Buddhism's definitive guide to meditation techniques, that "in order to perfect the supernormal faculties, the task must be undertaken by a yogin who has attained the fourth *jhāna*"[13]. Aśvaghoṣa is also clear that there are five such supernormal faculties, and he lists them in the next verse. They are the psychic powers (*ṛddhi*)[14], knowing the thoughts of others, the memory of past lives, divine hearing and divine sight (16:2). Buddhaghosa lists the same supernormal faculties, though in a different order, and he points out that these five faculties are part of mundane or worldly knowledge (*lokikābhiññā*, Vism 373). Some Pali and mixed Sanskrit texts include one further supernormal faculty, to make a total of six. This is knowledge of the destruction of the *āśravas*[15] (Sanskrit *āsrava-kṣaya-jñāna*, Pali *āsava-kkhaya-ñāṇa*). Such knowledge is supramundane, since it conduces to liberation, and it is the result not of *jhānic* attainment, but of insight (*vipassanā*). Aśvaghoṣa's understanding is that knowledge of the destruction of the *āsrava*s represents the next level of attainment after mastery of the supernormal powers. Thus it is not included in the list of five powers in 16:2, but mentioned immediately thereafter:

> *ataḥ paraṃ tattva-parīkṣaṇena*
> *mano dadhāty āsrava-saṃkṣayāya* | (16:3a)

> Henceforth, by an examination of reality, he positions his mind for the destruction of the *āsrava*s.

---

[13] *abhiññā sampādetum ... adhigata-catuttha-jjhānena yoginā yogo kātabbo*, Vism 373. Buddhaghosa devotes considerable attention to the *iddhi*s, which are the subject of *Visuddhimagga*'s Chapter 12, and the remaining *abhiññās*, which are described in Chapter 13.

[14] The *ṛddhi*s (Pali *iddhi*) are generally ten in number and include such psychokinetic powers as being able to form multiple copies of one's body, to become invisible, fly through the air and so forth. There are two displays of the *ṛddhi*s in the *Saundarananda*: the first is when the Buddha returns to Kapilavāstu and performs a series of such feats in front of King Śuddhodana (3:21-4), and the second is when he transports Nanda to the Himalayas, from thence to heaven, and home again (10:3, 10:18, 10:64).

[15] These are mental tendencies that bind one to rebirth. Destruction of the *āsrava*s equates to liberation.

In summary, Aśvaghoṣa's position seems to be that proficiency in the meditative states can result in the attaiment of the supernormal powers, but the basis for acquiring liberating knowledge is the scrutiny of reality (*tattva-parīkṣaṇena*), that is, by the techniques of insight meditation.

The gold-refining metaphor in the *Paṃsu-dhovaka Sutta* has the same outcome as the *Saundarananda* verses under consideration in that the finished gold product is likened to the supernormal powers. It differs, however, in that it includes knowledge of the destruction of the *āsava*s as a sixth supernormal faculty. The *Paṃsu-dhovaka Sutta* is not the only text to link gold imagery with the supernormal faculties. Either the psychic powers on their own (*iddhi*) or supernormal faculties as a group (*abhiññā*) are associated with refined gold in many of the Pali Canon's metaphorical uses of the gold manufacturing process.[16] Aśvaghoṣa is therefore presenting a familiar association in his verses. The full significance of the descriptions of the Buddha at 3:24 (page 190 above) and 10:4 (page 192 above) can now be appreciated. In light of the fact that it represents the supernormal faculties, refined gold (*tapta-kanaka*, 3:24, and *kanakāvadāta*, 10:4) is particularly appropriate to the Buddha's display of *ṛddhi*s.

In view of the foregoing comments on the dependence of the five supernormal powers on the mastery of the fourth level of meditation, it is natural to read Aśvaghoṣa's analogy of dirt-washing as a progression through the four increasingly subtle meditation levels. As the meditator masters one level of meditation, he drops certain factors of that level as relatively gross in order to proceed to the next level. For instance, Buddhaghosa describes how initial and applied thought are constituents of the first level of meditation, but when they appear to the meditator as coarse (*oḷārikata*) and he determines to be rid

[16] DN i.78, DN i.209, MN ii.18 and AN iii.16-19 all make this connection, as does AN i.256-8. SN v.92 connects the gold imagery only to the sixth supernormal power, the destruction of the *āsravas*. MN i.39 and MN iii.243 are exceptions in that they use the imagery of gold refining without connection to the supernormal powers. However, the latter in particular strikes me as an incomplete analogy.

of such coarse factors (*oḷārikaṅgaṃ pahānāya*, Vism 155), he then proceeds to the second level of meditation. Similarly, when happiness, a consituent of the second level of meditation, is seen to be coarse, then it too is abandoned and the meditator proceeds to the third level of meditaiton (Vism 159). The meditator next abandons bliss and finally attains the fourth level of meditation, which is characterised by equanimity and purity of mindfulness *(upekkhā-sati-pārisuddhi*, Vism 165). Aśvaghoṣa perceives in the dirt-washer's procedure of discarding dross in reverse order of size a model for the elimination of ever more subtle mental defilements.

Aśvaghoṣa has condensed a great deal of information on mental cultivation into the four verses that I have been considering. I have tried to draw out their meaning by unpicking the conceptual metaphor that underlies the passage. The preparation of gold by washing and smelting until it is malleable enough to be made into jewellery functions as the source of a number of apt parallels with the target domain, which is the gradual development of the practioner's mind until it is flexible enough to experience the supernormal faculties. The concrete nature of the gold refining source domain almost inevitably gives rise to a correspondence between gold and the mind, with the resulting danger of the reification of the mind. More accurately, gold corresponds to a state of mind. To summarise this and the other correspondences of the gold refining metaphor at 15:66-69 they are presented here in tabular form:

Table 2: Summary of the Metaphorical Correspondences of Verses 15:66-9

Source Domain	**Reference**	**Target Domain**	**Reference**
dirt-washer (*pāṃsu-dhāvakaḥ*)	15:66a	one with a focused mind (*yukta-mānasaḥ*)	15:67a
large bits of grit (*pāṃsūn bṛhataḥ*)	15:66b	major faults / gross flaws in meditation (*doṣān bṛhataḥ*)	15:67b
tiny bits of grit (*sūkṣmān*)	15:66c	subtle faults / subtle flaws in meditation (*sūkṣmān*)	15:67c
gold particles (*hemāvayavān*)	15:66d	constituents of the dharma (*dharmāvayavān*)	15:67d
goldsmith (*karmāraḥ*)	15:68b	practitioner of yoga (*yogācāraḥ*)	15:68c
gold (*kanakam*)	15:68a	the mind (*manas*)	15:68d
washed (*śuddham*)	15:68a	purified (*viśodhya*)	15:68d
cooks and turns (*pacati, āvartayati*)	15:68b	calms and concentrates (*śamayati, saṃkṣipati*)	15:68d
as he wishes (*svacchandād*)	15:69a	as he wishes (*yathecchaṃ*)	15:69d
types of ornaments (*alaṃkāra-vidhiṣu*)	15:69b	supernormal powers (*abhijñāsu*)	15:69c

5.4 Choosing the Right Method (Verses 16:65-7)

A second extended engagement with the metaphor of gold refining occurs at 16:65-7. These three verses take the same conceptual understanding of mental development as akin to gold production, but the emphasis in this case does not fall on the creation of the supernormal powers:

ulkā-mukha-sthaṃ hi yathā suvarṇaṃ
suvarṇakāro dhamatīha kāle |
kāle pariprokṣayate jalena
krameṇa kāle samupekṣate ca || (16:65)

dahet suvarṇaṃ hi dhamann akāle
jale kṣipan saṃśamayed akāle |
na cāpi samyak paripākam enaṃ
nayed akāle samupekṣamāṇaḥ || (16:66)

saṃpragrahasya praśamasya caiva
tathaiva kāle samupekṣaṇasya |
samyaṅ nimittaṃ manasā tv avekṣyaṃ
nāśo hi yatno 'py anupāya-pūrvaḥ || (16:67)

16:65 In this world a goldsmith at times blows the gold placed in the furnace, at times uses water to sprinkle, and at times watches it.

16:66 For in blowing at the wrong time he might burn the gold; casting it into water at the wrong time he would make it cool down; and (simply) observing it at the wrong time, he might not bring it to perfect readiness.

16:67 Likewise the correct meditational subject of an energy, calm or equanimity meditation should at times be mentally reviewed, for even diligence is destructive if it accompanies the wrong method.

These three verses emphasise actions taking place at the proper time. Timing – knowing what to do under certain circumstances – is critical to the success of the procedures described in both the source and target domains. Hence 'at the [right] time', 'under the [right] circumstances' (*kāle*) appears four times in the three verses, and 'at the wrong time', 'under the wrong circumstances' (*akāle*) three times. Like the gold-refining verses that end Canto 15, the three verses here are concerned with the process of mental development. In Canto 16 the Buddha continues his instruction to Nanda, emphasising the importance of the Four Noble Truths both as a group and individually (16:3-43). Thereafter, following a brief discourse on the elimination of the defilements (16:44-48), a long passage is devoted to the importance of choosing a suitable subject for meditation according to varying circumstances (16:49-81). The practitioner should select a subject after reflecting on the time and place of meditation and on his own strengths and weaknesses (16:52). Aśvaghoṣa forcefully makes the point that meditating on the wrong subject entails lack of success and bad consequences (*anartha*, 16:49). On no account should a practitioner persist in an unsuitable meditation - even sleeping is better than this (16:78). This section's preoccupation with suitable meditation is reflected by the frequent occurrence of the word *nimitta*, which refers to an object or theme selected for concentration in order to secure a particular type of meditation. The message of this long section is that the practitioner should monitor his progress at all times, carefully assessing the efficacy of his chosen subject of meditation, and switching when necessary to another more suitable subject.

The Buddha's directions that Nanda should apply himself to whichever of the three types of meditation is most appropriate under a particular set of circumstances is aptly demonstrated by the image of the goldsmith undertaking three different activities whilst working at his craft. The goldsmith has placed the gold at the entrance of the furnace (*ulkā-mukha*, 16:65a, though this can also mean a crucible or smelting pot. At any rate the gold would be in some heat-resistant container). On occasion (*kāle*) he blows the gold (*suvarṇaṃ ... dhamati*, 16:65b). I assume he is using either a pair of bellows or a blowpipe to blow not at the gold itself, but at the fire underneath it, in order to increase the temperature of the gold. Doubtless the goldsmith must continue to do this until melting point is reached, which in the case of gold is 1063 degrees centigrade. On occasion the goldsmith sprinkles on water (*pariprokṣayate jalena*, 16:65c). The object of his action is probably the fire, though he may be sprinkling water onto the melting gold. In either case, the result of the action would be to bring down the temperature of the gold. Sometimes the goldsmith merely watches the gold (*samupekṣate*, 16:65), but doesn't actively intervene. The crucial aspect of the process is that the goldsmith must accurately estimate the heat being applied to the gold and take action only when he judges that an adjustment is necessary. Verse 16:66 describes what would happen if the goldsmith were to perform each of these three actions under inappropriate conditions. If he blows at the wrong point in the procedure, so that the fire emits too great a heat, then the gold would burn. If he throws it in the water at the wrong time, it is cooled (*saṃśamayet*) – cooled too early, that is, before the requisite melting point has been reached. It is not easy to reconcile the fact that the previous verse speaks of sprinkling **with water** (*jalena*), while this verse speaks of throwing **into water** (*jale*). Molten gold can indeed be poured into water in order to set it, though it seems illogical to introduce a new activity into a verse that is supposed to illustrate the perils of mistiming actions presented in the preceding verse. Be that as it may, the third possible source of error in the gold refining process is sitting by and observing at a time when active intervention is necessary. In this case the gold will not reach the desired level of purity – it will not be 'properly cooked' (*samyak paripākam*).

The *upameya* of the gold-refining simile is given in just one verse, 16:67, in which each of the three actions undertaken by the goldsmith in bringing the gold to a perfect state is matched by one of the three types of meditation already described. The goldsmith's first activity, that of blowing, is implicitly equated to the first meditation mentioned in the sequence, the energy meditation (*sampragraha*). Sprinkling with water (or casting into water) is likened to the calm meditation (*praśama*), and the goldsmith's observation of the process is parallel to the equanimity meditation (*samupekṣaṇa*). However, there is no elaboration of the results of the practitioner's inappropriate development of a meditation that would correspond to the description of the results of the goldsmith's inappropriate actions. The last *pāda* of the verse is merely a general warning against faulty methods. Immediately preceding the gold-refining verses are the six medical similes on the correct treatment of humoral imbalance (16:59-64)[17], which, though related to the theme of correct meditational method, deal with entirely different meditations and states of mind. Neither does the remainder of the canto (16:68ff.) following the gold-refining verses yield any further information about the consequences of taking up an unsuitable energy, calm or equanimity meditation. It is not typical of Aśvaghoṣa's style to supply a detail in the source imagery that is not matched by a corresponding level of detail in the target situation.

In fact, Aśvaghoṣa does speak elsewhere of the consequences of undertaking an energy, calm or equanimity meditation under inappropriate circumstances, though to find this passage one must go back before the intervening medical similes, to 16:53-8. Here Nanda learns that the types of meditation that are to be carefully chosen and balanced are those that promote energy (*pragrāhaka*, 16:53 and 16:56), tranquillity (*śama* or *praśama*, 16:54 and 16:55) and equanimity (*aupekṣika*, 16:57 and 16:58), appearing in the same order as they do in 16:67. The first, the energy meditation, is not to be undertaken when the practitioner's spirits are already excited (*uddhanyamāne hṛdi*, 16:53b), for then his mind does not become peaceful (*cittaṃ praśamaṃ na yāti*, 16:53c). The calming meditation is not to be used for a torpid mind (*cetasi līyamāne*, 16:55b), as it would be further lowered by such treatment (*bhūyo layam eti*, 16:55c). The equanimity meditation is not to be used when the mind is either over-excited or depressed (*layaṃ gate cetasi soddhave vā*, 16:57b), since this would give rise to serious mishap (*tīvraṃ janayed anartham*,

[17] These are discussed in Chapter Four.

16:57c). Certainly this expansion on the nature of mismanaged meditation would work very well as part of the target domain for the gold-refining metaphor. The goldsmith blowing at the fire at the wrong moment and burning the gold would be like the practitioner overstimulating his mind with an energy meditation and failing to achieve tranquillity. The goldsmith throwing the gold into water at the wrong moment and prematurely cooling it would be like the practitioner depressing his mind with inappropriate calm meditation. The goldsmith sitting by and observing the gold so that if fails to become properly refined would be like the practitioner ruining his chance of a successful outcome with an inappropriate equanimity meditation.

The question remains as to why Aśvaghoṣa chose not to overtly draw out these potential corollaries as part of the gold-refining metaphor at 16:65-7, but instead slips them in at an earlier point in the canto, at 16:53-8. One answer might be that the results of inappropriate meditation were obvious and therefore did not need to be spelled out. Alternatively, gold refining as a metaphor for mental development was familiar in all its correspondences. Another possible answer is suggested by the Pali *Nimitta Sutta* at AN i.256-8. The *Nimitta Sutta* also develops the activity of gold refining as a model for mental development, but it presents a far tighter mapping between the details in the source domain and those in the target domain. The monk engaged in higher thought (*adhicittam anuyutta* - the commentary specifies *samatha* and *vipassanā*) is presented at the outset. From time to time he should set a subject for concentration in his mind (*kālena kālam samādhi-nimittaṃ manasi kātabbam*), or a subject for energy (*paggāha-nimittam*), or a subject for equanimity (*upekkhā-nimittam*). The *sutta* goes on to explain that if the monk should set only (*ekantam*) a subject for concentration in his mind; this would conduce to indolence (*kosajja*), energy alone would conduce to excitement (*uddhacca*), while if he cultivates only equanimity his mind would not be perfectly constituted for the destruction of the *āsavas* (*na sammā samādhiyeyya āsavānaṃ khayāya*). The *sutta* then brings in the comparison to the goldsmith, who places the crude gold (*jātarūpa*) in the furnace (*ukkā-mukhe*), and now and then blows it (*kālena kālaṃ abhidhamati*), or spinkles it with water (*udakena paripphoseti*), or observes it (*ajjhupekkhati*). If he performed only (*ekantam*) the first, the gold would burn (*daheyya*), just sprinkling with water would cool it down (*nibbāyeyya*), while in just observing the gold would not be properly prepared (*na sammā paripākaṃ gaccheyya*). However, if he carries out each action from time to time, then the gold becomes soft, workable, radiant, unbreakable, and perfect for working into whatever ornament he wishes. This successful conclusion is also then applied to the monk. If the monk from time to time cultivates each of the three types of meditation, then his mind becomes soft, workable, radiant, unbreakable and perfectly constituted for the destruction of the *āsava*s. He can then realise any of the supernormal powers (*abhiññā*) that he wishes.

This summary of the *Nimitta Sutta* shows that it has much in common with Aśvaghoṣa's reworking of the gold refining metaphor, from figurative detail to shared vocabulary. However, it is the differences between the two that are of greater interest. One point of difference between the two is that the *Nimitta Sutta* takes the gold refining metaphor to its habitual conclusion, which is that just as the goldsmith can make items of jewellery out of properly prepared gold, so can the practitioner turn his properly prepared mind to the supernormal powers. Perhaps Aśvaghoṣa found it unnecessary to repeat the outcome of the gold-refining process, since it is incorporated into the four verses at the end of Canto 15. Alternatively, he may not agree that these types of meditations result in the attainment of the supernormal powers.[18] Aśvaghoṣa also lays a slightly different emphasis on the balance required of the goldsmith in accomplishing his actions, since an action carried out at the wrong time (*akāle*) brings an undesirable result, while for the *Nimitta Sutta* the undesirable result occurs when that action

[18] It is also possible that the section on the supernormal powers was bolted on to the end of the *Nimitta Sutta* by later redactors in order to harmonise the text with the preceding *Paṃsu-dhovaka Sutta*.

alone (*ekantam*) is carried out. A third point of difference between the *Nimitta Sutta* and the *Saundarananda*'s restatement of the same material is relevant to the question raised previously: why does Aśvaghoṣa not spell out the consequences of inappropriate meditation at the same time as he spells out the consequences of mismanaged gold refining? When the *Nimitta Sutta* introduces the three types of meditation, it specifies concentration (*samādhi*)) instead of Aśvaghoṣa's calm (*praśama*), and places it first in the series of meditations rather than second. During the course of the *Nimitta Sutta* the types of meditation are mentioned six times in total, and always in the order concentration, energy, equanimity. Aśvaghoṣa mentions the three types of meditation twice, both times in the order energy, calm, equanimity. Yet both the *Nimitta Sutta* and Aśvaghoṣa present the list of the goldsmith's activities in the same order, blowing, sprinkling with water, and observation. This means that the *Nimitta Sutta* correlates the goldsmith's activities with different types of meditation than does Aśvaghoṣa. If we accept the ordering of the *Nimitta Sutta*, then the blowing of the goldsmith (which raises the temperature of the gold) would correspond to concentration, sprinkling with water (which cools the temperature of the gold) would correspond to the energy meditation, and observation would correspond to the equanimity meditation, while if we accept Aśvaghoṣa's ordering, then the blowing of the goldsmith corresponds to the energy meditation, sprinkling with water corresponds to the calm meditation, and observation corresponds to the equanimity meditation.

The *Nimitta Sutta* appears to have been a popular text, yet neither its commentary nor any of the later works that quote it[19] take issue with the nonsensical pairing of the blowing action, which results in burning the gold if done to excess, with meditative concentration, which is said to result in indolence if over-cultivated. The action of sprinkling water, which results in the gold cooling if done to excess, and the energy meditation,

---

[19] Vism 246-7, *Vibhaṅga Aṭṭhakathā* 229-30, and the *Ṭīkā* on AN i.9.

which results in excitement if over-cultivated, are an equally ill-matched pair. Burning is not an apt metaphor for a lethargic mind, nor cooling for over-excited mind, for the simple physiological reason that when one is agitated one's body temperature is generally higher than normal. It is therefore very likely that the *Nimitta Sutta* is corrupt. Possibly the term *samādhi* was employed in a general sense and originally covered a further three - *paggāha*, *sama* or *samatha*, and *upekhā*. The middle term (*sama-nimittam*) subsequently dropped out, with the resultant confusion.[20] Possibly Aśvaghoṣa knew an earlier, as yet uncorrupted version of the *Nimitta Sutta*, or he noticed the *sutta*'s confusion and unobtrusively rectified the analogy by switching the order in which the meditations are listed, both in the main statement of the metaphor at 16:65-6, and in the supplementary information provided at 16:53-8. Thus Aśvaghoṣa makes blowing the equivalent of an energy mediation, which seems more natural, and the water-sprinkling the equivalent of a calm meditation. However, presumably prompted by discretion, he does not set out the consequences of inappropriate meditation in the main statement of the metaphor, but instead inserts these consequences at 16:53-8 and separates them from the main statement by six verses based on entirely different imagery. Aśvaghoṣa's circumspection does not permit him to expose a weakness in a well-known teaching and his own variance from it, though neither would his poetic sensibility tolerate an awkward metaphorical 'fit'. Hence he finds a discreet way to adjust the metaphor's correspondences.

I have shown above how Aśvaghoṣa turns to the example of the goldsmith working at his craft in order to illustrate the practitioner's mental cultivation. In the case of the goldsmith, negligence or ignorance of an effective balancing and sequencing of activities would result in defective gold, while a similar failure on the part of the practitioner would result in a less-than-perfect mental state. Emerging from a study of the metaphor are two suggestions: firstly, that Aśvaghoṣa consciously emended the material contained in the *Nimitta Sutta*,

---

[20] I am indebted to Richard Gombrich for this suggestion.

and secondly, that a full expression of the metaphor is split across two connected passages, at 16:65-7 and 16:53-8. The correspondences set up across the two passages are summarised in Table 3 below.

Table 3: Summary of the Metaphorical Correspondences of Verses 16:65-7 and 16:53-8

Source Domain	Reference	Target Domain	Reference
goldsmith (*suvarṇakāraḥ*)	16:65b	~	
gold (*suvarṇam*)	16:65a	~	
at the right time (*kāle*)	16:65b,c,d	at the right time (*kāle*)	16:67b
blows (*dhamati*)	16:65b	energy (*sampragraha*)	16:67a
sprinkles with water (*pariprokṣayate jalena*)	16:65c	calm (*praśama*)	16:67a
observes (*samupekṣate*)	16:65d	observation (*samupekṣaṇa*)	16:67b
The gold would burn (*dahet*) if blown at the wrong time (*akāle*).	16:66a	The mind does not reach tranquillity (*cittaṃ praśamaṃ na yāti*) if an energy meditation (*pragrāhaka*) is developed in the wrong circumstances.	16:53c
The gold would cool down (*jale kṣipan*	16:66b	The mind becomes more depressed (*bhūyo*	16:55c

saṃśamayed akāle) if placed in water at the wrong time.		*layam eti cittam*) if a calm meditation (*śama*) is developed in the wrong circumstances.	
The gold would not reach perfection (*na samyak paripākam*) if observed when intervention is required.	16:66cd	Serious calamity might ensue (*tīvraṃ janayed anartham*) if an equanimity meditation (*aupekṣikam*) is developed in the wrong circumstances.	16:57c

In this chapter I have explored how the traditional connotations of gold as rare, valuable and pure mark the enlightened condition of both the Buddha and, eventually, Nanda. The noble metal, as characterised by its resistance to tarnishing and corrosion, is appropriately associated with the unchanging, irreversible state of liberation of the noble mind. Aśvaghoṣa also adopts the specialised activity of gold refining as a model for the mental development of the Buddhist practitioner, to which it offers several excellent parallels. It demonstrates that the kernel of enlightenment is buried within the mind of all, like gold within ore, and that knowledge, attentiveness and determined effort can turn the potential for liberation into the real attainment of *nirvāṇa*. The metaphor also captures the gradual and painstaking nature of the task, the careful attention to a variety of tasks, the increasing level of skill required, and the delicate balance that must be struck in order for the mind to be fully developed. Finally, the malleability and ductility of refined gold well reflect the flexibility and lack of rigidity in the mind of the advanced practitioner, while the comparison of a finished gold article to the supernormal powers is suggestive of beauty, rarity and, perhaps, a little showiness.

CHAPTER SIX

NANDA UPLIFTED

This chapter examines Aśvaghoṣa's creative use of a metaphor based on spatial orientation. The metaphors explored in the preceding chapters – Nanda as an elephant requiring training, Nanda as a sick man requiring treatment, the cultivated mind as refined gold – all have their source in the everyday cultural life of ancient India, and as such they are relatively easy to detect in the poem. Spatial metaphors, however, are less immediately obvious. In English such metaphors often depend on prepositions, as in the expressions "leave out the detail" or "she was beside herself with grief". Spatial or orientational metaphors are derived from basic bodily experience of the physical world, in this case, something being inside or outside a container. Other orientational metaphors hinge on spatial relations such as front/back, on/off and central/peripheral. The spatial relation investigated in this chapter is up/down, or verticality, which is used subtly but to great effect in the *Saundarananda.*

Metaphorical expressions of verticality derive from the assumption that the intrinsic value of something can be measured on a vertical scale on which a high reading is good and a low reading is bad. The positive connotations of 'up' and the corresponding negative connotations of 'down' have a wide range of applications, for instance to emotional states (on top of the world, feeling down), consciousness (wake up, fall asleep) sickness and death (rise from the dead, sink into a coma), status (top dog, low rank), moral behaviour (upright, underhand) and any other situation that requires a positive or negative evaluation (top notch, down-market).[1] These connotations are not confined to English, but appear to be universal. The Pali *Puggala Sutta* of the *Saṃyutta Nikāya* provides a nice illustration of the verticality metaphor in an ancient Indian context. In this *sutta* the Buddha explains to King Pasenadi that someone "going from darkness to

---

[1] See Lakoff and Johnson (1980:14-21) for a further discussion of orientational metaphors.

light" (*tamo-joti-parāyano*) is born in a low family (*nīce kule*),and is poor, wretched or diseased, but virtuous in thought, word and deed. Such a person is reborn in a happy condition in heaven (*sugatiṃ saggaṃ lokaṃ upapajjati*). The Buddha explains in a simile that this process is "as if a man were to climb into a litter from the ground, or climb onto a horse's back from a litter, or climb onto an elephant's shoulder from horseback, or climb to a terrace from an elephant's shoulder." (*Seyyathāpi, mahārāja, puriso pathaviyā vā pallaṅkaṃ āroheyya, pallaṅkā vā assa-piṭṭhiṃ āroheyya, assa-piṭṭhiyā vā hatthi-kkhandhaṃ āroheyya, hatthi-kkhandhā vā pāsādam āroheyya.*) The same simile is given in reverse order to illustrate a man who is born into good fortune, but who has a bad rebirth due to wicked thoughts, words and deeds (S.i.93-5). It is obvious from this extremely straightforward simile that upward movement was widely understood to imply an improvement in one's fortune, while downward movement signified 'declining' fortunes. Also obvious from the Buddha's simile is that heaven, a better state, was conceptualised as a higher place.

In the *Saundarananda*, verticality has both spatial and metaphorical applications. To begin with, the relative height of the characters is sometimes adjusted for a particular purpose, as when Nanda bows to the Buddha to demonstrate reverence. Furthermore, the altitude of the setting in which the action unfolds often has a significance beyond the literal. Thus the mountains, heaven and the palace rooftop are not merely interesting or picturesque locations but also representative of certain values. Finally, there is abundant figurative usage of phrases that normally denote vertical movement. Aśvaghoṣa uses such phrases to expose the characters' emotional state, to expound the doctrine of rebirth, to demonstrate the Buddha's agency with regard to Nanda and to mark the latter's spiritual progress. The *Saundarananda*'s metaphorical expressions of verticality can be identified by the non-literal usage of words derived from roots such as √*bhraṃś* (fall, drop), √*pat* (fall), √*cyut* (fall), √*lamb* (sink), √*nam* (bow) and √*ruh* (climb, ascend), sometimes with the addition of prefixes such as *ut-* (up) and *ava-*

(down). This chapter will explore each of these applications of verticality.

6.1 Relative Height

In the *Saundarananda*, as in countless other Buddhist texts, people bow to the Buddha to show their respect. Such acts of obeisance are physical manifestations of the age-old understanding that worthy persons, such as teachers, parents or rulers, should be placed at a higher level than their relatively inferior pupils, subjects or devotees. Hence the citizens of Kapilavāstu dismount from their horses when they see the Buddha approaching and bow to him (5:1). Spiritual pre-eminence takes precedence over temporal power, so the Buddha's father, King Śuddhodana, bows to him as to a guru (3:27). Though Nanda is in any case slightly shorter than the Buddha,[2] he nevertheless lowers himself before the Buddha, especially in Canto 5. When he first catches up with the Buddha he bows (*nanāma nandaḥ*, 5:6), holds his body in a semi-stoop (*vinatārdha-kāyaḥ*, 5:7) and bends forwards (*pra + nam*, 5:10 and 5:11). From this lowered position his eyes are raised to the Buddha (*unmukha-locanena*, 5:10). His positioning is indicative of his inferiority. Ironically, he had just thrown himself at Sundarī's feet in mock humility (4:17), but now he feels true reverence. When the Buddha later questions him about his longing for his wife, Nanda's failing is reflected by his posture: he is "bowed down with shame" (*hrī-vinata*, 10:2). After he has attained liberation, Nanda bows his head in recognition of his indebtedness to the Buddha, though the latter is not even present at this moment (17:73). When Nanda approaches the Buddha in person in the final canto in order to express his gratitude, he prostrates himself on the ground, his head at the Buddha's feet (18:20). This time, the Buddha is quick to raise him up (18:22); Nanda's spiritual standing is now much higher than it was.

In all the cases cited above, people lower themselves in recognition of their own inferior standing in comparison to the

---

[2] According to the Pali *Vinaya*, Nanda was four finger-breadths shorter than the Buddha (*catur-aṅgulomako bhagavatā*, Vin 4:173).

Buddha's spiritual stature. The *Saundarananda* also has three instances of a sage lifting himself into the air, an ability that can only be attained through the development of the psychic powers (*ṛddhi*)[3]. In each instance such a display is undertaken for the sake of conferring a benefit on others. In Canto 1 the sage Kapila, who in several respects foreshadows the Buddha, rises into the air in front of the princes in order to mark out the site of the future Kapilavāstu with drops of water. He is motivated to do so by "the wish for their prosperity" (*teṣāṃ vṛddhi-cikīrṣayā*, 1:28). The princes react appropriately by bowing their heads (1:30). The Buddha in due course perfects the action initiated by Kapila. The citizens of Kapilavāstu may owe their city to the generous instincts of Kapila, but they owe their moral and spiritual well-being to the Buddha. When he flies into the air in front of them and displays his psychic powers to them, his intention is to convert them to the dharma: "with the intention of guiding them [to insight], he flew up into the air (*vininīṣayā gaganam utpapāta ha*, 3:21). The desiderative here derives from *vi* + √*nī*, which is a standard way of indicating spiritual guidance in the *Saundarananda*.[4] The citizens react appropriately by bowing down (3:25), mirroring the actions of their forbears who bowed to Kapila. The effect on King Śuddhodana is immediate: "perceiving that his accomplishment of the psychic powers had made the king a suitable recipient [of instruction]" (*atha bhājanī-kṛtam avekṣya manuja-patim ṛddhi-sampadā*, 3:26), the Buddha preaches dharma to him and he reaches stream entry (3:27).

When the Buddha next rises into the air, it is again with the object of conferring a favour. Holding Nanda by the hand, he lifts him up, first to a mountainside and then to heaven, in order to teach him a hard lesson about the nature of desire. The adjective that qualifies the Buddha at the outset of the journey is *ujjihīrṣu* (10:3), which means both "desiring to lift up" and "desiring to uplift", so that the verticality metaphor is already

---

[3] See Chapter Five, page 200 above.

[4] For instance, the Buddha is referred to as *vināyaka* in 3:26, 5:50, 13:3 and 17:70.

built into the vocabulary. Unfortunately the simile in *pāda* d of this verse, which might have further explained the Buddha's intentions, is very uncertain. Johnston suggests *pāṇau gṛhītvā viyad utpapāta mīnaṃ jale madgur ivojjihīrṣuḥ* and translates accordingly: the Blessed One "grasped his hand and flew up into the sky to rescue him, like a cormorant which has caught a fish in the water and, wishing to bring it up, comes to the surface".[5] However, this not entirely satisfactory since the cormorant is more likely to eat the fish than do it a good turn. Once lifted to the vantage point of the mountainside, Nanda observes the ugly monkey on the mountainside and robustly asserts the superiority of his wife. The journey now continues to Indra's pleasure-grove, since the Buddha has "a further motivating illustration in mind" (*hetv-antaraṃ kiṃcid avekṣamāṇaḥ*, 10:18). The Buddha's intention in transporting Nanda up to heaven is to find another cause or reason (*hetu*) that will impel Nanda to work towards liberation. In each of these cases the superiority of a sage is demonstrated by his ability to ascend into the air at will, though this feat is only performed to facilitate prosperity or spiritual growth in the onlookers.

6.2 Mountains

While characters in the *Saundarananda* are physically positioned at lower or higher levels in relation to each other, the action as a whole is set in locations that vary in their altitude. The connotation that 'up' is better than 'down' holds true in each circumstance. One setting that benefits from the traditional Indian association of altitude with sanctity is the mountainside. In the popular imagination, mountains (especially the Himalayas) not only yielded health-giving herbs (as in 15:28) and precious metals (as in 10:5), but were also inhabited by rigorously ascetic sages. The convention that sages retire to the mountains to practise austerities is incorporated into the description of Kapila's hermitage in Canto 1. The sage Kapila has his hermitage "on the bright slopes of the Himalayas" (*pārśve himavataḥ śubhe*, 1:5). Naturally it is a beautiful place,

[5] Johnston (1932:54) has reservations about the simile.

abundant in fruit, flowers and lotus pools (1:6-9). Kapila himself is strenuous in his asceticism (1:1) and his disciples, who live on fruit and wild rice (1:10), are assiduous in their ritual practices (1:11). The hermitage seems like a cloud with its covering of smoke from sacrificial fires (*havir-dhūma-vitānena*, 1:6), a description which emphasises its altitude. The deer sleep undisturbed (1:12) and even the wild beasts wander around peacefully (1:13). The aura of piety that hangs over the mountain is also evident in Canto 10, when the Buddha and Nanda fly up "to the Himalayas with their gold ore and divine seers" (*dhātumantaṃ deva-ṛṣimantaṃ himavantam*, 10:5) and find themselves standing "on that pure mountain frequented by celestial singers and perfected beings, blanketed in smoke from sacrificial fires" (*tasmin girau cāraṇa-siddha-juṣṭe śive havir-dhūma-kṛtottarīye*, 10:6). Since holy people were believed to reside in the mountains, it is natural for the Buddhist tradition that its founder's home town should lie close to the Himalayas. Hence Kapilavāstu's association with mountains is stressed. Kapilavāstu is like a valley in the mountains (1:43); it has ramparts as great as mountains (1:42) and it resembles Mandara thronged with *kiṃnaras* (1:48) (of these mythological figures more will be said shortly). Mandara, a residence for various deities, is the name of a sacred mountain that served as a churning-stick at the churning of the ocean. An interesting simile in Canto 2 uses geomorphological features to reflect the relative height and spiritual standing of King Śuddhodana's two sons:

> *tayoḥ sat-putrayor madhye śākya-rājo rarāja saḥ |*
> *madhya-deśa iva vyakto himavat-pāriyātrayoḥ ||* (2:62)

> Between those two good sons the king of the Śākyas was resplendent like the Middle Country between the Himalayas and the western Vindhya mountains.

The Pāriyātra is a low range of hills forming the western Vindhya and marking the southern limit of the Madhya-deśa.

The Himalayas are not only considerable higher than the Pāriyātra but are also in the more auspicious northern direction. It is therefore appropriate that the Buddha should be associated with the Himalayas, and Nanda with the lesser mountain range.

As well as the ascetics and seers who were thought to lead ascetic lives in their pure mountain retreats, a number of other human and semi-divine beings were popularly supposed to inhabit the mountains. Celestial singers (*cāraṇa*, 10:6), accomplished beings of great purity (*siddha*, 10:6), hermits (*vanaukas*, 10:7) and mountain tribespeople (*kirāta*, 10:12) add colour to the episode of the mountainside visit (10:5-17), as do a number of animals. More important than these are the strange mythological beings known as *kiṃnara* or *kiṃpuruṣa* (m.) and *kiṃnarī* (f.), whose appearances in the *Saundarananda* are not confined to the scene of the mountainside visit. A *kiṃnara*, literally a "what-do-you-call-it man", is a semi-celestial being, sometimes half man and half animal, or half man and half bird. They were thought to live in the range of mountains north of the Himalayas, serving Kubera, god of riches and ruler of the northern quarter. In later times they were associated with the Gandharvas and celebrated as musicians.[6] A *kiṃnarī* is very beautiful and sings exquisitely. The attractiveness of the *kiṃnarī* as well as the ambiguous identity of this group of beings is apparent from the *Mahāvastu*'s *Kinnarī Jātaka*. It relates how a king gathered one of every type of animal for a huge sacrifice, but when all the invited sages arrive they say that one thing is missing – a *kinnarī*. A competent hunter is sent to the Himalayas to find a *kinnarī*, whom he duly tracks down by her sweet singing. The *kinnarī* is captured by a spell – the speaking of her name, which is Manoharā (mind-transporter) – and brought back for the sacrifice. There the son of the neighbouring king sees her and immediately falls in love with her. He preaches on the evil of sacrificing living creatures, which are all then released, and marries Manoharā. Further tribulations ensue as the prince neglects his state duties due to his enchantment with his wife. At

---

[6] MW (1899:283); Jones (1949:54).

the end of the *Jātaka*, Manoharā is identified as Yaśodharā, and the prince as the Buddha.[7]

It will be noted from this summary that the *Jātaka* incorporates these various stock attributes into its portrayal of a *kiṃnarī*: she lives in the mountains, she is heart-stoppingly lovely, and she is an object of sexual fascination for human men. Hence the hunter who is sent to capture the *kinnarī* enquires of a sage "Sir, I have heard that there are some human beings who play and disport with the Kinnarīs" (*bhagavaṃ śruṇīyati asti kecit manuṣyā kinnarīhi sārdhaṃ krīḍanti paricārenti*).[8] Furthermore, Manoharā's father is ruler of a city named Nirati, meaning "delight", especially sexual delight. It is clear that the *Jātaka* associates *kiṃnarī*s with sex, as too does the *Saundarananda*:

> *darī-carīṇām ati-sundarīṇāṃ*
> *manohara-śroṇi-kucodarīṇāṃ* |
> *vṛndāni rejur diśi kiṃnarīṇāṃ*
> *puṣpotkacānām iva vallarīṇāṃ* || (10:13)
>
> A number of excessively lovely cavern-dwelling *kiṃnarī*s with gorgeous hips, breasts and bellies appeared on all sides, like creepers with flowers as coiled hair.

Since *kiṃnarī*s (and their fortunate partners, the *kiṃnara*s) represent sexual pleasure, it is appropriate that they should function as the *upamāna* in several similes that describe Sundarī and Nanda in the earlier parts of the poem. In Canto 4, they are "like a *kiṃnarī* and a *kiṃpuruṣa* standing in a mountain waterfall intent on love" (*bhāvānuraktau giri-nirjhara-sthau tau kiṃnarī-kiṃpuruṣāv ivobhau*, 4:10ab). At this point Sundarī and Nanda are enjoying the pinnacle of their sexual happiness together. Hence the *kiṃnarī* and the *kiṃpuruṣa* are envisaged together,

---

[7] Mvu 2:94-115.

[8] Mvu 2:97, trans. Jones (1952:94).

and both are located in the mountains (*giri*). However, when Nanda and Sundarī are separated by the Buddha, this image of togetherness no longer applies. Instead, Sundarī's ladies-in-waiting "climbed anxiously from inside the house to the palace [roof], like *kiṃnarīs* climbing to the top of a mountain" (*antar-gṛhād āruruhur vimānaṃ trāsena kiṃnarya ivādri-pṛṣṭham*, 6:35). Since Sundarī's serving women are compared to *kiṃnarīs*, clearly Sundarī herself is indirectly likened to a *kiṃnarī*. The word *vimānam*, which calls to mind the aerial palaces of the gods, underscores Sundarī's semi-celestial identification.

What has happened to the *kiṃnarī*'s lover? She remains in her mountain fastness, but he has come down from the mountain, and is wracked with unmet sexual needs:

> *tad idaṃ śṛṇu me samāsato*
> *na rame dharma-vidhāv ṛte priyāṃ* |
> *giri-sānuṣu kāminīm ṛte*
> *kṛta-retā iva kiṃnaraś caran* || (8:12)

> So listen to this. To be blunt, I do not enjoy the prescriptions of dharma without my beloved, but am like a *kiṃnara*, his semen ready, wandering the mountain plateaux without his lover.

Nanda makes this frank admission to the unnamed *śramaṇa* who has asked to be taken into his confidence. Johnston's translation of the simile, "like a passionate Kinnara wandering on the mountain peaks without his love" is euphemistic and also suggests that the *kiṃnara* is very high up. Although *sānu* can mean 'peak, summit', it can also mean 'tableland', and even 'forest'.[9] 'Plateaux' seems the best option as it retains the idea of elevation as well as the suggestion that the *kiṃnara*'s lover remains further up the mountain. Thus interpreted, the simile better replicates the situation between Sundarī, who is very

---

[9] MW (1899:1202) and Apte (1970:597) list these and other defiinitions.

specifically located at a height, and Nanda, who is now living a life of enforced continence at ground level.

6.3 Heaven

From the above it can be seen that Aśvaghoṣa worked into the *Saundarananda* the popular view that mountains were inhabited by both sages and sirens. Piety, represented by the sages, and sex, represented by the *kiṃnarīs*, are both associated with mountains, but these two seemingly incompatible ideals are resolved only when one moves higher still – to heaven. From the *Saṃyutta Nikāya*'s description of progressive ascent – from the ground to a litter, from a litter to a horse – as a simile for the attainment of heaven, mentioned at the beginning of this chapter, it is clear that heaven was conceptualised as a place far above the earth. This is true of the *Saundarananda* too, since the Buddha and Nanda have to fly beyond the mountains to get there. Buddhist cosmology in its developed stage envisaged 26 heavens arranged in a vertical hierarchy, comprehensively investigated by Collins (1998) in his book *Nirvana and other Buddhist Felicities.* According to Collins (1998:301), who draws most of his information from the Pali *Vibhaṅga*, each heaven is twice as high as the one below it, and a large rock dropped from the lowest one would take a year to reach the earth. The heavens are populated by deities of increasing purity and longevity. The particular heaven visited by Nanda and the Buddha is identified in the *Saundarananda* as the one ruled by Indra.[10] Thus the Buddha and Nanda make their way to "the pleasure-grove of the thunderbolt-wielding king [i.e. Indra]" (*krīḍāvanaṃ vajra-dharasya rājñaḥ*, 10:18d), where Nanda gazes at Indra's forest (*aindraṃ vanaṃ tac ca dadarśa nandaḥ*, 10:35a).

Indra's heaven is the second lowest heaven in the Buddhist cosmological system. It is part of the sensory realm in which desire continues to operate, unlike higher heavens, which were

---

[10] Indra's realm was generally known as the *Trayastriṃśat* (Pali *Tāvatiṃsa*) heaven, the heaven of the Thirty-three. The number 33 refers to the 33 gods of the pre-Buddhist Vedic pantheon that was adopted by the Buddhist tradition.

conceptualised as free of desire. It is a very beautiful though rather artificial world of great visual splendour. Aśvaghoṣa describes multi-coloured birds, jewel-bearing trees and golden lotuses with diamond stems, all of which entrance Nanda. The defining feature of this heaven though, at least for the purposes of the Nanda legend, is the presence of the Apsarases. These heaven-dwelling nymphs are even more beautiful and desirable than the mountain-dwelling *kiṃnarīs* that foreshadow them. They approach Nanda with undisguised eroticism:

> *tāsāṃ jagur dhīram udāttam anyāḥ*
> *padmāni kāścil lalitaṃ babhañjuḥ* |
> *anyonya-harṣān nanṛtus tathānyāś*
> *citrāṅga-hārāḥ stana-bhinna-hārāḥ* || (10:37)
>
> Some sang in low, some in high tones, some pulled playfully at lotuses, and others danced exuberantly with each other, through their vivid gestures breaking their pearl necklaces on their breasts.

The Apsarases are haughty (*sa-garva*, 10:35), eternally youthful (*sadā yuvatyaḥ*, 10:36), flirtatious (*laḍantyaḥ*, 10:33), and make teasing gestures (*lalitāś ca ceṣṭāḥ*, 10:40). Lovemaking is their only occupation (*madanaika-kāryāḥ*, 10:36). They do not age (*ajara*, 10:61), unlike Sundarī, whose youth and fertility will soon dry up along with her *viśeṣaka*, the cosmetic mark that she applied so carefully in Canto 4. The Apsarases are so desirable that Nanda's mind would burn up were it not for the Buddha's power (10:46), and he quickly conceives such a longing for them that he thinks he will die of it (10:54).

However, the Apsarases are not sexually available to Nanda, but only to those who have won a heavenly rebirth after a life of restraint:

sadā yuvatyo madanaika-kāryāḥ
sādhāraṇāḥ puṇya-kṛtāṃ vihārāḥ |
divyāś ca nirdośa-parigrahāś ca
tapaḥ-phalasyāśrayaṇaṃ surāṇām || (10:36)

Eternally youthful and occupied solely with lovemaking, they were a communal pastime for heaven-dwellers who had earned merit. Possession of these heavenly women was no fault, but an acceptance of the rewards of asceticism.

In this verse Aśvaghoṣa expresses ancient India's fusion of the antithetical ideals of ascetic renunciation and sensual excess. In contrast to St. Augustine's wish to be chaste later, Indian sages are chaste first and are later rewarded with the fleshpots of heaven. This ancient Indian juxtaposition of a marked interest in sexual matters and a piety consisting of asceticism, celibacy and adherence to ritual practice has often been noted.[11] It is just this juxtaposition that allows the Buddha to strike a bargain with Nanda: "If you desire these women, practise the highest asceticism in this life to pay their purchase price" (*imā yadi prārthayase tvam aṅganā vidhatsva śulkārtham ihottamaṃ tapaḥ*, 10:59cd).

The paradox that celibacy, discipline and self-control in this life (*iha*) can be exchanged for an after-life of sexual abundance is presaged by the behaviour of Kapila's ascetics in Canto 1, whose minds strain heavenwards (*svargāyodyukta-cetasaḥ*, 1:17b) to such an extent that "they seemed to do violence to dharma with their passion for asceticism" (*tapo-rāgeṇa dharmasya vilopam iva cakrire*, 1:17cd). This is an early hint that ambitions of heavenly rebirth, however lofty in the popular

[11] Siegel (1983:4-5) for instance explores these two polar ideals through the persons of the great teacher Śaṅkara and the erotic poet Amaru, starting with the popular story that Śaṅkara assumed the body of Amaru in order to experience sex whilst remaining chaste. Doniger O'Flaherty (1973) scrupulously traces ascetic and erotic motifs in Śiva mythology.

estimation, fall short of the Buddhist ideal.[12] From the Buddhist perspective, heaven is neither a true 'up' nor a truly noble aspiration, though it seems so to Nanda. However, while heaven represents the summit of sensual experience and is thus an unworthy final goal, it is also part of Nanda's ongoing spiritual education in that it functions as a staging post on his way to liberation.

6.4 At the Top of the Palace

Having noticed the beautiful *kiṃnarīs* who live in the mountains and the seductive Apsarases that wait in heaven, there is one more highly-placed lady to consider. She of course is Sundarī, whose beauty is evident not least from her name. Sundarī, her palace and her serving women are strongly associated with the heaven and the Apsarases. When we first meet her, for instance, she is likened to "a divinity wandering in the garden of delight" (*sā devatā nandana-cāriṇīva*, 4:6a). *Nandana* is the name of the divine garden in Indra's heaven, so the Apsarases too are referred to "wandering in the garden of delight" (*nandana-cāriṇīḥ*, 11:1). Nanda's only concern is making love with his wife (*madanaika-kāryaḥ priyā-sahāyaḥ*, 4:1), and the Apsarases are qualified with the same phrase (*madanaika-kāryāḥ*, 10:36). Sundarī and Nanda are so beautiful and blissful in each other's company that they are accorded semi-divine status, as though created "greater than mortals, though not yet god-like" (*atītya martyān anupetya devān*, 4:6). The word *vimāna*, referring to Nanda's palace but also evoking the aerial chariots of the gods, appears five times in Canto 6 (6:3 (x2), 6:20, 6:30, 6:35). Just as Apsarases and the *kiṃnarīs* are associated with high places, so is Sundarī associated with the upper levels of her home.[13] Thus after Nanda has left her we are told that "though she remained in the same place high in the palace, Sundarī no longer seemed herself "*tatraiva harmyopari vartamānā na sundarī saiva tadā babhāse*, 6:1cd). This implies

[12] The Buddha's middle way famously eschews both asceticism and sensuality.

[13] Basham (1967:201) notes that multi-storeyed houses with flat roofs were common among the wealthy.

that both Nanda and Sundarī's lovemaking of Canto 4 and Sundarī's despair in Canto 6 take place in the upper reaches of the palace. The upper part of the palace is accessed by a flight of stairs (6:6-8) and comes complete with a flock of pigeons (6:8, 6:30), an earthly equivalent to the paradisal birds that delight the Apsarases (10:31). The same network of associations – heaven, the top of a palace, sex and meritorious action – is found in the *Buddhacarita* to describe the Bodhisattva's early life in his palace:

tataḥ sa kāmāśraya-paṇḍitābhiḥ
strībhir gṛhīto rati-karkaśābhiḥ |
vimāna-pṛṣṭhān na mahīṃ jagāma
vimāna-pṛṣṭhād iva puṇya-karmā || (AśvBC 2:32)

Then, a captive to the women, who were skilled in the accessories of love and indefatigable in sexual pleasure, he did not descend from the palace to the ground, just as one who has won Paradise by his merit does not descend to earth from the heavenly mansion.[14]

The point of Sundarī's repeated identification with the Apsarases is twofold; firstly, it shows that Nanda's life as depicted in Canto 4 is the equivalent of heaven on earth. When the Buddha intervenes in his life, he is not a desperate man being rescued from dreadful suffering, but young, rich, healthy and living in Nandana with a wife who is like a celestial nymph in her beauty and desirability. Even so, the Buddhist *summum bonum* is preferable by far. The sum of ordinary human happiness when compared to the bliss of liberation is like an ugly old monkey compared to a beloved and radiant wife. Secondly, the identification serves to show that Nanda makes the same mistake twice. Having initially believed that life with Sundarī is the highest good, he then believes that an after-life with the Apsarases is the highest good. He is mistaken in both cases, and

[14] trans. Johnston (1936:26).

Aśvaghoṣa demonstrates that there is trouble in paradise by introducing images of falling and sinking. The emphasis on downward movement is most prevalent in Canto 6, which presents the downside of earthly utopia, and in Canto 11, which presents the downside of heaven.

Canto 6 portrays Sundarī's grief at the loss of her husband with pathos and psychological accuracy. Ironically, Sundarī is at the top of her palace, but has been struck low by Nanda's departure. Her depression and low spirits are indicated by a vocabulary of hanging, leaning, falling and so on. At first she "leant out from the palace roof, her earrings hanging across her face" (*harmya-talāl lalambe | mukhena tiryaṅ-nata-kuṇḍalena*, 6:2). Her pearl necklace dangles down (*vilamba-hārā*, 6:3), and she falls on a sofa (*paryaṅka-tale papāta*, 6:5) with her slipper half-hanging off her foot (*sapādukaikārdha-vilamba-pādā*, 6:5). She hears footsteps on the stairs and leaps up, only to sink back onto the sofa (*bhūyaḥ śayanaṃ prapede*, 6:9) when she realises that it is not Nanda. With her face propped up by her hennaed hand, she resembles a lotus bending over its own reflection (6:11). She is like a statue of Lakṣmī that has toppled over (6:26). Finally, the sight of Nanda's *vīṇā* and other belongings triggers a complete breakdown: "howling loudly, she entered a state of darkness, collapsing as though sinking into mud" (*tamo viveśābhinanāda coccaiḥ paṅkāvatīrṇeva ca saṃsasāda*, 6:32cd). The verticality metaphor is not the only means whereby Aśvaghoṣa illustrates Sundarī's grief – he also employs a vocabulary of restless movement, skewness and loss of colour to express her emotion – but it is particularly effective since her emotional prostration contrasts with her physical elevation at the top of the palace. Canto 6 is both a sympathetic and delicate depiction of disappointed love (*vipralambha-śṛṅgāra*), an amatory situation beloved of *kāvya*, and a clear statement that the sort of life that Sundarī represents, in which happiness is staked on a particular person or set of circumstances, is extremely fragile.

6.5 Falling

Heavenly happiness may last a little longer than earthly happiness but is essentially no less fragile. The loss of heavenly happiness is presented in Canto 11 in terms of the verticality metaphor, as was the reversal of earthly happiness in Canto 6. In fact, Canto 6 predicts the theme of Canto 11 early on:

vilamba-hārā cala-yoktrakā sā
tasmād vimānād vinatā cakāśe |
tapaḥ-kṣayād apsarasāṃ vareva
cyutaṃ vimānāt priyam īkṣamāṇā || (6:3)

As she bent down from the palace with her necklaces of pearls dangling and their strings awry, she seemed like the best of the Apsarases watching her lover fall from her celestial abode when he had used up [the merit acquired through] his austerities.

Here is one further identification of Sundarī as an Apsaras, but the verse has a broader scope in that it equates the loss of earthly happiness with the loss of heavenly happiness. Nanda, for whom Sundarī is on the lookout from her vantage point on the palace roof, is implicitly likened to a heaven-dweller who has earned a stay in heaven through ascetic practices but whose time there has run out. The verse encapsulates the entire topic of Canto 11 as well as surmising what would happen were Nanda to stick to his bargain with the Buddha and practise *tapas* solely for the sake of heaven. The lesson that this verse teaches so succinctly, that heaven is a temporary estate from which one falls (just as earthly happiness is a temporary and precarious matter) is repeated over and over again in Canto 11. This verse also serves to inform us in advance that heaven and the delightful Apsarases that live there are a temporary reward, just in case we share Nanda's astounding naivety and remain unaware of celestial closing times.

Some versions of the Nanda legend describe Nanda's visit to hell following his visit to heaven. There he is confronted with the terrors that await him on completion of his sojourn with the Apsarases. Aśvaghoṣa's poem contains no such gruesome spectacle, but Ānanda's stern warnings in Canto 11 function as a conceptual equivalent. Thus the high of Canto 10 is succeeded by the inevitable low of Canto 11. In line with its topic of painful rebirths following a heavenly one, Canto 11, especially the second half, makes much use of the verticality metaphor and is replete with vocabulary formed from roots that denote downward movement, such as √*bhraṃś*, √*pat* and √*cyut*. This last in particular was a common euphemism for the death of a deity throughout the literature of ancient India, as in verse 6:3 just quoted. Ānanda produces a number of arguments in Canto 11 to convince Nanda that striving for heaven is unsatisfactory and foolish, culminating in the revelation that when a man's time in heaven expires, he is reborn as a human (11:39) or worse:

> *yadā bhraṣṭasya kuśalaṃ śiṣṭaṃ kiṃcin na vidyate* |
> *tiryakṣu pitṛ-loke vā narake vopapadyate* || (11:40)

> When the descending man has nothing good left, he is reborn among the animals, or in the world of the ancestors, or in hell.

In other words, how far down a man falls after his stay in heaven depends on whether anything good (*kuśalam*) still accrues to him. The concept of verticality provides a convenient structure on which to fit the schema of rebirth: unpleasant births are low, pleasant ones are high, and middle-ranking births, presumably, are in the world of mankind. Ānanda adduces a series of examples (*dṛṣṭānta*) of heroic, virtuous and compassionate figures who won heaven only to lose it again. Śibi, for instance, gave his own flesh to hawk, but even he fell from heaven (*svargāt paribhraṣṭaḥ*, 11:42). King Mandhātṛ had half of Indra's throne, but he too "returned below again" (*adhaḥ punar yayau*, 11:43). Nahuṣa ruled the gods, but thereafter fell to earth (*papāta nahuṣo bhuvi*, 11:44). Such a reversal of fortune is endemic, says Ānanda, for "great Indras have fallen in their hundreds" (*mahendrāḥ śataśaḥ petur*, 11:48). The former denizens of heaven cry out in regret as they fall to earth (*ity ārtā vilapanto 'pi gāṃ patanti divaukasaḥ*, 11:50cd). Indeed, they have much to regret, since their suffering as they depart from heaven is greater than that of mortals at the point of death (11:51). Their loss of heaven is heralded by tell-tale signs: their clothes become dusty, their wreaths wither, they begin to sweat, and they no longer feel pleasure (11:52). These are the signs of the sky-dwellers' imminent fall from heaven (*etāny ādau mimittāni cyutau svargād divaukasām*, 11:53ab). A fall from heaven is inevitable and occurs willy-nilly, but an ascent to a better birth is far harder. The famous Buddhist simile of the turtle and the yoke is based on the common perception that unpleasant births are lower than pleasant births, and Aśvaghoṣa in his rendering of the simile stresses the vertical element: "for one who has gone [down] comes up from below with difficulty, like a turtle swimming up to a hole in yoke" (*udeti duḥkhena gato hy adhastāt kūrmo yuga-cchidra ivārṇava-sthaḥ*, 18:27cd).

Nanda's ignorance concerning his post-heaven existence is conveyed in a simile that maintains the theme of falling:

> *yathā paśyati madhv eva na prapātam avekṣate |*
> *paśyasy apsarasas tadvad bhraṃśam ante na paśyasi ||*
> (11:29)
>
> Just as a man looking for honey does not notice a precipice, so in your focus on the Apsarases you do not see your resulting fall.

The man looking for honey is Nanda looking for the Apsarases, and the precipice over which he is about to tumble equates to the inevitable fall from heaven. Other metaphors are at play here – seeing stands for wisdom, and the sweet Apsarases are the honey that disguises the fact that a medicine is being administered – but the verticality metaphor stands out as the most obvious. Another simile featuring a precipice, but with a different perspective, is as follows:

vyathante hy apunar-bhāvāt prapātād iva bāliśāḥ || (12:22cd)

Fools shrink from not coming to birth again, just as they shrink from a precipice.

These two similes, both sharing as *upamāna* a fall from a cliff, are interesting in that they contrast a popular belief about rebirth with the Buddhist view of rebirth. The common misconception is that not being born again is like falling over a cliff, that is, a descent to some kind of lesser state. However, it is precisely the opposite - *saṃsāra*, the continuous round of birth and death - that precipitates the fall from one life to another.

The verticality metaphor is indispensable to the logical portrayal of pleasant and unpleasant births. Aśvaghoṣa also has other uses for the metaphor. The notion of downwards motion as a deterioration, lapse or failure is found in several other contexts. For instance, death is preferable to life for a monk who has allowed the disciplinary code to slip (*cyuta-vinaya*, 8:57). A close parallel, though in a lay rather than monastic situation, is found in the description of King Śuddhodana, who would prefer to die if he had fallen from the truth (*cyutaḥ satyāt*, 2:13). Nanda decides that he will go home because monastic life does not suit someone like himself who has "fallen from the path of dharma" (*dharma-pathāt cyutasya*, 7:47). After the Buddha's intervention and Nanda's committed efforts, it turns out that Nanda need not count himself as someone who has fallen from dharma (*bhraṣṭasya dharmāt*, 18:31). In every example, any conduct that does not match up to an ideal is considered a fall from a high point. Such individual lapses are no doubt a reflection of the fact that we live in a declining age (*bhraṃśini ... yuge*, 3:37).

Examples such as those above demonstrate the fluidity of the verticality metaphor, since the same source domain (up, down) is applied to a number of different target domains (asceticism, sex, rebirth, ethical behaviour). In all cases, though, the basic terms of the verticality metaphor hold true in that up represents something good and down represents something bad. The verticality metaphor has an especially important application in the context of the relationship between the Buddha and Nanda. Here the familiar metaphor with its simple and well-understood source domain of up and down contributes to Aśvaghoṣa's justification of the Buddha's intervention in Nanda's life. Thus Aśvaghoṣa takes care to show that while Nanda is enjoying what might be regarded as a high old time, with Sundarī up in the palace and potentially with the Apsarases up in heaven, from the Buddhist perspective he is actually sunk in carnality. The verticality metaphor reveals a conflict between what the world evaluates as worthwhile and good (and therefore ranks highly), and what Buddhism evaluates as worthwhile and good. Hence while the world locates the Apsarases in heaven, the *kiṃnarīs* on the mountainside and Sundarī on her rooftop, from the Buddhist perspective Nanda is at a low point, trapped in "the mire of love" (*paṅka-sneha*, 5:18). Lust is perceived as a condition that sucks Nanda down and prevents his spiritual rise. When he watches the Apsarases and feels that he is about to die of desire, he begs the Buddha for help: "Please save me, O sage, I am sinking" (*prasīda sīdāmi vimuñca mā mune*, 10:54a). Sundarī is similarly afflicted, though in her case the cause is disappointed love rather than desire, when "she collapsed as though sinking into mud" (*paṅkāvatīrṇeva ca saṃsasāda*, 6:32d).

6.6 Spiritual Uplift

Since the verticality metaphor is used to illustrate Nanda's low spiritual condition, it is logical that the pressure applied by the Buddha to Nanda should be envisioned as an upward force. The verticality metaphor is therefore expanded to incorporate the action of pulling someone up in order to take account of the Buddha's uplifting of Nanda. Thus in the important justificatory passage at 5:15-18, the Buddha is described as "wishing to lift him out of the mud of love" (*taṃ sneha-paṅkān munir ujjihīrṣan*, 5:18d). In the *Saundarananda* a form frequently indicates the Buddha's agency with regard to Nanda. The prefix *ut* with √*hṛ* means 'lift up', 'lift out', 'extricate', 'save' or 'rescue', and this combination is one of Aśvaghoṣa's favourite ways of denoting the Buddha's intentions towards Nanda. Exactly the same word occurs a little later in Canto 5, when we hear of the Buddha "wishing to lift him out of heedlessness" (*atha pramādāc ca tam ujjihīrṣan*, 5:34a).

The appeal to the persuasive power of the verticality metaphor is noticeable in Canto 5 because it is in this canto that the Buddha spirits Nanda away from his home. Likewise in Canto 10, when the Buddha exposes Nanda to the inflammatory beauty of the Apsarases, the verticality metaphor is again summoned to the Buddha's defence. Canto 10 opens with this verse:

> *śrutvā tataḥ sad-vratam utsisṛkṣuṃ*
> *bhāryāṃ didṛkṣuṃ bhavanaṃ vivikṣum |*
> *nandaṃ nirānandaṃ apeta-dhairyaṃ*
> *abhyujjihīrṣur munir ājuhāva ||* (10:1)

> Hearing that Nanda intended to give up his excellent observances and return home to see his wife, the sage summoned him, wishing to uplift one lacking joy and constancy.

Here three consecutive desideratives express Nanda's wilfulness; he wishes to leave off his vowed observances (*sad-vratam utsisṛkṣum*), see his wife (*bhāryāṃ didṛkṣum*) and live at home (*bhavanaṃ vivikṣum*). In contrast to these unskillful desires, the Buddha's one intention is to uplift (*abhyujjihīrṣu*) Nanda. The root *hṛ* prefixed by *abhi* and *ut* means 'lift up', 'elevate' or 'render prosperous'. Since the Buddha's intention is related to upwards movement, and since the inner logic of the verticality metaphor dictates that such movement always has positive connotations, it is obvious that Nanda's contrary wishes represent a lower, negatively-viewed position. Two verses later this interpretation is corroborated when the Buddha, wishing to uplift (*ujjihīrṣu*) Nanda, takes him by the hand and flies upwards (*utpapāta*, 10:3). The Buddha's desire to give Nanda spiritual uplift is paralleled by the physical motion of flying upwards.

Frequently in the *Saundarananda*, Nanda is not merely lifted up, but lifted out of something, generally mud. Mud invariably betokens love, attachment and desire, not only because it impedes progress, but because it is dirty. The *Saundarananda*'s many images of someone being pulled out of mud therefore tap into both the verticality metaphor and the purity metaphor, one of Buddhism's core conceptual metaphors. An example of the combination of mud and forced upward motion has already been encountered in verse 5:18. On two occasions, Aśvaghoṣa compares Nanda to an elephant being pulled out of the mud. In one of these, Nanda is raised or delivered (*uddhṛta*) by the Buddha like a young elephant pulled from the thick mud (*bahu-paṅkāt*, 8:17), while in the other, Nanda is dragged up from the worthless mud (*anartha-paṅkāt utkṛṣya*, 17:72) like a feeble-footed elephant from the mud. These two verses are discussed in Chapter Three and nothing further need be said about them here other than to note that verbal formations from √*kṛṣ*, like those from √*hṛ*, are typically used to define the Buddha's actions towards Nanda.

The root *kṛṣ* is also found in the complex verse preceding the one about the feeble-footed elephant:[15]

> *yenāhaṃ girim upanīya rukma-śṛṅgaṃ*
> *svargaṃ ca plavaga-vadhū-nidarśanena* |
> *kāmātmā tri-diva-carībhir aṅganābhir*
> *niṣkṛṣṭo yuvati-maye kalau nimagnaḥ* || (17:71)

> I was taken to the golden-peaked mountain and to heaven, where, lustful for the women who wander the triple heaven, and sunk in the evil of young women, I was dragged out [of that condition] by his example of the female monkey.

[15] Verse 17:71 forms a grammatical unit with 17:72, but has been isolated in the translation for the sake of clarity.

This verse is spoken by Nanda after he has attained liberation. In the context of the verticality metaphor it is an interesting one, since it superimposes two perspectives on Nanda's carnal ambitions. In the world's opinion he aspires to a delightful state marked by attractive things such as a "golden-peaked mountain" or "women who roam the triple heaven", phrases that have about them a hint of *kāvya* artifice. From a Buddhist perspective, though, he is "sunk" (*nimagna*) in the evil, strife or discord (*kali*) consisting of young women, and is therefore at a low point rather than at a high point. Furthermore, Aśvaghoṣa chooses the particularly strong word *kali*, meaning discord, strife, or the worst of any kind, to define the young women to whom Nanda is so attracted. The verse is an important one too in that Nanda in effect sanctions the Buddha's action in exposing him to the Apsarases because he is aware of its heuristic purpose. Nanda recognises that his lustful nature (*kāmātmā*) was keeping him in a low position. His ascent from that low position equates to the destruction of his lustful nature.

This network of associations finds fulfilment in the final canto:

> *aho viśeṣeṇa viśeṣa-darśiṃs*
> *tvayānukampā mayi darśiteyaṃ* |
> *yat kāma-paṅke bhagavan nimagnas*
> *trāto 'smi saṃsāra-bhayād akāmaḥ* || (18:40)

> Oh, you have here shown me compassion with distinction, you who see distinctions! Because of it I am free of lust, and have been saved from the danger of *saṃsāra*, O Lord, when I was [previously] submerged in the slime of lust.

Nanda's acknowledgement that his previous condition was a low one is repeated in his assertion that he was sunk (*nimagna*) in a state of carnality. He is aware that his former lustful nature is more appropriately likened to mud, the mud of lust (*kāma-paṅka*), than to heaven. Following the Buddha's compassionate intervention, Nanda has been pulled out of this mud and is now without lust (*a-kāma*). The process of saving Nanda from the mud of lust is identical to saving him from the danger of interminable rebirth (*saṃsāra-bhayāt*). In the final analysis, then, it is desire or lust (*kāma*) that is equivalent to *saṃsāra*, and to be free of lust is to be liberated. It is this process that is envisioned in the *Saundarananda* as an ascent from an inferior state, aided by the Buddha, who exerts the upwards force. Conscious of his debt, Nanda asks how he could possibly compensate the Buddha, "by whom I was pulled out of the sea of existence, like a man rescued from the great ocean when his boat has been smashed by waves" (*samuddhṛto yena bhavārṇavād ahaṃ mahārṇavāc cūrṇita-naur ivormibhiḥ*, 18:48cd). In this simile the state of *saṃsāra* from which Nanda has been plucked is likened to the ocean. The favourite verb for demonstrating the Buddha's agency, *ut* + √*hṛ*, is here compounded with *sam*, perhaps suggesting the perfectness or completion of his action.

I have shown in this chapter how Aśvaghoṣa uses the verticality metaphor to represent two conflicting world views. Both incorporate the conventional evaluation of something higher as better, and of something lower as worse. In the first instance, the verticality metaphor is used to illustrate Nanda's emotional and sexual desires. The more desirable the object of his longing, the higher that object is located in space. Three high places are shown in the poem, each of them home to sexually desirable women. However, something is amiss with each of these high places. The mountains harbour the pious Kapila and the beautiful *kiṃnarīs*, but also ascetics who follow wrong doctrines, princes who behave badly, and an ugly monkey. The same spot at the top of Nanda's palace is the scene of both his joyous lovemaking and Sundarī's intense grief. Indra's heaven is home to the ravishing Apsarases, but it is also where Nanda experiences the greatest discomfort of his life. These 'highs' are obviously no guarantee of tranquillity and peace. This fact is verified by the second usage of the verticality metaphor, since it simply inverts the target domain. Thus the fulfillment of Nanda's desires no longer represents the top of the scale of pleasant states of existence, but the bottom. The Buddha drags Nanda upwards from this nadir.

The foregoing assessment of the verticality metaphor would seem to require that the ultimate aim of *nirvāṇa* be presented as the highest estate. Yet this is not the case. The *Saundarananda* is very clear about what Nanda has been lifted **from** – he has been lifted from the mud of lust, and with it, from the round of rebirth – but altogether less clear about what he has been lifted **to**. A host of epithets are given to *nirvāṇa*, including the very frequent *śreyas*, 'the best', *parama* 'the supreme', and *mokṣa* 'liberation', deriving from the metaphor of freedom from bondage. A metaphor of height, though, is never explicitly applied to *nirvāṇa*. Possibly Aśvaghoṣa felt that if he were to use a metaphor of height to describe the state of liberation, it could easily be confused with heaven. Certainly the verticality metaphor cannot adequately convey the conception of *nirvāṇa*, since *nirvāṇa* cannot be contained within the normal categories of space. For this reason, perhaps, Aśvaghoṣa explicitly denies that the liberated man actually "goes" anywhere, "not to the earth, not to the sky, nor to any of the directions or intermediate directions" (... *naivāvaṇiṃ gacchati nantarikṣaṃ | diśaṃ na kāṃcid vidiśaṃ na kāṃcit* ..., 16:29bc). These lines are taken from one of the *Saundarananda*'s few passages (16:26-29) that attempt to describe the state of liberation. Another verse from the same passage qualifies the state of liberation as follows:

> *yasmin na jātir na jarā na mṛtyur*
> *na vyādhayo nāpriya-saṃprayogaḥ |*
> *necchā-vipan na priya-viprayogaḥ*
> *kṣemaṃ padaṃ naiṣṭhikam acyutaṃ tat ||* (16:27)

> In it there is no birth, no old age, no death, no sicknesses; no association with anything unpleasant, no failure of wishes, no separation from anything pleasant; it is a dependable, unfallen state of ease.

For the purposes of this chapter, the most interesting word in this list of attributes in *acyuta*, 'not liable to fall'. This is the closest that Aśvaghoṣa gets to assigning *nirvāṇa* a role in the verticality metaphor. With reference to the liberated state, *acyuta* means that once the state of liberation is attained, it is irreversible. It cannot be taken away or lost, in stark contrast to a precarious and transient heavenly existence. Unfortunately, people are ignorant of the impermanence of heaven. Just as fish happily swim about in a net, unaware of the disaster about to befall them,

> *antar-loka-gatāḥ kṛtārtha-matayas tadvad divi dhyāyino manyante śivam acyutaṃ dhruvam iti svaṃ sthānam āvartakam* || (11:61cd)

> ... likewise people within the world believe they have achieved their end. They are engrossed in heaven and think it benign, unfallen and certain, yet their own stay there is reversible.

Here people falsely believe heavenly existence to be *acyuta*, a permanent state that is not liable to fall, but as the end of the verse makes clear, their condition is reversible (*āvartakam*). In due course they will almost literally drop like stones back down to earth, or even to hell. One inevitably falls from heaven, however high heaven may be, but one cannot fall from *nirvāṇa*, because it cannot be located on a vertical scale.

The aim of this chapter has been to reveal the ubiquitous yet subtle manifestations in the *Saundarananda* of a very basic conceptual metaphor, that 'up' represents something good while 'down' represents something bad. No doubt the traditional narrative, which finds Nanda transported up to heaven, inspired the play with the vertical dimension. I have shown how the height of various characters is indicative of their worth. Ordinary people bow to gurus, while the gurus can levitate above ordinary people, always for their benefit, of course. Even more telling is the altitude at which the action takes place. An examination of the three high places presented in the poem reveals that they are all associated with what might be regarded as a good life. The ascetics who perform austerities in the mountains are renowned for their piety, but ultimately their goal and everyone else's is to reach heaven, where they will enjoy sex of a celestial quality with the Apsarases. Other bestowers of sexual favours are also located in high positions – the *kiṃnarīs* on the mountainside, and Sundarī at the top of her palace. These ladies are stacked hierarchically along a vertical axis of desirability. Thus the verticality metaphor is useful in presenting the false highs that initially beguile Nanda, and in drawing attention to the inevitable decline that succeeds such a high. Sundarī droops with grief after experiencing a temporary joy, and heaven-dwellers fall to a lower rebirth after a brief stay in heaven. The mistake that Nanda makes in equating ever greater bliss with the attainment of ever more desirable objects is artfully communicated by a number of similes that liken Sundarī to both an Apsaras and a *kiṃnarī*, and Nanda to a *kiṃnara*. Even more clearly is his mistake revealed when the verticality metaphor is inverted, so that the high estate to which Nanda aspired, either with his wife, or with the Apsarases, is shown to be a low and muddy place from which he must be extricated by the Buddha. Throughout its many formulations, then, the main purpose of the verticality metaphor is to record Nanda's spiritual growth, even though the ultimate aim of *nirvāṇa* cannot be encompassed within the vertical or any other orientational dimension.

CHAPTER SEVEN
NANDA REROUTED

The preceding chapter discussed how a vertical dimension serves as an indicator of positive or negative worth in the *Saundarananda*. The topic of the present chapter is again an orientational metaphor, though this time concerned with movement on a horizontal plane. This is a complex though universally recognisable metaphor in which a purpose, goal or aim appears as a destination, while the action undertaken in order to achieve that goal is envisaged as travelling along a certain route. The metaphor stems from the infantile experience of seeing a desirable object at a remove, and having to make some effortful movement, such as crawling, to reach it. Dozens of English idioms grow from this metaphor, such as on track, off-course, reaching a crossroads, a rough ride, living in the fast lane. Frequently life itself is conceptualised as a journey, with the person living that life as a traveller. This core metaphor can be enriched by numerous other correspondences. A crossroads, for example, could signify a decision that has to be made, being lost might represent a failure or disappointment, a wise friend could appear as a guide, and a set of moral principles or religious beliefs might be viewed as a map or itinerary.

7.1 Life as a Journey

As well as idiomatic expressions of the type mentioned above, entire works of literature derive from the concept of a traveller journeying towards a known or unknown destination as representative of a person either proceeding through life or developing a new understanding. In its simpler form, the metaphor imparts chronology, functioning as a timeline against which milestones in a person's life can be marked off. Of greater interest is the metaphor's ability to connote maturation and psychological development. Within a religious context, a journey can signify a growing understanding of religious truths. Thus the metaphor provides the allegorical underpinning for Bunyan's *Pilgrim's Progress*, and also for the *Divine Comedy*, at the beginning of which Dante presents himself as a traveller on his life's journey, lost in a dark wood because he has missed the right way. Jäkel (2002) points out that many biblical passages visualise righteous conduct as God's path, a path that is characterised as straight, smooth and level. Unlike an earthly road, God's path does not reach an end but is everlasting. In contrast, sinners travel a multitude of wicked ways that always lead to death. The paths taken by the wicked are crooked, dark, slippery and thorny. In the Old Testament, God is envisaged as supporting and leading the righteous in their journey, while in a particularly well-known New Testament manifestation of the path metaphor, Jesus himself is identified as the path by which God may be reached (John 14:4-6).

In Buddhist as in Christian literature, the journey metaphor is an ordinary way of expressing a central religious idea. It is unquestioningly understood that the dharma is a path (Sanskrit *mārga*, Pali *magga*), so that following the path equates to living a wise, virtuous and meditative life according to Buddhist principles. A related *sine qua non* is that the Buddha is the knowledgeable guide who points out the path. Thus in the Pali Canon the Buddha is the one who tells the way (*magga-kkhāyin*, MN iii.6, *Mahāniddesa* 1.33, Sn 85) and points out the way (*magga-desaka*, Sn 84). In the layperson's formulaic expression of Buddhist commitment, the Buddha explains the dhamma "as though pointing out the path to one who is lost" (*seyyathāpi ...mūḷhassa vā maggaṃ ācikkheyya*, DN i.252; MN i.24, i.39, i.184 etc.). All other disciples are followers on this path, as Ānanda observes: "The Blessed One made the way arise that had not arisen ... he is a knower of the way, wise in the way, skilled in the way ... At present the disciples continue as followers in the way, and later acquire it" (*bhagavā anuppannassa maggassa uppādetā... maggaññū magga-vidū magga-kovido. Maggānugā ca pana etarehi sāvakā viharanti pacchā samannāgatā ti*, MN iii.8). There are a number of potential spin-offs from this fertile metaphor, for instance that the path leads to *nirvāṇa* (*nibbāna-gāmī maggo*, MN iii.4), or that those who fall short of Buddhist values are either lost or follow an entirely different path. The path metaphor is just as deeply embedded in later forms of Buddhism, so that Chapter Seven of the *Lotus Sūtra*, for example, likens the goal of early Buddhism to an illusory city conjured up by a compassionate guide to encourage weary travellers. Indeed, Buddhism in this later development defines itself as the great vehicle (*mahā-yāna*) in which its adherents travel. It becomes difficult to speak of Buddhist topics without resorting to the path metaphor, which together with its logical extension of *nirvāṇa* as a destination is quickly adopted even by modern interpreters of Buddhism. For instance, Sangharakshita (1957:42-3) speaks of honouring the Buddha as one who "without a teacher and without a guide breaks through the obstacles which block the road to Nirvana and throws it open once more to the traffic of humanity."

By the time of Aśvaghoṣa, the Buddhist habit of conceptualising the dharma as a path was already well-established, and the rest of this chapter will focus on the specific application to the *Saundarananda* of this conventionalised understanding. The discussion will incorporate several examples from the poem, including instances in which the path metaphor is extended into a scenario of travel as commercial enterprise. The main purpose of the chapter is to demonstrate that in Aśvaghoṣa's hands the path metaphor serves as a viable metaphor for conversion. Since Nanda is rerouted from a life of sensual indulgence to one of ascetic containment, it is clear that a directional vocabulary is needed to map his reorientation. Words that mean 'turn round', 'facing' and 'drag' have a special import in this connection, as will be shown.

The simple metaphor of life as a journey, which envisages life stretching out before one and along which one travels towards one's end, is of minor interest in the *Saundarananda*. It is the basis of a few verses in Canto 15, but is not found elsewhere. In order to accommodate the cyclical nature of life as it is understood in Indian thought, the metaphor does however receive an interesting twist. Hence a path is likened not to one life alone, a life that ends in death, but to a countless series of lives. Eventually the path comes to represent *saṃsāra* itself, rather than one individual life. The following two verses occur within the framework of a warning against attachment to friends and family:

> *atīte 'dhvani saṃvṛttaḥ sva-jano hi janas tava |*
> *aprāpte cādhvani janaḥ sva-janas tu bhaviṣyati ||* (15:32)
> ...
> *pratiśrayaṃ bahu-vidhaṃ saṃśrayanti yathādhva-gāḥ |*
> *pratiyānti punas tyaktvā tadvaj jñāti-samāgamaḥ ||* (15:34)
>
> For on the road already travelled, someone who is now family was then a stranger, and on the road to come a stranger will be family ... Just as travellers shelter together in various rest-houses, and leave them and part again, so it is with a group of family-members.

In the first example, previous lives are conceptualised as that portion of the road that lies behind one (*atīte 'dhvani*), while lives still to come are described as the road ahead (*aprāpte cādhvani*), literally the road not [yet] taken. Our friends and family are our current travelling companions on our life's journey, but we did not know them whilst we were on the earlier part of our journey, nor will we retain the same familial group in the future. This is a clear-cut example of the metaphor of life as a journey, in which the path functions mainly to mark time. The second example elaborates on the journey idea with a simile that effectively conveys the brevity of life and the arbitrariness of our affections. Here, family members are likened to a group of travellers who share temporary lodgings only to go their separate ways in the morning. The word *adhva-ga* for 'traveller' (literally 'going on a road'), reminiscent of the *adhvan* of 15:32, points to the underlying conceptual metaphor despite the verse's ostensible simile format. Johnston's translation of 15:32 completely ignores the path metaphor, with resulting impoverishment for both verses.

Several other verses in this section expound on the nature of the endless and repetitive journey through *saṃsāra*. The journey has no goal; instead, the traveller is dragged through *saṃsāra* by the consequences of his own actions (*svena karmaṇā*, 15:31). He may travel to a different country (*janapada*, 15:42 or *deśa*, 15:46, 15:48 and 15:49), only to find himself prone to the usual afflictions of thirst, hunger and tiredness (15:44), and old age, sickness and death (15:46). There is no way (*gati*) that does not distress the man who takes it (15:47). In fact, he can find no safe place anywhere in the world (15:49). Finally, death with murderous intent stalks (*jighāṃsur anugacchati*) him as he journeys through life (15:59). Most of these verses work on both the literal and the metaphorical level, such that a person is visited by these afflictions not just wherever he goes, but also whenever he goes. The physical action of moving along embodies the abstract notion that *duḥkha* pervades time as well as place. In short, life in *saṃsāra* is envisaged as an undirected and virtually never-ending journey that never leads to a safe place.

This understanding of *saṃsāric* existence as a path is relatively rare in the *Saundarananda*, occurring only in a few isolated examples, some of which are given above. On the other hand, a great number of verses are founded on the enduring Buddhist convention of the dharma as a path. Numerous similes embodying all the traditional correspondences spring from this deeply embedded conceptual metaphor. In its most startling and original manifestation, the metaphor is brought vividly to life when the Buddha literally blocks Nanda's path. More will be said about this symbolic action in due course. As a preliminary, the next few paragraphs will investigate Aśvaghoṣa's general characterisation of the right path and its final destination, the presentation of the Buddha as guide and path-knower, and what constitutes the wrong path. Thereafter, the metaphor's application to Nanda's personal situation will be investigated.

7.2 The Path of Dharma

First and foremost, the right path is the path of dharma, the path that righteous persons wish to travel. King Śuddhodana, the model of a wise and virtuous layman, "wishes to proceed along the footpath of dharma" (*yiyāsur dharma-paddhatim*, 2:6). After the Buddha has preached the dharma in Kapilavāstu, even a previously lax citizen "did not swerve from the true path" (*na cacāla sat-pathāt*, 3:40). Even more does dharma present itself as a path for the ordained; therefore "the insignia [of monkhood] are inappropriate for someone who has slipped from the path of dharma" (*na ... liṅgaṃ kṣamaṃ dharma-pathāc cyutasya*, 7:47). The right path is benign and pure (*śive śucau vartmani*, 5:46). It is the true path, and unlike the *saṃsāric* path which entails repeated death, it is the only path by which deathlessness can be found: "when he has lost the true path, the deathless condition disappears for him too" (*pranaṣṭo yasya san-mārgo naṣṭaṃ tasyāmṛtaṃ padam*, 14:44). If he stays the course, though, he is "liberated ... by the noble path" (*āryeṇa mārgeṇa ... muktaḥ*, 17:34). Other verses confirm that the right path is noble and liberating. Specifically, one who understands the first three Noble Truths "proceeding together with wise friends, reaches peace by the noble path" (*āryeṇa mārgeṇa sa śāntim eti kalyāṇa-mitraiḥ saha vartamānaḥ*, 16:39). The present participle *vartamāna*, from √*vṛt*, to proceed or continue, suggests that the good friends are co-travellers. The path here considered is the Eightfold Path, which has already been described two verses earlier in *yamaka*-enriched terms as having three divisions and eight branches, and as being straight, irremovable, and noble (*tri-skandham etaṃ ... mārgaṃ praspaṣṭam aṣṭāṅgam ahāryam āryam*, 16:37).

The right path, then, is noble, true, pure, benign, liberating, distinct, and accords with dharma. Additionally, and in contrast to the goalless path of *saṃsāra*, this path does have a destination. The word *śiva*, meaning benign, auspicious or blissful, appears as an attribute both of the path and of the path's destination, so that by applying oneself to the Eightfold Path, "one reaches the condition of utter bliss" (*prāpnoti cātyanta-śivaṃ padam*, 16:37). Alternatively, *śreyas*, the excellent, is the object of the path (18:41, 13:9). The path is also said to lead to deathlessness (14:44) or, more frequently, peace (8:28, 16:29, 16:39):

> *spṛhayet para-saṃśritāya yaḥ*
> *paribhūyātma-vaśāṃ sva-tantratām* |

upaśānti-pathe śive sthitaḥ
spṛhayed doṣavate gṛhāya saḥ || (8:28)

The man who scorns self-reliance and independence and craves the support of another would yearn for home, with all its defects, when standing on the benign path that leads to peace.

This verse posits two mutually exclusive ways of life. The domestic life desired by those of a dependent nature is defective (*doṣavat*). It is explicitly opposed to the right path, which is benign or blessed (*śiva*), leads to peace, and is favoured by those of an independent nature. One can deduce that a domestic life never leads to peace, while the right path has no defects. Nanda is situated in the path of peace because by this point he has become, at least superficially, a follower of the Buddha.

In a further characterisation of the path's destination, Nanda is said to stand as though at the gateway to the city of *nirvāṇa* (*dvārīva nirvāṇa-purasya tasthau*, 17:41d). While other words that qualify the destination of the path are abstract and refer to the target domain, likening it to peace, deathlessness or happiness, here is one example in which the source domain is elaborated. In fact, it is the *Saundarananda*'s only example of the end of the path envisioned as a place. If the concept of *nirvāṇa* as a city is merely implied in Pali canonical texts, but is commonplace in later commentarial literature, as Steve Collins (1998:224-9) asserts, then this verse must serve as one of the earliest explicit examples of this correspondence.

The Buddha, as Nanda's spiritual director, is naturally viewed as the guide who shows the way along the path. This extension of the basic path metaphor incorporates the notion of a guide who has travelled a particular route before and is familiar with the final destination, and who by virtue of his specialised knowledge can guide others along this same route. The Buddha's designations as *daiśika* (3:42, 18:41, 18:50), someone who knows a place (*deśa*), and as *su-daiśika* (18:50), stress the Buddha's familiarity with the destination, that is, with enlightenment. Other terms stress the Buddha's knowledge of the route, so that the Buddha is said to be knowledgeable, skilled or expert in the path (*mārga-kovida*, 3:3). The same compound appears in the *Majjhima* extract quoted on page 243 above. Similarly, he is said to be a knower of the true path (*san-mārga-vid*, 5:6). Finally, just as a guide is familiar not just with the final destination but also with the smaller stages into which a journey can be broken down, so too does the Buddha know the steps (*krama-jña*, 13:9) that mark out a gradual progression to liberation. Occasionally an abstract quality such as regulated conduct (*śīla*, 13:28) or mindfulness (*smṛti*, 14:39) is personified as the guide who helps the traveller cross dangerous territory.

Since practising the Buddha's dharma is conceived as following the right path, logic dictates that living according to an alternative norm may be conceptualised as following the wrong path. A wrong path is recognised and avoided by a virtuous person such as King Śuddhodana, who "did not proceed down a contemptible path" (*nāvṛtad garhite pathi*, 2:26). The Buddha-to-be leaves his teachers Ārāḍa and Uḍraka because he recognises that what they preach is "not the path" (*amārgaḥ*, 3:3). In his search for liberation he goes on to experiment with strenuous asceticism, but rejects this too on the grounds that "this is not the path" (*naiṣa mārgaḥ*, 3:5). The word *mārga* in its technical sense refers to the Buddhist dharma[1], but in a looser sense it indicates any lifestyle, as in 3:16, when the Buddha is said to dispel the ignorance "of sensual people who follow a wide variety of paths" (*viṣayātmakasya hi janasya bahu-vividha-mārga-sevinaḥ*). Here, as so often, a predilection for sensory experience is the hallmark of a person who has embarked on wrong paths. That these paths are many (*bahu*) is in itself a condemnation, for the path of dharma is one only.

---

[1] In a specialised meaning, path (*magga*) also refers to the moment of entering one of four progressive stages of spiritual development – stream-enterer, once-returner, non-returner and *arahant* – as conceived in the Pali Canon. When the disciple has completed the work required of each level, he realises the corresponding fruit (*phala*) of that path.

While the alternative to practising the dharma may be conceptualised as following a wrong path or various different paths, it is also occasionally presented as an undemarcated tract of land where there is no path at all. Such undeveloped land suggests a rawness and wildness that is at odds with the Buddhist predilection for discipline and cultivation, which is better represented by the urban geography of Kapilavāstu with its well-kept gardens and wide boulevards. Thus a mind lacking mindful awareness (*smṛti*) is likened to a poor-sighted man walking over rough ground without a guide (14:39), while ethical conduct (*śīlam*) is likened to a guide in a wilderness (*kāntāra iva daiśikaḥ*, 13:28). The notion that a pathless terrain represents a lack of control is found also in the following verse:

> *alabdha-cetaḥ-praśamaḥ sarāgo*
> *yo na pracāraṃ bhajate viviktaṃ* |
> *sa kṣaṇyate hy apratilabdha-mārgaś*
> *carann ivorvyāṃ bahu-kaṇṭakāyām* || (14:47)

> The passionate man who has not achieved emotional peace and who does not adopt solitary habits gets hurt in his failure to find the path, as though he were walking over thorny ground.

The simile in this verse takes as *upamāna* for excitable and gregarious habits not a wrong path, but simply "ground" (*urvī*), which is unlike a path in that it lacks definition and leads nowhere. It is also beset by thorns, representing its lack of cultivation and maintenance. In such inhospitable terrain it is inevitable that sooner or later the rambler will step on a thorn and be injured (*kṣaṇyate*). The positioning of this verb in the third *pāda* is an example of semantic and metrical disalignment, a technique rarely found in Aśvaghoṣa (Pollock 1977:229). It induces slight tension and imbalance as the reader momentarily waits to discover what happens to the passionate man. Thorny terrain is not a path at all, let alone the right path, though it is not clear from the verse whether the thorns represent emotional disturbances, a passionate nature, the company of worldly people, or all three. In a repetition of the image three verses further on, it is definitely the last: "he who avoids the company of others as a thorn ... is known to have accomplished his object" (*kṛtārthaḥ sa jñeyaḥ ... pareṣāṃ saṃsargaṃ pariharati yaḥ kaṇṭakam iva*, 14:50).[2] Interaction with anyone other than a *kalyāṇa-mitra* is evidently a thorn in the side for a dedicated follower of the right path.

The examples in the preceding paragraphs paint a general picture of the path metaphor with all its traditional correspondences. The terms chosen to convey the picture are by and large bland and conventional, with occasional interest generated by the more concrete images, such as *nirvāṇa* as a city or society as a thorn. The habit of presenting the dharma as a path is so ingrained in Buddhist culture that the word *mārga* has in most instances become a technical term, and consequently fails to inspire much metaphorical development. However, the path metaphor is by no means dead, for it furnishes substance and depth to the depiction of Nanda's ongoing conversion; its very familiarity is put to service in structuring Nanda's progress. Every Buddhist reader, familiar with the constructs of the path metaphor on a subconscious level at least, knows in an instant that it is an excellent thing for someone to be consigned to the path, or that someone who has comes off the path has lapsed in their monastic training. The path metaphor is an extremely useful conversion metaphor, furnishing Aśvaghoṣa with a handy mechanism for tracing Nanda's initial false direction, his redirection by the Buddha, and his eventual successful completion of the journey. The specific application of the path metaphor to Nanda's particular situation is examined in greater depth in the following paragraphs.

As discussed above, Aśvaghoṣa has two ways of extending the path metaphor to make room for the notion of wrong living – the wrong path or paths being one alternative, an unmarked wilderness the other. Both extensions are used to refer to

---

[2] This differs from the *Udāna* version, quoted in Chapter Two, in which Nanda is said to have crushed the thorn of desire.

Nanda's profligate early life of sensual indulgence. Nanda's admission that his former life was unsatisfactory occurs late in the poem, after he has attained enlightenment. At this point he invokes the metaphor of the wrong path in retrospective recognition of his waywardness, saying of himself that "I was being pulled down the path of suffering by ignoble physicality" (*ahaṃ hy anāryeṇa śarīra-jena duḥkhātmake vartmani kṛṣyamāṇaḥ*, 17:64). This brief statement has several points of interest. Firstly, the path of which Nanda speaks is clearly not the right path, since it is in essence suffering (*duḥkhātmake*). Though Nanda's love scene with his wife in the early part of the poem is full of charm, and though he considered himself happy at the time, from the perspective of liberation his early life was unsatisfactory at best. We are reminded of the Four Noble Truths, the second of which is the fact of *duḥkha*, and the fourth of which provides an exit in the form of the right path, the Noble Eightfold Path. Also of interest in Nanda's statement is his dramatisation of 'that which arises from the body' (*śarīra-jena*) – sensual desires as well as a misplaced sense of his enduring physical robustness – as a force powerful enough to render him passively 'dragged along' (*kṛṣyamāṇaḥ*). Nanda here acknowledges his former characteristic lack of volition as well as the infelicity of his circumstances at that time.

Nanda may not recognise the misdirection of his former life until Canto 17, but the Buddha, with his superior wisdom, has known it all along. Nanda formulates his admission of wrong living in terms of a wrong path, while the Buddha, at a much earlier point in the narrative, poses a rhetorical question founded on the equation of wrong living and a wilderness:

saṃsāra-kāntāra-parāyaṇasya
śive kathaṃ te pathi nārurukṣā | (5:40ab)

How can you be so preoccupied with the wasteland of *saṃsāra* that you have no urge to venture upon the good path?

The path of which the Buddha speaks is obviously the right path, qualified as it is by *śiva*, a term that has been previously noted in reference to the right path. The Buddha contrasts the right path with the endless round of *saṃsāra* conceptualised as a large forest, wilderness or wasteland (*kāntāra*). In Pali works the equivalent term *kantāra* is used both literally and figuratively to convey the wilds of ignorance or false views.[3] The etymology of the word *parāyaṇa*, from *para* + *āyaṇa*, a final end or aim, or principal destination, relates to the path metaphor and supports the Buddha's analysis of Nanda's mental state: at this stage in the story, Nanda is not on the right path, but continues to aim at a jungle life. The Buddha is quick to diagnose Nanda's customary lack of volition as an important factor in his failure to better himself. He therefore takes a substantive derived from the desiderative form of *ā* + √*ruh*, to mount or ascend, when he declares that Nanda has 'no inclination to set out on' (*nāruruksā*) the good path.

7.3 Blocking Nanda's Path: An Analysis of Canto 5

Such is the state of affairs when Nanda first encounters the Buddha in Canto 5, a powerful and closely argued canto that is a highlight of the *Saundarananda*. Nanda at this point lacks the ambition or motivation to free himself from a perpetuity of wandering through the wilds of *saṃsāra*, but the Buddha has higher aspirations for him. The interplay between the Buddha's imprecations to Nanda and Nanda's continuing resistance to them is very skillfully managed in Canto 5, especially in the form of path symbolism. Since Nanda is evidently on the wrong path, a fact that is recognised by the Buddha now, and later also by Nanda himself, then he must be taken off his current path and redirected to the right path. This reconfiguring of Nanda's destiny barely features in other versions of the legend, which tend instead to focus on the visit to heaven and the celestial nymphs. The *Udāna* account omits the leading forth episode entirely. The Pali *Udāna*, *Dhammapada* and *Aṅguttara* commentaries have the Buddha visit Nanda's house on the dual

[3] PED, p. 186.

occasion of the latter's wedding and consecration as heir apparent, hand Nanda his bowl, then leave again, forcing Nanda to follow the Buddha in order to return the bowl. A similar, though condensed account is provided by the *Theragāthā* commentary, while the *Jātaka* has just a passing reference to Nanda's wife calling out to Nanda "at the time when he was leaving the house together with the *Tathāgata*, after he had taken the Blessed One's bowl."[4] The Chinese *Abhiniṣkramaṇa Sūtra* gives more detail, having Nanda follow the Buddha through the streets from the palace to the monastery, all the while carrying the bowl full of rice and honey which the Buddha has refused to accept.[5] The commentaries are of a later date than the *Saundarananda*, as is the Chinese translation of the *Abhiniṣkramaṇa Sūtra*, but in any case they and the other versions of the story contain no more than a bare account of the encounter which in the *Saundarananda* is brilliantly fleshed out over the course of an entire canto. The events of Canto 5 – the Buddha besieged by enthusiastic followers on the road, Nanda struggling to reach him, the Buddha noticing Nanda in the throng and disappearing down a side-road to shake off his followers whilst retaining Nanda, then stepping into Nanda's path to block his exit, and finally turning him over to Ānanda to be manhandled towards tonsure – all these are Aśvaghoṣa's own invention, and they all take place on paths. Additionally, Aśvaghoṣa is careful to place the onus for Nanda's initial departure on Nanda himself. So while other versions of the legend describe the Buddha as entering Nanda's palace, congratulating him, and then forcing his departure through the stratagem of handing his bowl to Nanda before leaving the palace, Aśvaghoṣa has the Buddha leave the palace without seeing or speaking to Nanda. Shortly afterwards Nanda voluntarily sets out to find the Buddha, having first received the requisite permission from his spouse to do so. The Buddha hands his bowl to Nanda much later, not in the palace but in a

---

[4] *Bhagavato pattaṃ ādāya Tathāgatena saddhiṃ gehā nikkhamana-kāle*, J 182.
[5] Beal (1875:369-70).

deserted side-road. Thus the force of the Buddha's initial intervention is considerably softened.

Canto 5 of the *Saundarananda* takes place outdoors, in and around the city of Kapilavāstu. The subject matter, as indicated by the canto title *nanda-pravrājanam*, is Nanda's ordination, the event described in the Pali texts as "the going forth from home to homelessness".[6] This is the first step in what will be an ongoing process of conversion, not complete until Nanda reaches liberation in Canto 17. *Pravrājanam*, from *pra* + √*vraj*, has a general meaning of 'proceeding', 'departing from' and 'setting out for' as well as its more specialised meaning 'to become a monk', and therefore already contains within its etymology the notion of a journey. In his portrayal of this important event, Aśvaghoṣa builds the conceptual metaphor of the path into the actual narrative, so that the streets literally walked by Nanda also take on a figurative function, symbolising the different ways of life available to him. This juxtaposition of *mise-en-scène* and figurative function commences in the last verse of Canto 4, when Nanda, after delaying his departure from his palace because he cannot tear himself away from Sundarī, at last catches sight of the Buddha ahead of him:

> *atha sa pathi dadarśa mukta-mānaṃ*
> *pitṛ-nagare 'pi tathāgatābhimānaṃ* |
> *daśa-balam abhito vilambamānaṃ*
> *dhvajam anuyāna ivaindram arcyamānam* || (4:46)

> Then on the road he saw him of the Ten Powers, free from pride even in his father's city because he had the disposition of a Tathāgata, stopping everywhere and being worshipped like Indra's banner in a procession.

The Buddha too has been delayed, in his case due to the number of people on the road who wish to honour him. The road in question is thronged with people, as at a festival. The opening verses of Canto 5 provide further information about the road:

---

[6] *agārasmā anagāriyaṃ pabbajjā*, Vin 2.253, MN ii.56 etc.

athāvatīryāśva-ratha-dvipebhyaḥ
śākyā yathā-sva-rddhi gṛhīta-veṣāḥ |
mahā-paṇebhyo vyavahāriṇaś ca
mahā-munau bhakti-vaśāt praṇemuḥ || (5:1)

Then the Śākyas, clothed according to their wealth, got down from their horses, chariots and elephants, and the merchants came from their large shops, and overcome by devotion to the great sage, they bowed low.

The road is a major thoroughfare, wide enough to accommodate horses, chariots and elephants. Resolving the compound *mahāpaṇa* as *mahā* + *āpaṇa*, one could further speculate, as does Johnston, that the road is lined with large shops. It is certainly lined with houses; the next verse confirms that while some citizens followed the Buddha for a while, and others departed straight after paying their respects, "some, having made *añjali* to him, stood [in the doorways] of their own houses with their eyes absorbed in gazing at him" (*kecit svakeṣvāvasatheṣu tasthuḥ kṛtvāñjalīn vīkṣaṇa-tat-parākṣāḥ*, 5:2cd). *Āvasatha* is a habitation or dwelling, so people clearly live alongside this road. Such is the crush in the street that the Buddha can hardly pass:

buddhas tatas tatra narendra-mārge
sroto mahad bhaktimato janasya |
jagāma duḥkhena vigāhamāno
jalāgame srota ivāpagāyāḥ || (5:3)

Then the Buddha went along the royal highway, making his way with difficulty through the great stream of devoted people there, as if through a streaming monsoon river.

The Buddha is probably walking along Kapilavāstu's most impressive street, the one used by the king (*narendra-mārga*).

This urban road, beset with traffic, associated with government, and surrounded by residential and commercial premises, provides a snapshot of quotidian life and as such can be taken as representative of *saṃsāra*, despite the presence of the Buddha. The simile of the river in flood supports this interpretation, since a river or flood is a familiar Buddhist image of *saṃsāra*, crossing which one reaches liberation.

Allowing the busy main road this symbolic value, it stands to reason that Nanda, who is currently in the thick of *saṃsāra*, is stuck in the road and can make no real progress towards the Buddha.

atho mahadbhiḥ pathi saṃpatadbhiḥ
saṃpūjyamānāya tathāgatāya |
kartuṃ praṇāmaṃ na śaśāka nandas
tenābhireme tu guror mahimnā || (5:4)

Because of the large numbers on the road flocking to pay homage to the Tathāgata, Nanda was not able to pay his respects, but he rejoiced in the greatness of the guru.

Circumstances and possibly his own lack of volition ensure that Nanda cannot reach the Buddha. Nanda is content to stay in the background and witness the Buddha's charismatic presence from a distance. His strong attachment to domestic life soon persuades him to retreat:

svaṃ cāvasaṅgaṃ pathi nirmumukṣur
bhaktiṃ janasyānya-mateś ca rakṣan |
nandaṃ ca gehābhimukhaṃ jighrakṣan
mārgaṃ tato 'nyaṃ sugataḥ prapede || (5:5)

Wishing to dismiss his own followers whilst retaining the devotion of people of other persuasions, and intending to catch hold of Nanda who was turning towards home, the Sugata set out along a different road.

Nanda is described as *gehābhimukha*, literally facing homewards, indicating his inclination to return to his wife without making further efforts to greet the Buddha. The Buddha has noticed him, however, and he initiates a development that is typical of his role as the agent of Nanda's conversion. The adjective *nirmumukṣu* and the present participle *jighrakṣan*, deriving from the s of *nir* + √*muc* and √*grah* respectively, point to the Buddha's control of the situation. The Buddha shakes off most of the crowd by turning into another road (*mārgam* ... *anyam*). He wishes to nurture the devotion of those who are not his committed followers, whose minds are on other things (*anya-mati*), presumably by granting them free access to him now that the bulk of the crowd has dispersed. He also wants to catch hold (*jighrakṣan*) of Nanda in order to persuade him against returning home. This other road, then, is reserved for those whom the Buddha singles out for special attention, and it represents a progression along the Buddhist path. There follows a verse rich in suggestiveness and *double entendre*:

> *tato viviktaṃ ca vivikta-cetāḥ*
> *san-mārga-vin mārgam abhipratasthe* |
> *gatvāgrataś cāgryatamāya tasmai*
> *nāndī-vimuktāya nanāma nandaḥ* || (5:6)

> Then the judicious knower of the right path reached an isolated [stretch of] road. Nanda went in front and bowed down to him, the foremost man, who was free from [attachment to] delight.

The other road has now become secluded, presumably as the Buddha moves further away from the centre of Kapilavāstu. Alternatively, reading *abhipratasthe* as 'set out on', the Buddha takes a third, yet quieter path. Whichever option is the case, the route taken by the Buddha, and which Nanda follows, is marked by increasing isolation (*viviktam* ... *mārgam*). The repetition of the word *vivikta*, used literally in connection with the physical isolation of the road and figuratively in connection with the

Buddha's faculty of mental discrimination (*vivikta-cetas*), confirms that the characters' physical movement around the physical terrain symbolises their mental and volitional states. In later cantos, especially in Canto 14, the concept of *viveka*, which means emotional detachment and the ability to think discriminately as well as physical solitude, becomes increasingly important. The assumption that the habit of correct mental discrimination is best cultivated in solitude, noticeable here in verse 5:6 and in later cantos, is openly stated in 14:46 when the Buddha tells Nanda that "once physical separation is achieved, mental discrimination is easy to reach" (*kāyasya kṛtvā hi vivekam ādau sukho 'dhigantuṃ manaso vivekaḥ*). Hence Nanda's progression along an ever quieter road points to his later mental development.

The repetition of the word *mārga* also draws attention to the symbolic value of the action. Just at the moment when the Buddha, followed at a short distance by Nanda, is walking along an isolated path (*mārga*), the Buddha is described as 'knower of the good path' (*san-mārga-vid*). This is an obvious pun, for it is apparent that the good path known to the Buddha is not so much the quiet side-road as the path of Buddhist discipline that is looming for Nanda, though of course the former is emblematic of the latter. There is further wordplay when Nanda steps in front (*agrataḥ*) of the Buddha to at last pay his long overdue respects. Nanda had been behind the Buddha on the path, so perhaps the Buddha has turned towards Nanda, though it is more likely, in view of the Buddha's subsequent actions, that Nanda first overtakes the Buddha and then turns to face him. Just as Nanda overtakes him, the Buddha is described as 'foremost' (*agryatama*). Nanda may be ahead on the quiet side-road, but the Buddha is first on the metaphorical path. We are also reminded that the Buddha is Nanda's *agrya*, older brother. A further attribute of the Buddha is his lack of 'delight' (*nāndī-vimukta*). The only other occurrence of the word *nāndī* in the *Saundarananda* is at 4:8, where it is associated, within the context of Nanda and Sundarī's mutual besottedness, with Kāma, the god of love, and his partner Rati. The Buddha is free of sexual infatuation of this type, but not so Nanda, whose very name resonates with it.

When Nanda at last catches up with the Buddha, he salutes him, invites him for a meal, and is refused (5:7-10). He then decides to go home, but the Buddha forestalls him by presenting him with his bowl (5:11). This is awkward for Nanda, since placing it on the ground or attempting to thrust it back at the Buddha would be highly disrespectful. However, Nanda's longing for home is so great that he tries to extricate himself from this delicate situation:

> *parāṅmukhas tv anya-manaskam ārād*
> *vijñāya nandaḥ sugataṃ gatāsthaṃ* |
> *hasta-stha-pātro 'pi gṛhaṃ yiyāsuḥ*
> *sasāra mārgān munim īkṣamāṇaḥ* || (5:13)

> But Nanda realised that the Sugata had his mind on other things and was not concentrating [on him], so with his head turned to keep his eye on the sage he moved away from the road, intending to go home, though he still had the bowl in his hands.

Nanda decides to seize the opportunity of the Buddha's preoccupation and make off, even though that means taking the bowl with him. The depiction of the Buddha as momentarily distracted is unusual, but necessary for the storyline if Nanda is to be presented as attempting to escape unnoticed. Nanda's efforts to flee are much developed in other versions of the tale, even to comical effect, but in the *Saundarananda*, though Nanda voices his desire to go home frequently enough, this is the only time that he physically tries to do so. Impelled by his wish to go home (*gṛhaṃ yiyāsuḥ*) to Sundarī and his other domestic comforts, Nanda moves or even runs away from the path (*sasāra mārgāt*). The literal path once again coincides with the metaphorical one; the quiet path down which the Buddha has led

Nanda represents the Buddhist path that Nanda will shortly be made to tread, but which he seeks to avoid.

The Buddha, though seemingly distracted, notices that Nanda is trying to slip away and takes immediate preventative action:

bhāryānurāgeṇa yadā gṛhaṃ sa
pātraṃ gṛhītvāpi yiyāsur eva |
vimohayām āsa munis tatas taṃ
rathyā-mukhasyāvaraṇena tasya || (5:14)

Just as he was intending to go home out of love for his wife, though he had accepted the bowl, the sage confused him by blocking the entrance to the street.

This has to be the Buddha's single most controversial act in the entire poem, and the next four verses (5:15-18) are devoted to its analysis and justification by reason of Nanda's passivity. The Buddha physically blocks Nanda's way so that he cannot rejoin the main street. Since the word *rathyā* means 'carriage-way', it is more than likely that it refers to the large and busy thoroughfare, crammed with carriages, horses and elephants that is the setting for the events of 5:1-4. The Buddha's forceful action also has obvious symbolic value, since he is preventing Nanda from returning to the household life. The bustling main street, representative of life in the world, leads back to Nanda's palace, but the quiet side-road leads to the monastery, and it is in this direction that Nanda most unwillingly now wends his way:

nandas tu duḥkhena viceṣṭamānaḥ
śanair agatyā gurum anvagacchat | (5:19ab)

Nanda, moving with difficulty, followed the guru slowly and helplessly.

Nanda follows because he has no choice, *agati* here meaning that there is no escape.

Just as the monastery is approached via the quiet side-road, so is monastic living a logical concomitant of following the path of dharma. The monastery is the end of the road for Nanda in that his life as a householder and husband has finished, but it is also the beginning of his spiritual journey towards liberation. This dual connotation is stressed by the repetition of the triple *vihāra* and a play on its meaning in verse 5:20:

> *tato munis taṃ priya-mālya-hāraṃ*
> *vasanta-māsena kṛtābhihāraṃ* |
> *nināya bhagna-pramadā-vihāraṃ*
> *vidyā-vihārābhimataṃ vihāraṃ* || (5:20)
>
> Then this lover of garlands and necklaces, who was familiar with the assaults of Spring, was led by the sage to the monastery, where pleasure in women was destroyed and which was considered the abode of knowledge.

The emphatic repetition of *vihāra*, a word which includes such definitions as monastery, recreation ground and pleasurable pastime in its wide semantic range, makes the point that Nanda has arrived at a place where his old life is forced to give way to a new life. This is the place (*vihāra*) where finding pleasure in the company of women (*pramadā-vihāra*) is broken (*bhagna*). The usual accoutrements of romantic love – necklaces, garlands, the spring months – signify Nanda's sexually-charged life, Vasanta (Spring) being often personified and considered a friend or attendant of Kāma, the god of love. These are to be replaced by chastity and understanding. Thus this verse, with its skillfully managed collision of *kāvya* convention and the imperatives of dharma, marks an important point on Nanda's trajectory towards liberation.

The first half of Canto 5 shapes the familiar story of Nanda led forth by the Buddha through a conscious conflation of real and metaphorical paths; the physical terrain traversed by Nanda functions as a map of his past and future lives. So long as Nanda remains on the busy main road that represents workaday life in the world, the Buddha remains inaccessible to him – a powerful visual statement of the impossibility of making spiritual progress while engrossed in domestic affairs. Once on the quiet side-road that represents a life of seclusion, Nanda can approach the Buddha with ease; this shows that Buddhist practice requires withdrawal. Furthermore, this is the way to the monastery, where Nanda's attachment to his 'man in the street' life will be eradicated. His disinclination for his new path, his preference for his former life, and the Buddha's intervention to keep him on the straight and narrow are all plain to see in Aśvaghoṣa's deployment of the path metaphor. The preoccupation with the path metaphor lessens during the second half of Canto 5, which consists mainly of the Buddha's efforts to persuade Nanda of the wisdom of leaving home (5:21-32 and 5:37-49). Naturally the Buddha is aware that Nanda is averse to a life of self-restraint and seclusion, but in Canto 5's final appeal to the path metaphor he maintains that it is in Nanda's best interests. Unpalatable but healthy food is better for you than unhealthy sweetmeats, explains the Buddha, and "for the same reason, I commit you to a benign and pure path, though you don't like it" (*yasmād ahaṃ tvā viniyojayāmi śive śucau vartmani vipriye 'pi*, 5:46cd). Thus is Nanda consigned to the Buddhist path by his guide, and his ordination soon follows (5:51).

7.4 Turning Around

After Canto 5, there is no longer an actual path to symbolise Nanda's conversion, but there are frequent verbal manifestations of the metaphorical path in the remainder of the *Saundarananda*. Nanda's post-ordination progress is hardly swift, and by Canto 7 things are looking bad. Nanda's continuing obsession with Sundarī and his inability to spend time in meditation (unlike the meditating monk whom he notices in 7:20) lead him to declare that he has "fallen from the path of dharma" (*dharma-pathāt cyuta*, 7:47). In conjunction with his fall from the path, he notices that his senses are agitated (*calendriya*, 7:47) and that his thoughts are elsewhere (*anya-citta*, 7:47). Despite his low self-appraisal, however, there is evidence of some new-found awareness in Nanda, since now he at least recognises that he was on the path of dharma; he also knows that the mental restlessness resulting from romantic passion is incompatible with such a path. He realises that he is a monk in appearance only, comparing himself to a lamp in a painting that is not actually real (7:48). As Nanda feels that he cannot view himself as a true monk who is truly travelling on the path of dharma, he decides to disrobe and go home. But he has no time to act on his decision, for he is approached by the unnamed ascetic who has noticed his distress and who lectures him throughout Cantos 8 and 9. Among the ascetic's strongly worded criticisms is the assertion that Nanda, in refusing to follow the path on which the Buddha has placed him, is heading in the wrong direction. The ascetic asks Nanda "You, so proud of your physique, travelling to your ruin, what **are** you thinking of?" (*kṣayaṃ vrajan kiṃ bala-dṛpta manyase*, 9:8d), or more colloquially, "What on earth do you think you're doing?" The ascetic's admonitions have little impact, whereupon Nanda is summoned to the Buddha:

> *taṃ prāptam aprāpta-vimokṣa-mārgaṃ*
> *papraccha citta-skhalitaṃ sucittaḥ* | (10:2ab)
>
> When he arrived, his mind faltering and the path to liberation untaken, the noble-minded one questioned him.

Nanda's earlier self-diagnosis that he has fallen from the path of dharma is confirmed by the pointed refrain in this verse, for although he has managed to get to the place to which he was summoned (*prāpta*), he has not taken the path to liberation (*aprāpta-vimokṣa-mārga*). Just as Nanda has previously associated his lapse from dharma with the restless movement of his sense perceptions (*calendriya*, 7:47), so is his lack of path attainment here accompanied by skittish thoughts (*citta-skhalita*) – which of course contrast with the good thoughts (*su-citta*) of the Buddha. Sensory and mental restlessness are indicative of, perhaps even responsible for, Nanda's failure to pursue the path to which he was consigned in Canto 5. It is clear from the metaphor that at this point in the narrative Nanda cannot be considered as following the Buddhist path, though he has not formally disrobed.

Until the beginning Canto 12 Nanda has been ruled by his senses. He has settled for discipline and self-restraint merely as currency to buy time with the Apsarases, and it is only Ānanda's lesson in Canto 12 on the transience of heaven that finally persuades him to replace his goal of pleasurable sensory experience with the Buddhist goal of liberation. His mental reorientation to the dharma is presented in a powerful and vivid simile:

> *tasya svargān nivavṛte saṃkalpāśvo mano-rathaḥ* |
> *mahā-ratha ivonmārgād apramattasya sāratheḥ* ||
> (12:5)

> The chariot of his mind with its horses of fancy turned away from heaven, as a great chariot is turned back from the wrong path by its attentive charioteer.

In terms of the path metaphor, Nanda had been heading in the wrong direction, towards heaven rather than towards liberation. Now, under the impetus of shock (*saṃvega*, 12:4, 8 and 9), he changes his mind, a crucial moment that is dramatised in this verse as a large carriage veering away from a false turning. Two interpretations are possible, depending on the weight of meaning that the verb *ni* + √*vṛt* (turn back, turn away, stop, retreat) is made to bear: the more likely option is that the chariot was already on the wrong path and now turns round to rejoin the right path, or alternatively, a turn down the wrong road is narrowly avoided at the last moment. The verse is an example of a particular technique of Aśvaghoṣa's noted on page 18 above, in which both a simile and a metaphor are used in conjunction to amplify each other's meaning. Thus in the *upameya* the term chosen to denote Nanda's mind is *mano-ratha*, with its connotations of desire and delight, while the engine which powers this vehicle is the metaphorical *saṃkalpāśva*, the horses of imagination, volition, or fanciful notions. The phrase reveals Nanda's motivation – until now he has allowed himself to be carried away by wishful thinking. The wrong path (*unmārga*) of the *upamāna* obviously represents Nanda's former goal of heaven (*svarga*), but the *upamāna*'s heedful charioteer has no match in the *upameya*. It may be Ānanda, who has just spoken to Nanda about the unsatisfactoriness of heaven, or it may be the Buddha, who is frequently referred to as a charioteer in Buddhist literature, or it may be Nanda himself, since two verses earlier we are told that the *hetu*, his impulse to liberation, has matured sufficiently to prevent him from ignoring Ānanda's words (*paripāka-gate hetau na sa tan mamṛṣe vacaḥ*, 12:3cd).

The extension of the path metaphor to include the image of horse and chariot appears a second time in Canto 12, when the Buddha congratulates Nanda on his conversion:

> *ciram unmārga-vihṛto lolair indriya-vājibhiḥ* |
> *avatīrṇo 'si panthānaṃ diṣṭyā dṛṣṭyāvimūḍhayā* || (12:20)

> For a long time the restless horses of the senses have carried you the wrong way. How wonderful that through clear-sightedness you have alighted on the [right] path!

Here is a similar image of Nanda travelling along the wrong path, though the instrument of his propulsion is slightly different. The metaphorical horses by which Nanda is pulled along correspond in this instance to his senses (*indriya*) rather than to his wishful thinking, referring to his constant desire for pleasurable sensory experience. As has already been noted, a fall from the right path or travel along the wrong path is frequently associated with restless motion; here too the wayward[7] sense horses are qualified as fidgety (*lola*). Nanda's recent arrival on the Buddhist path is attributed in this verse to clear vision (*dṛṣṭyā avimūḍhayā*), which stands of course for unclouded judgement. Nanda's *volte-face* is the result of his greater wisdom.

[7] The English word 'wayward' as the aphetic form of 'awayward', is particularly apt in this context.

Now that Nanda has turned to face the right way and has reconciled himself to his monastic situation, his progress is fast. The Buddha ends his exhortations to Nanda in Canto 16, and in the next verse, which opens Canto 17, Nanda is described thus:

athaivam ādeśita-tattva-mārgo
nandas tadā prāpta-vimokṣa-mārgaḥ |
sarveṇa bhāvena gurau praṇamya
kleśa-prahāṇāya vanaṃ jagāma|| (17:1)

Then, having had the way to reality thus pointed out to him, Nanda took the path to liberation; with deep affection he bowed to the guru and set out for the forest in order to abandon his defilements.

The Buddha has been acting as a knowledgeable guide for several cantos, instructing Nanda in self-restraint and meditation. These instructions are directions to Nanda to help him find his way along the path to liberation, so Nanda is aptly qualified as 'one to whom the way to truth has been pointed out' (*ādeśita-tattva-mārga*). Now that he has willingly accepted the directions, he is able to set out on the right road. The phrase 'taken the path to liberation' (*prāpta-vimokṣa-mārga*) is a deliberate recall of 10:2, when Nanda, prior to his visit to heaven and his subsequent disenchantment with it, had not yet taken the path to liberation (*aprāpta-vimokṣa-mārga*). Since Nanda does not achieve liberation until 17:60, and indeed does not acquire stream-entry until 17:27, it seems that this phrase does not refer to any specific level of attainment or non-attainment. Rather, it refers to Nanda's motivation, which in 10:2 was contra-liberation, but which by 17:1 is pro-liberation. Nanda no longer wishes to counter the Buddha. Indeed, Nanda now recognises that the Buddha was instrumental in converting his initial reluctance into decisive and ultimately successful action:

kathaṃkathā-bhāva-gato 'smi yena
chinnaḥ sa niḥsaṃśaya saṃśayo me |
tvac-chāsanāt sat-patham āgato 'smi

su-deśikasyeva pathi pranaṣṭaḥ || (18:8)

That hesitation which made me full of uncertainty has been cut away, O you who are without hesitation. Because of your instruction I have arrived at the true path, like a lost man who finds his way through the directions of a good guide.

In this classic exposition of the path metaphor, the doubting Nanda correlates to the man who was lost (*pranaṣṭa*), the Buddha equates to the good guide (*su-deśika*), and his teaching functions as a set of directions (*śāsana*) that enable Nanda to make his way along the correct route (*sat-patha*). Thus fortified, Nanda was able to 'go the distance' and reach the end of the course (*parāṃ gatim gataḥ*, 18:54). Finally, Nanda adopts the position with regard to other people that the Buddha had formerly adopted towards him; he helps others who are on the wrong path, who are still wandering in *saṃsāra*, without despising them (*naivonmārga-gatān parān paribhavan*, 18:62).

The extensive instructions provided by the Buddha from Cantos 12 to 16 form a set of directions that function for Nanda as a kind of blueprint for action, or as a plan, road map or itinerary that he is to follow. The Sanskrit word *nyāyaḥ* embraces this concept of methodical advance. The Buddha warns that "humanity is damaged by the lack of a plan (*anyāyena manuṣyatvam upahanyāt*, 15:26). The word is specifically related to path metaphor in Canto 14:

āryo nyāyaḥ kutas tasya smṛtir yasya na vidyate |
yasyāryo nāsti ca nyāyaḥ pranaṣṭas tasya sat-pathaḥ || (14:43)

Where is the noble plan of a man who is not mindful? And the right path is lost to a man who has no noble plan.

Someone who does not have the appropriate route directions will not find the good path that leads to liberation. The possession of a map to the right destination is linked here with mindfulness (*smṛti*). This is the case also in verse 16:33, when the Buddha enjoins Nanda to practise "perfect mindfulness in conjunction with a map to reach the truth" (*nyāyena satyādhigamāya yuktā samyak smṛtiḥ*). A little later the authorial voice summarises the Buddha's lengthy exhortations as directions for Nanda to follow:

> *ity evam anyāya-nivartanaṃ ca*
> *nyāyaṃ ca tasmai sugato babhāṣe* | (16:68ab)
>
> In this way the Sugata spoke to him concerning the right method and retreat from the wrong method.

Nanda is advised to turn away (*nivartanam*) from inappropriate directions (*anyāya*), presumably those that conflict with the guidelines supplied by the Buddha.

7.5 Orientational Vocabulary

Words formed from the root *ni* + √*vṛt*, such as *nivartanam* above, are an example of an orientational vocabulary used in conjunction with the path metaphor to supply spatial relations between the traveller, his route, pitfalls along the way, and his ultimate destination. Such words of spatial logic occur regularly in the *Saundarananda* to chart progress along the path. Verbal and nominal formations from *ni* + √*vṛt* indicate a turning away, turning back or retreating from a certain path, and by extension, desisting from a certain action. These formations are used in the figurative sense frequently enough; hence the Buddha turns away from asceticism (3:2), the meditating monk has turned away from curiosity and pride (7:22), the Buddha refers to a time when desire and passion will be turned back by Nanda (15:51), and in the example above, Nanda is to turn away from faulty methods. Similarly, Nanda eventually turns away from his thirst for heaven (12:6). A more interesting occurrence is 12:5 quoted above, in which Nanda's desire-bound mind (*mano-ratha*) is compared to a chariot turned away (*nivavṛte*) from a wrong path by a vigilant charioteer. The same idea of a turning vehicle is found in the verse in which the Buddha predicts Sundarī's reorientation to the dharma, telling Nanda that when she hears of his stable mind, "with its desires for the various sense objects turned back" (*nivṛtta-nānā-viṣayair mano-rathaiḥ*), she will preach dispassion to the women (18:59). Verbal formations from *ni* + √*vṛt* are linked to the Fourth Noble Truth, when the Buddha tells Nanda to "understand the path as turning away" (*nivartakaṃ cāpy avagaccha mārgam*, 16:42d). This definition of the Noble Eightfold Path is based on the familiar opposition between *pravṛtti*, active engagement with the world, and *nivṛtti*, cessation from such worldly endeavour. In fact, verse 16:42 equates *pravṛtti* with suffering, and *nivṛtti* with liberation. Thus the action of 'turning away' from wrong paths by keeping to the right path is viewed favourably throughout the *Saundarananda*.

One last example of turning aside from a wrong path, previously encountered in Chapter Three, has Nanda liken himself to an elephant:

> *ahaṃ hy anāryeṇa śarīra-jena*
> *duḥkhātkmake vartmani kṛṣyamāṇaḥ* |
> *nivartitas tad-vacanāṅkuśena*
> *darpānvito nāga ivāṅkuśena* || (17:64)

> For I was being pulled down the path of suffering by ignoble physicality, but I was turned back, hooked by his words, as a proud elephant is turned back with a hook.

Nanda acknowledges that he did not turn from the path of suffering – in other words, the path of *saṃsāra* – through self-generated volition, but because of the Buddha's exhortations (*tad-vacana*). Thus the past participle *nivartita*, formed from the causative of *ni* + √*vṛt*, reflects the fact that Nanda was made to turn round. Prior to the Buddha's intervention, Nanda was "being dragged" (*kṛṣyamāṇaḥ*), a usage that is typical of his characterisation. Verbal formations from the √*kṛṣ* and *ā* + √*kṛṣ*, to pull, drag, draw or attract, like those from *ni* + √*vṛt*, track Nanda's route from libertinism to liberation. In particular, they provide a spatial vocabulary for the forced push-pull motion centred on Nanda, exerted by the Buddha from one side and by Sundarī and Nanda's own sensual proclivities from the other side. So at the end of Canto 4, the two opposing forces exerted on Nanda are crystallised in two verbs from √*kṛṣ*:

> *taṃ gauravaṃ buddha-gataṃ cakarṣa*
> *bhāryānurāgaḥ punar ācakarṣa* | (4:42ab)
>
> Reverence for the Buddha drew him on, love for his wife pulled him back again.

Nanda's helpless seesawing indicates his lack of independence. Two verses later, he is still suspended between the two possibilities offered to him, "held back by his attachment to sensual pleasures, drawn forward by his attachment to the dharma" (*sa kāma-rāgeṇa nigṛhyamāṇo dharmānurāgeṇa kṛṣyamāṇaḥ*, 4:44ab). The balanced *pāda*s in both examples mirror the equal weight that Nanda grants these two important figures in his life. Nanda is aware that passion is a powerful drive, for when he observes a monk engaged in successful meditation, he comments: "I assume he has no lover tugging at his heart" (*śaṅke priyākarṣati nāsya cetaḥ*, 7:21d). But there is a lover tugging at Nanda's heart, hence the unnamed ascetic remarks that Nanda is "forcibly drawn by lust" (*madanena ca kṛṣyase balād*, 8:53c). On a more general note, the Buddha says that a man "is dragged" (*kṛṣyate*) to hell by the restless)senses (*capalair indriyaiḥ*, 13:33). According to Aśvaghoṣa's important justificatory passage at 5:15-18, Nanda's predisposition towards sensuality means that he cannot go willingly to liberation, but must be impelled: "for that reason, the sage pressurised Nanda" (*nandaṃ yatas taṃ munir ācakarṣa*, 5:15d). The controversial question of over-forceful conversion is subtly captured in verbs from √*kṛṣ* as their meaning shades from 'attract' into 'coerce'.

The same back and forth motion evinced by √*kṛṣ* is revealed by another item of vocabulary related to the path metaphor, the substantive *mukha*. Although the word has a literal meaning of mouth or face, it also has an orientational function, especially when prefixed by *abhi*, 'towards' and *parāñc*, 'away from'. In indicating which way Nanda is facing, *abhimukha* also suggests the direction that he intends to take and thus the future that he desires for himself. Prior to his visit to heaven, Nanda is oriented towards his home, where his wife waits, and away from the path to liberation. He is already turning "homewards" (*gehābhimukha*, 5:5) when the Buddha diverts him by turning down the quiet side-road. Later Nanda is described as "focused on his beloved wife" (*priya-bhāryābhimukha*, 8:14) and "inclining towards domestic pleasures" (*gṛha-sukhābhimukha*, 8:59 and 9:51). The word *parāṅmukha* shows an intention to proceed in the opposite direction, for it indicates what Nanda has turned his back on. So in Canto 8 Nanda explains that he is "averse to the delights of forest living" (*vana-vāsa-sukhāt parāṅmukhaḥ*, 8:13). However, once the Apsarases have replaced Sundarī as the object of his desire, Nanda is said to "turn away from passion for his wife" (*bhāryā-rāgāt parāṅmukha*, 11:8). Nanda finally faces in the right direction after Ānanda has rectified his misconceptions of heaven in Canto 11. At this point, the prospect of liberation, the excellent, is said to appear before him (*śreyaś caivāmukhī-bhūtam*, 12:18c). The Buddha can now address him as "dharma-facing man, you have put that kind of fiery passion behind you" (*rāgāgnis tādṛśo yasya dharmonmukha parāṅmukhaḥ*, 12:26cd).

7.6 The Travelling Merchant

Words deriving from *ni* + √*vṛt*, √*kṛṣ* and *mukha* are subtle verbal signposts that help the reader to identify Nanda's location on his route from *saṃsāra* to *nirvāṇa*. They barely hint at the underlying path metaphor. By way of a contrast, the poem also features several similes and metaphorical expressions in which the path metaphor is fully developed and easily discernible. Many of them have been mentioned in this chapter. There remain four lively instances of the genre, all featuring the conflation of the traveller figure with a character beloved of Buddhist story literature, the merchant-venturer. In this familiar scenario, a group of traders travel together for safety, hazarding the dangers of brigands, wild animals and food shortages for the chance of acquiring enormous riches. There is never a trace of the modern sensibility that turning an overly handsome profit might constitute an unworthy endeavour. Rather, financial gain is a regular simile for the attainment of liberation in the Pali Canon, and the Buddha himself is sometimes presented as a caravan-leader.[8] Hence the Buddha of the *Saundarananda* berates Nanda as a foolishly stubborn trader:

> *saṃsāra-kāntāra-parāyaṇasya*
> *śive kathaṃ te pathi nāruruksā* |
> *āropyamāṇasya tam eva mārgaṃ*
> *bhraṣṭasya sārthād iva sārthikasya* || (5:40)

> How can you be so preoccupied with the wasteland of *saṃsāra* that you have no urge to venture upon the good path, even when you have been set on that very path? It is as though a merchant separated from his caravan [would not wish to take the right road even when it was pointed out to him].

As has previously been stated, *saṃsāra* is equated to a wilderness (*kāntāra*). Nanda's obstinate refusal to follow the Buddha's path means he has no chance of escape from the repeated death of *saṃsāra*, just as the lone trader lost in hostile terrain stands little chance of survival, let alone of winning riches, when he refuses an offer of help. The lone trader is at particular risk because he lacks the protection afforded by travelling in convoy, just as Nanda's refusal to join the company of monks disqualifies him from the guidance they offer. Nanda's error, according to this verse, is threefold: he is lost in that he is

[8] J iii.62, for example.

not yet on the Buddhist path, he refuses help in finding the path, and he refuses the prospect of supportive companions.

By the end of the poem, the seemingly hopeless situation has, after all, turned out well:

> *diṣṭyāsi śāntiṃ paramām upeto*
> *nistīrṇa-kāntāra ivāpta-sāraḥ |*
> *sarvo hi saṃsāra-gato bhayārto*
> *yathaiva kāntāra-gatas tathaiva ||* (18:32)

> How wonderful that you, like a man who has come through the wilderness and found riches, have reached supreme tranquillity! For all who are in *saṃsāra* are prey to danger, just like people in the wilderness.

The Buddha is congratulating Nanda on having successfully negotiated his way through *saṃsāra* to win liberation. Once again, the activity of long-distance trade supplies the figurative material for this verse. In obtaining supreme peace, Nanda is compared to someone who has made his fortune (*āpta-sāraḥ*), while *saṃsāra* correlates to the now familiar wilds (*kāntāra*). In *pāda*s c and d the image broadens to include all of unliberated humanity as wanderers in *saṃsāra*, afflicted by various dangers. In responding to the Buddha's congratulations, Nanda recognises his debt of gratitude to the Buddha, and more surprisingly, to his parents:

> *bhrātrā tvayā śreyasi daiśikena*
> *pitrā phala-sthena tathaiva mātrā |*
> *hato 'bhaviṣyaṃ yadi na vyamokṣyaṃ*
> *sārthāt paribhraṣṭa ivākṛtārthaḥ ||* (18:41)

> I would have failed, like a man who falls behind his caravan and makes no money, if I had not been liberated by you, my brother and guide to excellence, by my father who is established in the fruit, and also by my mother.

The Buddha appears in his familiar role as the indispensable guide who points out the way to the excellent (*śreyasi daiśikena*). Nanda also pays tribute to the supportive company of other successful wayfarers, such as his father, whose attainment of the first stage or 'fruit' of the path to liberation is recounted in 3:27. Such forerunners are likened to a caravan of traders (*sārtha*) whose presence provides security and encouragement. If he had not kept up with them, Nanda would have perished (*hato 'bhaviṣyam*) because he would have remained in *saṃsāra*.

We can now summarise the correspondences by which the conceptual metaphor of the path is expanded into the more specialised metaphor of travel for the purposes of trade:

Table 4: Correspondences of the Travelling for Trade Metaphor

Target Domain	**Fundamental Source Domain**	**Specialised Source Domain**
Nanda	traveller	merchant
the Buddha	guide	guide
progress to liberation, the dharma	path	trade
saṃsāra	wilderness	wilderness
other practitioners	wise companions	caravan
liberation	destination, a city	great riches
new insight	turning round	~
code of discipline	map	~

The Buddha's acceptance of Nanda's gratitude completes the *Saundarananda*'s exposition of the trade metaphor:

idaṃ kṛtārthaḥ paramārtha-vit kṛtī
tvam eva dhīmann abhidhātum arhasi |
atītya kāntāram avāpta-sādhanaḥ
sudaiśikasyeva kṛtaṃ mahā-vaṇik || (18:50)

> Wise man, it is right that you, goal-achiever and successful knower of the ultimate truth, should say this, just as on passing through the wilderness and acquiring a fortune a great merchant properly declares the deeds of his guide.

In summary, the *Saundarananda* recognises two metaphors founded on the source domain of travel along a path. One is the universally recognised metaphor of life as a journey, which, in the Indian context, is a helpless and endless meandering down the path of *saṃsāra*. The other constitutes a goal-oriented journey by which the traveller reaches liberation from *saṃsāra*. In this specifically Buddhist working of the metaphor, the Nanda appears as a traveller who is unwillingly deposited on the path of dharma. He is aided by the Buddha as his guide, the presence of suitable travelling companions, and a good map. Others who are plodding along in *saṃsāra* are sometimes said to be on the wrong path, and sometimes seen as being off the path, trapped in the wilderness. Although over-familiarity with the path metaphor often renders its presence in Buddhist culture nondescript or even virtually invisible, Aśvaghoṣa remains deeply sensitive to the possibilities the metaphor suggests. This chapter has demonstrated a number of ways in which the path metaphor supports Aśvaghoṣa's portrayal of conversion. The poet's creative handling of the core metaphor is evident throughout, particularly in Canto 5, when he maps out Nanda's states of mind on physical terrain. Nanda's current spiritual orientation and the maturation of his volition is further indicated by an associated special vocabulary, with his intended direction of travel indicated by *mukha* and the forces that impel and attract him indicated by √*kṛṣ*, while the process of his conversion is traced by words deriving from *ni* + √*vṛt*. On occasion, Aśvaghoṣa further concretises the metaphorical path to liberation as a trade route that leads the merchant to fabulous wealth. The path metaphor in its various guises admirably depicts the shift from Nanda's enforced travel to his voluntary travail.

CHAPTER EIGHT

CONCLUSION

The subject of this book began by stating as its subject the metaphors for conversion found in Aśvaghoṣa's *Saundarananda*. The opening chapter contended that these conversion metaphors are best interpreted through an application of George Lakoff's understanding of conceptual metaphor, whereby a familiar experiential domain or area of human activity becomes the well-spring for a number of figurative expressions. The bulk of the book analyses many of the poem's figurative expressions on the assumption that they are not only linked by a common conceptual metaphor, but that they are enriched by such a connection. Alternative approaches whereby figurative expressions are analysed according to their stylistic form are deliberately eschewed. The canto-by-canto overview of the *Saundarananda* that forms the greater part of Chapter Two presents not merely the poem's ostensible narrative facts but also points out the poem's key motifs as they arise. Chapter Two also refers to other versions of the story of the uxorious Nanda, and suggests some ways in which the *Saundarananda* differs from these other accounts. Aśvaghoṣa's version is distinguished by its thematic integrity, coherent structure and psychological authenticity, virtues which are to no small extent due to the poet's sensitive use of metaphor.

Chapters Three to Seven examine Aśvaghoṣa's use of specific conceptual metaphors to delineate Nanda's ongoing conversion. Chapter Three concerns the conceptual metaphor of an elephant in an originally wild and unmanaged condition who is subjected to a training program or other assistance. Some of the *Saundarananda*'s elephant similes depict an elephant stuck in mud and then pulled out of the mud, others speak of an elephant suffering from the condition of *mada* who is then free of that condition, while the largest group of similes concern an elephant captured from the wild and trained for war. The tamed elephant is the main expression of the concept of spiritual development facilitated by the imposition of restraint and strict boundaries, though this concept is also reflected elsewhere, for instance in the story of the sage Kapila in Canto 1.

Chapter Four examines the *Saundarananda*'s numerous medical metaphors within the framework of a four-limbed medical paradigm consisting of a doctor prescribing treatment to a patient suffering from an illness. The Buddha is conceptualised as the wise physician, presented from the outset as the ideal medical practitioner who is endowed with the virtues of compassion, skill and specialist knowledge. Aśvaghoṣa proceeds to draw a careful parallel between the three psychological faults (*doṣa*) that hinder the attainment of liberation, and the three humoral faults (*doṣa*) that in the Āyurvedic medical system hinder perfect health. When the specific fault that gives rise to the illness has been diagnosed, then the appropriate remedial action can be taken. Medical treatment is matched to meditative exercise according to which *doṣa* is present. In Nanda's case, passion is responsible for his suffering. Nanda's deepening commitment to the Buddhist goal is expressed in terms of his gradual metamorphosis into the ideal patient, one who has insight into his own debility, unhesitatingly obeys his physician, and who actively participates in his own recovery. Finally, Chapter Four suggests that the Buddha's radical treatment of exposing Nanda to the Apsarases is justified by Aśvaghoṣa on medical grounds, with the possibility that Nanda is subjected to emetic therapy which purges him of passion.

Chapter Five investigates how the refining of gold is made a metaphor for the cultivation of the mind. Gold, prized for its high worth, purity and resistance to corrosion, becomes a natural metaphor for the state of liberation. Over the course of the poem Aśvaghoṣa therefore develops a progressively stronger association between Nanda and the noble metal. Drawing on the source domain of gold manufacturing, Aśvaghoṣa constructs an elaborate parallel between the techniques of gold refining and the refining of the mind through meditation. First, the meditator eliminates his faults in order of magnitude, just as the dirt-washer sifts pebbles and suchlike from the gold before tackling smaller particles of dust. The goldsmith's subsequent production of gold ornaments resembles the meditator's achievement of supernormal faculties. A further analogy is developed between the meditator who carefully monitors the effectiveness of his chosen form of meditation, and the goldsmith who carefully watches over the process of gold refining in order to ascertain which action is the most appropriate. In each case observation, good judgement and earnest application will eventually produce the desired result. The chapter also raises the possibility that Aśvaghoṣa rectified an anomaly in a corresponding Pali text.

Two orientational metaphors are explored in Chapters Six and Seven. Chapter Six explores the *Saundarananda*'s use of a vertical dimension, with the concept of 'up' evaluated positively and 'down' negatively. The chapter investigates the physical positioning of certain characters and important locations such as the Sundarī's roof-top, the mountains and heaven, all associated with sensual pleasures. The mountains, in a paradoxical juxtaposition of renunciation and sexuality, are inhabited by ascetics as well as by gorgeous *kiṃnarīs*. The Apsarases of heaven are even more alluring, and are promised to Nanda as a reward for a life of celibacy and ascetic restraint. Sundarī, whose domain is the upper levels of the palace, is frequently identified with the Apsarases. These places may represent Nanda's highest aspirations, but images of falling and sinking reflect their imperfect and transient nature. Nanda is in fact sunk in carnality, and the Buddha's endeavours to give him spiritual uplift are presented as the application of upward force. When Nanda eventually attains *nirvāṇa*, it is conceptualised as a place from which one cannot fall.

The subject of Chapter Seven is Aśvaghoṣa's utilisation of Buddhism's most common and therefore barely noticeable metaphor, the dharma conceived as a path. All the traditional correspondences set up in this familiar metaphor are to be found amongst its many manifestations in the *Saundarananda*. Thus the Buddha appears as the guide who knows the path and its destination, while his instructions serve as a map. When Nanda strives to realise the dharma within his life, he is portrayed as following the path towards the destination of liberation, but as long as he fails to do so, he is said to be following the wrong path or wandering in the undemarcated wilderness of *saṃsāra*. Canto 5 contains a particularly vivid and memorable dramatisation of the path metaphor. Aśvaghoṣa's stroke of genius in having the Buddha step forward to block Nanda's departure provides one of the *Saundarananda*'s most arresting moments. The metaphor proves of further value in charting Nanda's subsequent attainment of liberation, as in its provision of a vocabulary of spatial relations to plot his changing orientation. The crucial moment at which he changes his mind is conceptualised as a large chariot turning round. Nanda's journey towards liberation is also developed as a trader's venture through dangerous territory for the sake of enormous wealth.

The conceptual metaphors presented in this book share a common purpose. Each contributes to the poem's unity of theme by reflecting and recording Nanda's conversion, an event that is not any single moment but a long-term process of spiritual growth. As the metaphors engage with the same material, they also have a similar target domain, though the source domain, that experience or activity familiar to the poem's readers, differs in each case. Each metaphor to some extent incorporates into its target domain Nanda's initial state, his final state, and a converting action which produces the change from the former to the latter. These three elements are mirrored in the source domains in a variety of ways. Thus Nanda in the early stages of his conversion is portrayed as a wild or ruttish elephant, a recalcitrant patient, or a traveller separated from his caravan. At this point he has false aspirations and his mental state is like crude gold. Once he is approaching emancipation, or upon achieving it, he is viewed as cured, or as a successful merchant. His mind is like a well-trained war elephant, or refined gold, and his condition is unfallen. The converting action effecting these conversions is conceived as capturing and disciplining the elephant, arrow extraction or other medical treatment, the gold-refining process from discarding waste matter to smithing, upward motion, or indicating the path. This bare equation, systematised and greatly simplified in this conclusion, can only hint at the range of correspondences developed in the poem, but it is hoped that the remainder of this book has conveyed something of the full complexity and richness of Aśvaghoṣa's metaphoric thinking.

Many of the metaphors that have been explored here narrate not just Nanda's conversion, but also Nanda's characteristic passivity and the subsequent requirement for the Buddha to function as a catalyst. Aśvaghoṣa foregoes matter-of-fact reporting of the Buddha's agency, preferring to tussle with the possibility that Nanda's conversion may be considered too forceful. His justification for the Buddha's strong-arm tactics is conveyed in part through the conceptual metaphors, which regularly stress present pain for future gain. The elephant metaphor delivers the message that the removal of the elephant from its native habitat and its subjection to rigorous discipline are necessary in order to transform the once wild creature into a noble fighting machine. The medical metaphor in particular provides a persuasive justification for the Buddha's vigorous intervention in Nanda's life, presenting Nanda as a recalcitrant patient who doesn't know what is good for him, and the Buddha as a skilled physician who is obliged to inflict short-term suffering on his patient in order to save his life. Not only do the metaphors record the facilitation of Nanda's conversion by the Buddha, they also bring out the fact that Nanda's conversion, superficial to begin with, does not begin to take hold until his own volition gathers sufficient momentum. Nanda has to take charge of his own path to liberation, a change of heart which is surely difficult to convey. The metaphors are particularly useful in delineating such inner, psychological action. The path metaphor, for instance, provides an impressive image of a large vehicle turning round, while the medical metaphor portays Nanda's evolution from a disobedient patient who refuses to take medical advice to a patient who acknowledges that he is gravely ill and adapts his attitude accordingly. As the metaphors plot Nanda's mental journey, they are able to reveal the moment when Nanda, instead of countering the Buddha, begins to take charge of his own ongoing conversion.

The *Saundarananda* grants its audience a great boon with its conceptual metaphors. In reflecting an abstract, complex target domain in a concrete and more readily comprehensible source domain, the conceptual metaphors make vivid and visible the essentially private and invisible drama of conversion that is played out in Nanda's heart and mind. Aśvaghoṣa uses metaphor to concretise psychological events and abstract concepts as traditional relationships and familiar everyday activities, successfully achieving cultural resonance whilst avoiding cognitive dissonance. I hope that my investigations into the sources of the poem's metaphors have recovered forgotten aspects of these relationships and activities that enhance their connotative power. Where aspects of these relationships and activities remain familiar to us, I have highlighted their presence in the text, since over-familiarity can detract from their significance, especially when a conceptual metaphor is a particularly well-understood (though perhaps unconsciously understood) Buddhist cultural phenomenon. I hold that an appreciation of metaphor is essential not just for understanding the *Saundarananda*, but for understanding what Steve Collins (1998) has called the 'imaginaire' – the world as imagined by Buddhists. I also hope that the full harvesting of each conceptual metaphor's field of suggestion allows Aśvaghoṣa to emerge as a truly Buddhist poet, a poet who presses *kāvya* conventions into Buddhist service in his urgent concern for the dissemination of his message. Aśvaghoṣa's metaphors are always explanatory rather than merely decorative in function: they explain the conversion of Nanda and his reorientation to the Buddhist goal of liberation. And since metaphors can restructure the reader's ordinary ingrained patterns of thinking, a metaphor may have some power to convert of its own. Being powerful, persuasive and frequently repeated, the *Saundarananda*'s conceptual metaphors coerce us for our good, just as the Buddha did for Nanda when he stood in the road to stop him going home.

APPENDIX: VERSIONS OF THE NANDA LEGEND

References for various sources of the Nanda story together with bibliographical information where known are here listed by source type. This list is doubtless far from complete.

Pali Sources

1. Ud 3.2.21-4. Translation in *The Udāna* by Masefield, P. (1994). Oxford: PTS, pp. 39-43.
2. Dhp 13-14. Translation in *The Dhammapada* by Radhakrishnan, S. (1950). Oxford: Oxford University Press.
3. Th 157-8. Translation in *Poems of Early Buddhist Monks* by Norman, K.R. (1997). Oxford: PTS, p. 22.
4. SN ii.281. In this passage the Buddha rebukes Nanda for going out to beg with a glazed bowl, in pressed and ironed robes, and with his eyes anointed. Translation in *The Life of the Buddha* by Bhikkhu Ñāṇamoḷi (1972). Kandy: Buddhist Publication Society, p. 84.
5. VinMV 1:54. This is a very short mention of the Buddha calling at Nanda's house on his wedding day, giving his bowl to Nanda and leaving, Nanda's betrothed calling out to him, and his ordination. Translation in *The Life of the Buddha* by Bhikkhu Ñāṇamoḷi (1972). Kandy: Buddhist Publication Society, p. 77.
6. Vin 4:173. Here Nanda appears as handsome, almost as tall as the Buddha, and wearing a robe of the same measurement as the Buddha's, with the result that from a distance the other monks mistake Nanda for the Buddha. The other monks subsequently complain to the Buddha and he institutes the new rule against wearing a robe the same as his own. Translation in *The Life of the Buddha* by Bhikkhu Ñāṇamoḷi (1972). Kandy: Buddhist Publication Society, p. 196.
7. J 182. Translation in *Stories of the Buddha's Former Births* Volume II by Rouse, W. (1895). Cambridge: Cambridge University Press.

8. Ud-a 3.2. Translation in *The Udāna Commentary* Volume I by Masefield, P. (1994). Oxford: PTS, pp. 449-64.
9. Dhp-a I.9.i. Translation in *Buddhist Legends* Part I by Burlingame, E.W. (1921). Oxford: PTS, pp. 217-225.
10. Th-a 2.31-34. Translation in *Psalms of the Brethren* by Rhys Davids, C.A.F. (1964). London: Luzac & Co, pp. 126-127.
11. *Manorathapūraṇī* (Commentary on the *Aṅguttara Nikāya*) i.315-318. This gives a summary of the Nanda story in explanation of AN i:25, in which the Buddha pronounces Nanda the best amongst his disciples for guarding the doors of the senses. Translation in *Buddhist Parables* by Burlingame, E.W. (1922). New Haven: Yale University Press.

Chinese Sources

1. *Tch'ou yao king*, K24 in *Tch'ou yao king* Vol. IV, pp. 739b-740a, edited by Taisho Issaikyo. No translation.
2. *Tsa pao tsang king*, K8 (*Saṃyukta-ratna-piṭaka Sūtra*) in *Tsa pao tsang king* Vol. IV, pp. 485c-486c, edited by Taisho Issaikyo. French summary in *Cinq cents contes et apologues: Extraits du Tripiṭaka Chinois Vol. IV* by Chavannes, E. (1934). Paris: Librairie Ernest Leroux,, pp. 211-212.
3. *Fo pen hing tsi king*, K56 (*Abhiniṣkramaṇa Sūtra*) in *Fo pen hing tsi king* Vol. III, pp. 911b-914b, edited by Taisho Issaikyo. Translated in *The Romantic Legend of Śākya Buddha by* Beal, S. (1875). London: Trübner & Co., pp. 369-378.

Tibetan Sources

1. *Kṣudraka-vastu* of the *Mūla-sarvāstivāda-vinaya* (*Bkaḥ-ḥgyur, ḥdul-ba De* 114a-119a) in *The Tibetan Tripiṭaka (Peking Edition)* Vol. 44, pp. 47-49, edited by Suzuki, D.T. English summary in *The Life of the Buddha and*

the Early History of his Order by Rockhill, W. (1884). London: Trübner & Co., p. 55.

Sanskrit and Mixed Sanskrit Sources

1. Mvu 3.33-41, the *Puṇyavanta Jātaka*. One of the characters is the handsome Rūpavanta, who values beauty more than anything and who uses his good looks to extort money from a courtesan. He was Sundarananda (sic) in a previous life. Translation in *The Mahāvastu* Volume III by Jones, J.J. (1956). London: Luzac & Co.
2. *Sundarī-nandāvadāna*, no. 10 in Kṣemendra's *Bodhisattvāvadānakalpalatā*. Vaidya, P.L. (ed.) (1959). *Avadānakalpalatā* Volume II. Darbhanga: pp. 85-95. Translation in "The Story of Sundarī and Nanda" (1896). *Journal of the Buddhist Text Society of India* Vol. IV, part III, pp. 20-8. Calcutta.

Other Textual Sources

1. Unnamed medieval Sinhala manuscripts, translated in *A Manual of Buddhism* by Hardy, R. Spence (1880). London: Williams & Norgate, pp. 210-211.

Art Sources

1. Frescoes from the walls of cave 16 at Ajantā depict incidents from the Nanda story. See *Ajanta* Volume III by Yazdani, G. (1946). London: Oxford University Press, pp. 49-56 and *The Colour and Monochrome Reproductions of the Ajanta Frescoes, Based on Photography* by Yazdani, G. (1947). London: Oxford University Press, Plates LII-LV.
2. A series of bas-reliefs at Nāgārjunikoṇḍa, dating from the second half of the second century CE, depict the Nanda story.
3. Engraved panels of the Kuṣāṇa period, now in the Lucknow and Mathura museums, show Nanda handing his wife a garment and holding a mirror for her.

4. A jamb from Amaravati from the second half of the second century AD. See *Early Indian Sculpture* by Bachofer (1929). Paris: Pegasus Press, plate 128.
5. A Gāndhāran relief of Nanda's tonsure. See *L'Art Greco-Bouddhique du Gandhāra* Volume I by Foucher, A. (1905-1951). Paris: E. Leroux, p. 471, and figures 234 and 238. Also reproduced on p. 30 in "Identification of an Ajanta Fragment" by Begley, W. (1968). *Oriental Art* N.S. Volume 1, pp. 25-33.

Passing references to Nanda

1. AN iv.166-168. Translation in *The Book of the Gradual Sayings* Volume IV by Hare, E. M. (1935). London, PTS, pp. 112-114.
2. Mil 169. Here the Buddha's exposure of Nanda to the Apsarases is listed as one of a variety of methods for liberating different people. Translation in *Milinda's Questions* Volume I by Horner, I. B. (1963). London: Luzac & Co., pp. 237-8.
3. Mvu 3:176. Here it is explained that King Śuddhodana decrees that one man from each *kṣatriya* family should go forth. He himself has two sons, the Exalted One and Sundarananda. Sundarananda is excused because the Exalted One had already left home. Translation in *The Mahāvastu* Volume III by Jones, J. J. (1956).
4. *Śatapañcāśatka* 125. In this verse from the section on Skilful Means, Nanda, Mānastabdha and Aṅgulimāla are named as examples of sensuality, pride and violence respectively, now converted to their opposites. Translation in *The Śatapañcāśatka of Mātṛceṭa* by Shackleton Bailey, D. R. (1951). Cambridge: CUP, 1951

BIBLIOGRAPHY

Primary Sources: Texts and Translations

Ācārya, J. and Nārāyan, R. (eds.) (1980). *Suśruta Saṃhitā.* Varanasi: Chaukhambha Orientalia.

Bays, G. (tr.) (1983). *The Voice of the Buddha: The Beauty of Compassion. Lalitavistara.* Berkeley: Dharma Publishing. 2 volumes.

Bhatt, G. H. (ed.) (1960). *The Vālmīki-Rāmāyaṇa Critical Edition* Volume I. Baroda: Oriental Institute.

Burlingame, E. (tr.) (1921). *Buddhist Legends* Parts 1, 2 and 3. Oxford: PTS.

Chaṭṭasaṅgāyana Tipiṭaka (1999). [CD-ROM]. Igatpuri: Vipassana Research Institute. Version 3.

Cowell, E.B. (tr.) (1895-1907). *The Jātaka or Stories of the Buddha's Former Births* Volumes I-VI. London: Luzac & Company.

Edgerton, F. (tr.) (1931). *The Elephant-Lore of the Hindus.* New Haven: Yale University Press.

Fausbøll, V. (ed.) (1877-96). *Jātaka* Volumes I-VI. London: Luzac & Co.

Ganapati Śāstrī, T. (ed.) (1910). *The Mātaṅgalīlā of Nīlakaṇṭha.* Trivandrum Sanskrit Series No. X.

Horner, I. B. (tr.) (1963). *Milinda's Questions* Volume I. London: Luzac & Co.

Ingalls, D. (tr.) (1990). The *Dhvanyāloka* of Ānandavardhana with the *Locana* of Abhinavagupta. Cambridge, Massachusetts: Harvard University Press.

Johnston, E.H. (ed.) (1928). *The Saundarananda of Aśvaghoṣa.* London: Oxford University Press.

Johnston, E.H. (tr.) (1932). *The Saundarananda or Nanda the Fair.* London: Oxford University Press.

Johnston, E.H. (ed. & tr.) (1936). *Aśvaghoṣa's Buddhacarita or Acts of the Buddha.* New Delhi: Munshiram Manoharlal.

Jones, J.J. (tr.) (1949-56). *The Mahāvastu* Volumes I-III. London: Luzac & Co.

Kangle, R. P. (ed. and tr.) (1965-72). The *Kauṭilīya Arthaśāstra* Parts I-III. Bombay: University of Bombay.

Lamotte, E. (1976), rendered into English by Sara Boin. *The Teaching of Vimalakīrti.* Oxford: PTS.

Ñāṇamoḷi, Bhikkhu (tr.) (1956). *The Path of Purification – Visuddhimagga.* Colombo: A. Semage.

Ñāṇamoḷi, Bhikkhu and Bodhi, Bhikkhu (tr.) (1995). *The Middle-Length Discourses of the Buddha.* Boston: Wisdom Publications.

Narayana Ayer, V. (ed. & tr.) (1964). *Kāvyādarśa of Daṇḍin.* Madras: V. Ramaswamy Sastulu & Sons.

Norman, K.R. (tr.) (1997). *Poems of the Early Buddhist Monks.* Oxford: PTS.

Pollock, S. (tr.) (1986). *The Rāmāyaṇa of Vālmīki: Ayodhyākāṇḍa.* Princeton: Princeton University Press.

Radhakrishnan, S. (tr.) (1950). *The Dhammapada.* Oxford: Oxford University Press.

Radhakrishnan, S. (tr.) (1953). *The Principal Upaniṣads.* New Delhi: Harper Collins.

Sankara Rama Sastri, C. (ed.) (1956). *Kāvyālaṅkāra of Bhāmaha.* Madras: Sri Balamanorama Press.

Senart, É. (ed.) (1890). *Le Mahāvastu.* Paris: Societé Asiatique.

Shackleton Bailey, D. R. (ed. & tr.) (1951). *The Śatapañcāśatka of Mātṛceṭa.* Cambridge: Cambridge University Press.

Sharma, P. (1981-94). *Caraka-Saṃhitā: Agniveśa's treatise refined and annotated by Caraka and redacted by Dṛḍhabala (text with English translation).* Varanasi: Chaukhambha Orientalia. 4 volumes.

Shastri, Haraprasad (ed.) (1939). *Saundarananda Kāvya of Aśvaghoṣa.* Calcutta: Royal Asiatic Society of Bengal.

Srikantha Murthy, K. R. (1991-95). Vāgbhaṭa's Aṣṭāṅga Hṛdayam: text, English translation, notes, appendix, and indices. Varanasi: Krishnadas Academy. 3 volumes.

Srikantha Murthy, K.R. (1995). *Aṣṭāṅgasaṃgraha of Vāgbhaṭa* (text and translation). Varanasi: Chaukhambha Orientalia.

Vaidya, P.L. (ed.) (1958). *Lalitavistara.* Darbhanga: Mithila Institute.

Vaidya, P. L. (ed.) (1962). *The Vālmīki-Rāmāyaṇa Critical Edition* Volume II. Baroda: Oriental Institute.

Secondary Sources:

Abbott, J. (1847). "Account of the process employed for obtaining gold from the sand of the river Beyass". *JASB* 16, pp. 266-8.

Agrawal, D.P. and Margabandhu, C. (1975-6). "Ancient Gold Workings: Some New C^{14} Dates". *Purātattva* 8, pp. 138-9.

Apte, V.S. (1890). *The Student's Sanskrit-English Dictionary*. Delhi: Motilal Banarsidass. Second edition.

Basham, A.L. (1954). *The Wonder that was India*. New Delhi: Rupa & Co. Third revised edition.

Beal, S. (1875). *The Romantic Legend of Śākya Buddha*. London: Trüber & Co.

Begley, W. (1968). "Identification of an Ajanta Fragment". *Oriental Art* N.S. 1, pp. 25-33.

Benjamin B., Dirven R. and Ries J. (eds.) (1998). *Faith and Fiction. Interdisciplinary Studies on the Interplay between Metaphor and Religion: A Selection of Papers from the 25th LAUD Symposium of the Gerhard Mercator University of Duisburg on "Metaphor and Religion"*. Frankfurt: Peter Lang.

Bennett, A.A.G. (1964). "The Works of Aśvaghoṣa". *Mahabodhi* 72, pp. 244-248.

Bhattacharya, B. (1976). *Aśvaghoṣa: A Critical Study* Santiniketan: Bidyut Ranjan Basu.

Birnbaum, R. (1979). *The Healing Buddha*. London: Rider & Company.

Biswas, A.K. (1996). *Minerals and Metals in Ancient India*. New Delhi: D. K. Printworld (P) Ltd. 2 volumes.

Bohn, R. R. (1973). *Aśvaghoṣa's Saundarananda: A Poetic Study*. Unpublished PhD thesis. University of California, Berkeley.

Boswell, J. (1791). *Life of Johnson*. Oxford: Oxford University Press. New edition 1989.

Cautley, Lieut. (1835). "Note on the Gold Washings of the Gumti River". *JASB* 4, pp. 279-82.

Collins, S. (1982). *Selfless Persons*. Cambridge: Cambridge University Press.

Collins, S. (1998). *Nirvana and Other Buddhist Felicities: Utopias of the Pali Imaginaire*. Cambridge: Cambridge University Press.

Conze, E. (1959). *Buddhist Scriptures*. London: Penguin.

Coomaraswamy, A. (1977). "Saṃvega: Aesthetic Shock". In R. Lipsey (ed.), *Coomaraswamy I: Selected Papers. Traditional Art and Symbolism*. Princeton: Princeton University Press, pp. 179-85.

Cooper, D. (1986). *Metaphor*. Oxford, Basil Blackwell.

Cooper, D. (2002). "Emptiness: Interpretation and Metaphor". *Contemporary Buddhism*, 3, 1, pp. 7-20.

Covill, L. (2007). *Handsome Nanda*. New York: New York University Press and the Clay Sanskrit Library.

Cribb, J. (1999). "The early Kushan kings: new evidence for chronology. Evidence from the Rabatak inscription of Kanishka I." In M. Alram and D. Klimburg-Salter (eds.), *Coins, art and chronology. Essays on the pre-Islamic history of the Indo-Iranian borderlands*. Wien: Verlag der Österreichischen Akademie der Wissenschaften, pp. 177-205.

De, S.K. (1960). *History of Sanskrit Poetics*. Calcutta: K. L. Mukhopadhyay. Second revised edition.

Dongier O'Flaherty, W. (1973). *Asceticism and Eroticism in the Mythology of Śiva*. London: Oxford University Press.

Falk, H. (1997). "Refining Gold in Ancient India: ad JUB 3.17.3". *Acta Orientalia*, 58, pp. 47-51.

Frye, N. (1982). *The Great Code: The Bible as Literature*. London: Routledge & Kegan Paul.

Ghose, L. (1999). *Emotion in Buddhism: a case study of Aśvaghoṣa's Saundarananda*. Unpublished PhD thesis. McGill University, Montreal.

Gombrich, R. (1988). *Theravada Buddhism*. London: Routledge.

Gombrich, R. (1991). "*Pātimokkha*: purgative". In The Editorial Committee of the Felicitation Volume for Professor Dr. Egaku Mayeda (eds.), *Studies in Buddhism and culture in honour of Professor Dr Egaku Mayeda on his sixty-fifth birthday*. Tokyo: Sankibo Busshorin, pp. 31-8.

Gombrich, R. (1996). *How Buddhism Began: The Conditioned Genesis of the Early Teachings*. London: The Athlone Press.

Gupta, S. (1983). *The Elephant in Indian Art and Mythology*. New Delhi: Shakti Malik.

Gurner, C. W. (1927). "Aśvagoṣa and the *Rāmāyaṇa*". JASB new series, 23, 3, pp. 347-367.

Hakeda, Y. (1962). "Buddhist Hybrid Sanskrit Words in Aśvaghoṣa's *kāvyas*". *JAOS*, 82, pp. 150-63.

Halliwell, S. (1987). *The* Poetics *of Aristotle: Translation and Commentary*. London: Duckworth.

Hamilton, S. (2000). *Early Buddhism: A New Approach. The I of the Beholder*. Richmond: Curzon Press.

Hardin, G. (1974). "Living on a Lifeboat". [Online]. [Accessed 28th June 2005]. Available from World Wide Web: <http://www.garretthardinsociety.org/articles/art_living_on_a_lifeboat.html>.

Hardy, R. Spence (1880). *A Manual of Buddhism*. London: Williams & Norgate.

Jäkel, O. (2002). "Hypotheses Revisited: The Cognitive Theory of Metaphor Applied to Religious Texts". *Metaphorik*, 2. [Online]. [Accessed 28th June 2005]. Available from World Wide Web: <http://www.metaphorik.de/02/jaekel.htm>.

Jasper, D. (1989). *The Study of Literature and Religion*. Basingstoke: Macmillan.

Jenkins, F. (1838). "Native account of washing for gold in Assam". *JASB* 7, 2, pp. 621-8.

Lakoff, G. and Johnson, M. (1980). *Metaphors We Live By*. Chicago and London: University of Chicago Press.

Lakoff, G. and Johnson, M. (1999). *Philosophy in the Flesh: The Embodied Mind and its Challenge to Western Thought*. New York: Basic Books.

Lakoff, G. and Turner, M. (1989). *More than Cool Reason: A Field Guide to Poetic Metaphor*. Chicago: University of Chicago Press.

Lévi, S. (1896). "Notes sur les indo-scythes". *Journal Asiatique*, pp. 444-484. Translated Philips, W. R. (1903). "Notes on the Indo-Scythians". *Indian Antiquary*, 32, pp. 381-389.

Lienhard, S. (1984). *A History of Classical Poetry: Sanskrit-Pali-Prākrit*. In J. Gonda (ed.), *A History of Indian Literature*, Vol III, Fasc 1. Wiesbaden: Otto Harrassowitz.

Lüders, H. (1911). *Bruchstücke Buddhistischer Dramen*. Berlin: Georg Reimer. Reprinted (1979) as *Monographien zur Indischen Archäologie, Kunst und Philologie*, Volume 1. Wiesbaden: Franz Steiner Verlag.

McMahan, D. (2002). *Empty Vision: Metaphor and Visionary Imagery in Mahāyāna Buddhism*. London and New York: Routledge Curzon.

Monier-Williams, Monier (1899). *Sanskrit-English Dictionary*. Oxford: Oxford University Press.

Norman, K.R. (1983). *Pāli Literature: Including the Canonical Literature in Prakrit and Sanskrit of all the Hīnayāna Schools of Buddhism*. Wiesbaden: Otto Harrassowitz.

Obeyesekere, G. (1977) "The theory and practice of psychological medicine in the ayurvedic tradition". *Culture, Medicine and Psychiatry*, 1, pp. 151-181.

Passi, A. (1982). "Some Preliminary Considerations on Aśvaghoṣa's *Saundarananda*". *East and West*, 32, pp. 65-74.

Passi, A. (1996). "Nanda Revisited. Stanzas from the IV Canto of Aśvaghoṣa's *Saundarananda*". In E. Garzilli (ed.), *Translating, Translations, Translators from India to the West*. Harvard Oriental Series, Opera Minora, Volume I.

Pollock, S. (1977). *Aspects of Versification in Sanskrit Lyric Poetry*. New Haven, Connecticut: American Oriental Society.

Putri, B. (1946). "Toilet and Treatment of Hair in the Kuṣāṇa Period". *Indian Culture*, 12, pp. 166-7.

Pye, M. (1978). *Skilful Means*. London: Duckworth.

Rhys Davids, C. (1906-7). "Similes in the *Nikāyas*". *JPTS*, pp. 52-151.

Rhys Davids, T. W. and Stede, W. (1921-5). *Pali-English Dictionary*. Oxford: PTS.

Richards, I. A. (1936). *The Philosophy of Rhetoric*. New York: Oxford University Press.

Rohrer, T. (1995). "The Metaphorical Logic of (Political) Rape: The New Wor(l)d Order". [Online]. [Accessed 28th June 2005]. Available from the World Wide Web: <http://zakros.ucsd.edu/~trohrer/metaphor/brhtml.htm >.

Salomon, R. (1983). 'The Buddhist Sanskrit of Aśvaghoṣa's *Saundarananda*'. *WZKS* 27, pp. 97-112.

Sangharakshita (1957). *A Survey of Buddhism*. Bangalore: The Indian Institute of World Culture.

Scharfe, H. (1999). "The doctrine of the three humours in traditional Indian medicine and the alleged antiquity of Tamil Siddha medicine". *JAOS*, 119(4), pp. 609-29.

Schlingloff, D. (1975). 'Aśvaghoṣa's *Saundarānanda* in Ajanta' (sic). *WZKS* 19, pp. 85-102.

Sen, S. (1930). 'The language of Aśvaghoṣa's *Saundarananda-Kāvya'*. *JASB* 26, pp. 181-206.

Shastri, H. (1909). 'The Recovery of a Lost Epic by Aśvaghoṣa'. *JASB* 5, pp. 165-6.

Siegel, L. (1983). *Fires of Love, Waters of Peace: Passion and Renunciation in Indian Culture*. Honolulu: University of Hawaii Press.

Sontag, S. (1988). *AIDS and its Metaphors*. New York: Farrar, Straus & Giroux.

Soskice, J. (1985). *Metaphor and Religious Language*. Oxford: Clarendon Press.

Strong, J.S. (1995). *The Experience of Buddhism: Sources and Interpretations*. Belmont: Wadsworth.

Tatelman, J. (2000). *The Glorious Deeds of Pūrṇa*. Richmond: Curzon Press.

Valdes, M. (ed.) (1991). *A Ricoeur Reader: Reflection and Imagination*. Hemel Hempstead: Harvester Wheatsheaf.

Warder, A.K. (1974). *Indian Kāvya Literature* Volume II. Delhi: Motilal Banarsidass. Second revised edition 1990.

Williams, P. (1989). *Mahāyāna Buddhism*. London: Routledge.

Wujastyk, D. (1998). *The Roots of Āyurveda*. New Delhi: Penguin. Revised edition.

Zysk, K. (1991). *Asceticism and Healing in Ancient India: Medicine in the Buddhist Monastery*. New York: Oxford University Press.

GLOSSARY

anātman	*see* no self
alaṃkāra	"ornament" or poetic embellishemt; figures of speech and stylistic devices in literary Sanskrit
Apsarases	beautiful semi-divine women
Ānanda	well-known disciple of the Buddha
Ārāḍa	one of the Buddha's teachers
arhat	"worthy", person who has achieved liberation according to the teachings of early Buddhism
āsrava	mental tendencies that bind one to rebirth; their destruction equates to enlightenment
awakening	*see* liberation
bodhisattva	the Buddha prior to his enlightenment
brahmin	member of the priestly caste
Buddha, the	"awakened one", epithet of Sarvārtha-siddha Gautama after he attains enlightenment; Nanda's older half-brother
cakravāka	the ruddy sheldrake, a species of waterbird that signifies conjugal love in Sanskrit literature
conceptual metaphor	the transference of our understanding of our bodily, social or cultural experience to an abstract realm; Lakoff's insight that metaphor resides in thought, not just in a particular linguistic expression.
dependent origination	the Buddhist doctrine that phenomena arise and cease together in a mutually interdependent web of cause and effect
dharma	the doctrine expounded by the Buddha which leads to liberation

doṣa	in Buddhism, a fundamental character fault which prevents enlightenment. In Āyurveda, one of the three humours.
duḥkha	*see* suffering
Eightfold Path	the fourth of the Four Noble Truths consisting of a guide to overcoming suffering
enlightenment	*see* liberation
Four Noble Truths	core Buddhist doctrine concerning suffering, its origin and its defeat
Gandharvas	a class of semi-divine beings famed as musicians, and sometimes lovers of the Apsarases
Ikṣvāku	dynasty in northern India into which the Buddha was born
Indra	chief of the gods, and ruler of the heavenly realm visited by Nanda and thte Buddha
indriya	the senses, whose operation is to be carefully guarded
jhāna/dhyāna	Pali and Sanskrit terms for four progressively subtler meditative states
Kāmạ	god of love
kāma	sensual desire
Kapila	a sage, legendary founder of Kapilavāstu
Kapilavāstu	the city in which Nanda lives, and hometown of the Buddha
karma	past deeds which influence one's present circumstances
kāvya	refined type of Sanskrit literature
kiṃnara / kiṃpuruṣa (m) and *kiṃnarī* (f)	mythical mountain-dwelling beings famed for their beauty
kleśa	one's impurities and passions which one must seek to combat
kṣatriya	a member, or the mores, of the warrior and aristocratic class of society

liberation	the experience of *nirvāṇa* (*q.v.*) and the cessation of suffering, achieved by Nanda in Canto 17
mada	an elephant's periodic state of must or rut, during which he is excitable and difficult to train
Mandara	sacred mountain, residence of various deities
Māra	personification of evil and the passions, and representative of death. He tempts the Buddha-to-be to abadon his quest for liberation.
mārga	a path, both literally and metaphorically
Meru	sacred golden mountain at the centre of the word
Nanda	the Buddha's half-brother and hero of the *Saundarananda*
Nandana	gardens of heaven frequented by the Apsarases
nirvāṇa	"blowing out" desire, malice and ignorance; the end of suffering and rebirth.
no self	(*anātman*) the theory that the human being has no separate and independent self
pātimokkha	the set of rules observed by Buddhist monks and nuns
rasa	"taste"; the emotional flavouring carried by a literary work
rūpaka	a metaphor
samādhi	meditative concentration
saṃsāra	"going round", the continuous cycle of birth and death
śīla	moral self-restraint
skillful means	(*upāya kauśalya*) the application of different methods of teaching to

	different individuals according to their specific circumstances
smṛti	mindful awareness
source domain	area of human activity from which a conceptual metaphor is drawn
śramaṇa	religious ascetic
Śuddhodana	King of Kapilavāstu and father of Nanda and the Buddha
suffering	the basic fact of human experience; first of the Four Noble Truths
Sugata	the "well-gone", epithet of the Buddha
Sundarī	"Beauty", Nanda's wife
supernormal powers	(*abhijñā*) psychic powers, knowing the thoughts of others, remembering past lives, divine hearing and sight, acquired after intense meditative cultivation
target domain	the topic to which a conceptual metaphor is applied
Tathāgata	the realised one "who has gone thus"; epithet of the Buddha
Uḍraka	one of the Buddha's teachers
upamā	simile
upamāna	the object of comparison in a simile. For instance, in the simile "Sundarī's eyes are like bees", the bees are the *upamāna*.
upameya	the object of comparison in a simile. In the above simile, Sundarī's eyes are the *upameya*.
upāya kauśalya	*see* skillful means
vīṇā	Indian lute
viśeṣaka	cosmetic mark applied by Sundarī in Nanda's presence

INDEX

A

B

H

I

J

K

L

M

N

O

P

R

S

T

U

V

Y